Cavalier Capital

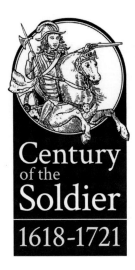

The Century of the Soldier series – Warfare c 1618-1721

www.helion.co.uk/centuryofthesoldier

'This is the Century of the Soldier', Falvio Testir, Poet, 1641

The 'Century of the Soldier' series will cover the period of military history c. 1618–1721, the 'golden era' of Pike and Shot warfare. This time frame has been seen by many historians as a period of not only great social change, but of fundamental developments within military matters. This is the period of the 'military revolution', the development of standing armies, the widespread introduction of black powder weapons and a greater professionalism within the culture of military personnel.

The series will examine the period in a greater degree of detail than has hitherto been attempted, and has a very wide brief, with the intention of covering all aspects of the period from the battles, campaigns, logistics and tactics, to the personalities, armies, uniforms and equipment.

Submissions

The publishers would be pleased to receive submissions for this series. Please contact us via email (info@ helion.co.uk), or in writing to Helion & Company Limited, 26 Willow Road, Solihull, West Midlands, B91 1UE.

Titles

No 1 *'Famous by my Sword'. The Army of Montrose and the Military Revolution* Charles Singleton (ISBN 978-1-909384-97-2)*

No 2 *Marlborough's Other Army. The British Army and the Campaigns of the First Peninsular War, 1702–1712* Nick Dorrell (ISBN 978-1-910294-63-5)

No 3 *Cavalier Capital. Oxford in the English Civil War 1642–1646* John Barratt (ISBN 978-1-910294-58-1)

Books within the series are published in two formats: 'Falconets' are paperbacks, page size 248mm x 180mm, with high visual content including colour plates; 'Culverins' are hardback monographs, page size 234mm x 156mm. Books marked with * in the list above are Falconets, all others are Culverins.

Cavalier Capital

Oxford in the English Civil War 1642-1646

John Barratt

 Helion & Company Limited

Helion & Company Limited
26 Willow Road
Solihull
West Midlands
B91 1UE
England
Tel. 0121 705 3393
Fax 0121 711 4075
Email: info@helion.co.uk
Website: www.helion.co.uk
Twitter: @helionbooks
Visit our blog http://blog.helion.co.uk/

Published by Helion & Company 2015

Designed and typeset by Bookcraft Ltd, Stroud, Gloucestershire
Cover designed by Paul Hewitt, Battlefield Design (www.battlefield-design.co.uk)
Printed by Gutenberg Press Limited, Tarxien, Malta

Text © John Barratt 2015
Illustrations © as individually credited
Maps © Helion & Company Limited 2015. Maps designed by Paul Hewitt,
Battlefield Design (www.battlefield-design.co.uk)

Front cover: King Charles reviews Sir John Owen's Regiment, c. 1643.
(Drawing by Peter Dennis © Helion & Company).

ISBN 978 1 910294 58 1

British Library Cataloguing-in-Publication Data.
A catalogue record for this book is available from the British Library.

For details of other military history titles published by Helion & Company Limited
contact the above address, or visit our website: http://www.helion.co.uk.

We always welcome receiving book proposals from prospective authors.

Contents

List of Illustrations

List of Maps

Introduction

For almost four years between 1642 and 1646, the city of Oxford was the defacto Royalist capital during the English civil war. Here for much of the time were King Charles and his Court, the leading officials of the Royalist administration, and hundreds of the King's sympathisers, often refugees from other parts of the country.

Oxford also housed major parts of the Royalist war effort, magazines and munitions manufacturing, artillery and stores. There were hospitals, prisons, fortifications, a garrison and all the other paraphernalia of war.

Oxford's streets and colleges were filled with courtiers, soldiers, citizens and all the daily alarms of war, for the Royalist capital frequently found itself in the forefront of the war and under attack.

This book tells the story of the events of this tumultuous time, and of the men and women caught up in Oxford's years as Cavalier Capital.

Thanks are due to all the team at Helion, the staff of The British Library, London, Bodleian Library , Oxford, and Shropshire Libraries, and to Rik Tyler for his cartographic skills.

Chronology

1642

13 August	King's Proclamation from York of 9 August, proclaiming Earl of Essex a traitor read in Oxford. Dr Pinke reviews arms of privileged men.
18 August	Privileged men, their servants and scholars begin military training.
20 August	Review in New Parks.
22 August	East Bridge fortified; King raises Standard at Nottingham
25 August	Another review in New Parks
28 August	Arrival of Royalist troops under Sir John Byron
1 September	Citizens prevent troops and scholars from demolishing bridge over Osney.
9 September	Dr Pinke arrested in Aylesbury and sent to London.
10 September	Byron leaves Oxford with consignment of University plate to join King.
14 September	Lord Saye arrives in Oxford to take control for Parliament.
15 September	Lord Saye disarms colleges and seizes hidden plate.
16 September	Review of City Trained Band in Brokenhayes.
20 September	Saye and his troopers leave.
22 September	Arrival of Parliamentarian troops from Thame.
23 September	Mutinous behaviour of Parliamentarian troops.
24 September	Lord Saye decides not to garrison Oxford.
27 September	Parliamentarian troops muster in New Parks.
30 September	Fighting amongst Parliamentarian troops in Oxford.
Mid-October	Parliamentarians quit Oxford.
23 October	Battle of Edgehill.
29 October	King enters Oxford.
1 November	Convocation begins conferring degrees on leading Royalists.
3 November	King leaves Oxford at start of advance on London.
4 November	Town disarmed.

5 November	Oxfordshire Trained Bands muster on Bullingdon Green and are disarmed.
13 November	Bonfires and celebrations for Royalist victory at Brentford.
22 November	New fortifications erected at East Bridge.
29 November	King and princes return to Oxford.
5 December	Work commences on defences.
9 December	Prisoners from Marlborough brought in.

1643

1 January	Skirmish at Burford.
3 January	Equipment of Shrewsbury Mint arrives.
10 January	Requisition of College plate.
12 January	Muster of 3,000 foot in New Parks.
13 January	Funeral of Lord D'Aubigny.
1-4 February	Visit of Parliament's Commissioners.
6 February	Arrival of 1,100 prisoners from Cirencester.
13-14 March	Systematic work on fortifications continues.
16 April	Earl of Essex begins siege of Reading.
24 April	King begins attempt relieve Reading; action at Caversham Bridge.
27 April	Reading surrenders.
May	Arrival of first munitions convoy from North of England.
8 June	Essex renews advance on Oxford.
10 June	Essex reaches Thame.
17 June	Bonfires to celebrate Hopton's victory at Stratton.
18 June	Action at Chalgrove.
25 June	Urry's raid on Wycombe
14 July	Queen Henrietta Maria arrives in Oxford.
22 August	Death of Sir William Pennyman
5 September	Royalists abandon siege of Gloucester.
20 September	First Battle of Newbury.
23 September	King returns to Oxford.
3 October	Royalists occupy Reading.
22 December	Sir Arthur Aston wounded in scuffle.

1644

22 January	First meeting of Oxford Parliament.
6 February	Prince Rupert leaves to take up command in Wales and the Marches.
16 April	Oxford Parliament porogued until 8 October.
17 April	Queen leaves Oxford on first stage of journey to the West.

18 May	Royalists quit Reading.
25 May	Royalists abandon Abingdon.
26 May	Waller occupies Abingdon.
27 May-3 June	Fighting around Oxford. King slips out of city.
4 June	King reaches Bourton on the Water.
5 June	King arrives at Evesham.
6 June	King reaches Worcester.
12 June	Gage takes Boarstall House.
29 June	Battle of Cropredy Bridge.
2 July	Royalist defeat at Marston Moor.
5 July	Bonfires lit in Oxford on false report of Royalist victory at Marston Moor.
14 July	King sets off to West in pursuit of Essex.
5 August	Unsuccessful attempt to surprise Abingdon.
3 September	Essex's foot surrender at Lostwithiel.
8 September	Bells and bonfires in Oxford celebrating victory at Lostwithiel.
9-13 September	Gage's relief of Basing House.
19 September	Sir Arthur Aston injured in riding accident.
6 October	Great Fire in Oxford.
27 October	Second Battle of Newbury.
1 November	King arrives in Oxford. Henry Gage knighted.
6 November	Review of Royalist forces on Bullingdon Green. Prince Rupert appointed Lieutenant General.
9-10 November	King retrieves ordnance from Donnington Castle.
19 November	Gage's second relief of Basing Horse.
21 November	Unsuccessful attempt to surprise Abingdon.
23 November	Army goes into winter quarters.
7 December	Aston's leg amputated. Gage becomes Governor, though not officially until 25 December

1645

10 January	Attempt on Abingdon.
11 January	Sir Henry Gage mortally wounded at Culham Bridge.
10 March	Oxford Parliament adjourned until 10 October.
23 April	Cromwell beats up Northampton's brigade at Islip.
24 April	Colonel Windebank surrenders Bletchingdon House to Cromwell.
25 April	Windebank sentenced to death.
27 April	Cromwell defeats Royalist force at Bampton in the Bush; summons Faringdon.
3 May	Windebank executed; Cromwell raises siege of Faringdon.
4 May	Rupert and Maurice reach Oxford.

7 May	King leaves Oxford on summer campaign.
22 May-5 June	Second Siege of Oxford.
7 June	Fairfax repulsed at Boarstall House.
14 June	Battle of Naseby.
28 August	King arrives in Oxford.
30 August	King leaves Oxford for Welsh Marches.
September	Action at Thame.
11 September	Surrender of Bristol.
15 September	Prince Rupert arrives in Oxford.
17 September	Rupert deprived of commission; Legge placed under house arrest.
8 October	Sir Thomas Glemham arrives in Oxford as Governor.
5 November	King arrives in Oxford.
9 November	Legge set at liberty.
9 December	Rupert and Maurice arrive in Oxford.

1646

18 March	Colonel Rainsborough lays siege to Woodstock.
21 March	Battle of Stow-on-the-Wold.
25 April	Prince Rupert's regiments disbanded.
26 April	Woodstock surrenders.
27 April	King leaves Oxford to go to Scots at Newark.
May-June	Siege and surrender of Oxford.

1

The City of Oxford

Situated about 60 miles west of London, in a semi-circle of low hills at the point where the rivers Cherwell and Isis become the Thames, Oxford dates back at least to Saxon times. It was important as a major crossing point of the Thames on an ancient east-west route, with several fords in its vicinity.

The town as we know it had its origins in the 8th century, and within two centuries grew to considerable significance. It was a Saxon "planned" town, as evidenced by the existing street pattern of central Oxford. The town was one of the fortified "burghs" established by the rulers of Wessex as a defence against the Danes, though it is unclear if the popular theory that King Alfred was responsible is correct.

By the early Middle Ages Oxford lay at the centre of a number of major English trade routes. In 1066 it was one of the largest English towns, though for reasons which are not entirely clear Oxford declined for a time after the Norman Conquest. It was burnt during the 12th century civil war between Stephen and Matilda, but recovery was steady, with signs of prosperity including mills of various kinds along the river banks, a growing wool and cloth trade, and an increasing number of monasteries and churches in the town. By the 13th century the university was increasingly influential in Oxford, though friction was to continue for centuries between "town and gown", leading to a succession of violent incidents.

From around this time Oxford was governed by a mayor and town council, with extensive privileges modelled on those of London.

Like all medieval towns and cities, Oxford, though for the most part spared the effects of war, suffered from frequent visitations of the plague and economic fluctuations. The population also varied. In 1377 the town had about 3,000 inhabitants, together with between 1,000-1,500 members of the university.

From the early 16th century onwards, Oxford's prosperity increased steadily. By 1562 it was the eighth largest town in England, and was granted city status in 1542. A rise in municipal confidence was reflected in the provision of some amenities such as piped water to conduits in the town, and one writer remarked "if God himself on Earth abode did make, he Oxford sure would for his dwelling take."[1] In the early 16th century the town itself still had a population of around 3,000. By 1580 this had grown to 5,000, and by 1660 the combined population of town and university would be double that number.[2]

By 1642 there had been much rebuilding in the town, especially by the colleges, but the city streets were generally in bad condition. They were generally narrow and badly paved and drained, and in 1640 the town ditch near to the North Gate was described as being an open sewer.[3] Butchers and other tradespeople dumped offal in the streets, and encroachments built illegally on the frontages of buildings, with overhanging signs and the like, often made the streets difficult to negotiate. There were frequent disputes between university and town regarding the alleged unauthorised building of cottages. The rapid development of the town was changing its nature, and Oxford was much less spacious than had been the case a few decades earlier.

The major expansion of the town was along its northern edge, where it was not restricted by the rivers, and at the same time there were major building projects at many of the colleges. The "poorer sort" often lived in quite squalid conditions, but the merchants, professional classes and other notables had timber-framed houses with the distinguishing feature of a massive stone fireplace, and were often quite grand and ornate.

As befitted a town which was such a bustling centre of trade and lying on several important cross-country routes, Oxford in 1642 had 11 major inns, including the Star, the Mitre and the Golden Cross and many smaller taverns and alehouses.

The poorer quarters, the abode of workers and employees in the various trades and industries of the town, were in the parishes of St Thomas, St Mary Magdalen, St Peter-le-Bailey and St Ebbes, whilst St Aldate's, St Martin's, All Saints St Mary's and St John comprised the more wealthy central area of the town. The university claimed, with some justice, that the prosperity of Oxford depended to a great extent on servicing the needs of the colleges, although this did minimise Oxford's importance as a market centre.

There was some industry in the town, notably the leather and clothing trades, which in the 1620s accounted for about 46% of Oxford's apprentices. Food and drink trades, which tended to be in the hands of the wealthier merchants, were highly dependent upon the custom of the university. By the 1630s the victuallers ranked third in importance to those involved in the leather and clothing trades. There was also significant numbers of cutlers and builders.[4]

---

1   Quoted Chance et al, *A History of the County of Oxford: Volume 4, the City of Oxford* (hereafter referred to as *V.C.H.*) (London, 1979) Volume 4, p.74.
2   Ibid.
3   Ibid., pp.76-78.
4   Ibid., p.80.

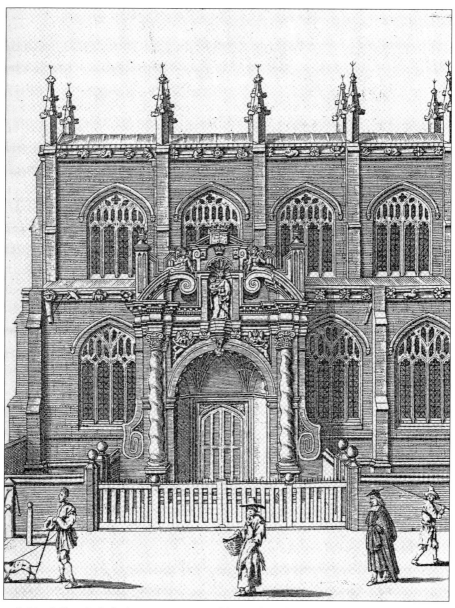

St Mary's Church, Oxford, seen as a centre of the Anglican high church of Archbishop Laud. (Author's collection)

Oxford had close links with London, with extensive commerce between the two cities. From London, often brought by barges along the Thames, favoured over the unreliable roads, came a huge range of goods, including salt fish, spices and other luxuries, and even basics, such as leather goods, which were presumably also produced in Oxford. Cattle were brought into Oxford from as far away as Herefordshire and Wales.

Brewers and maltsters were prominent in the ranks of the town councillors, as were goldsmiths, cutlers, glovers and shoemakers. The senior members of the council were drawn from a narrower, and wealthier, section of Oxford society. They included an overwhelming majority of men engaged in the food and drink and distributive trades.[5] The town council was divided into aldermen, bailiffs, chamberlains and common councillors. There were a group of eight assistants with special powers who with the mayor and aldermen formed an inner council called "The Thirteen", or mayor's council, who did most of the day-to-day running of municipal affairs. Although The Thirteen had the main executive power, the membership of the council increased steadily during the 16th and early 17th centuries to reach over 130 by 1630. The irregular meetings of the full council took place in the council chamber with great ceremony, councillors being expected to wear their robes. This concern for their dignity did not prevent council meetings being frequently stormy, with members, often drunk, evicted for "opprobrious words" and "saucy speeches."[6] The council was most visible to the ordinary citizens at times of great celebration, such as the reception and entertainment of visiting royalty, when it was the practice to fill the Carfax conduit with claret and distribute free beer to the poorer freemen of the town.

Throughout the later 16th and early 17th centuries, disputes between "town and gown" were frequent events. One of the main bones of contention was the status of "privileged persons", those who, whilst not scholars, were matriculated and enjoyed the privileges of the university. This meant that they were exempt from the jurisdiction of the city and could also practice a trade in Oxford without being a freeman. There were numerous complaints that the university had extended "privileged" status to a wide range of college servants and members of trades regarded as being of particular value to the university.

There were other grievances regarding monopoly of the city mills, responsibility for street cleaning and poor relief, the licensing of alehouses. The Privy Council was appealed to on several occasions, but nothing was resolved, whilst a new charter granted to the university in 1636 made matters worse by granting it extensive new powers. The dispute was still before the House of Lords on the outbreak of Civil War.

5   Ibid.
6   Ibid., p.81.

2

War comes to Oxford

Oxford had close links with London, both by road and river. In the 1630s, following many years of conflict with millers who wanted build weirs on the Thames, the river was made navigable with locks at Iffley and Sandford, enabling the first barge from London to reach Oxford in 1635. Unlike the roads, which were frequently almost impassable in bad weather, and with higher transport costs resulting from turnpikes and tolls, the river enabled bulky goods to be moved more easily, and allowed restrictions to be placed on the use of heavy wagons on the roads to London in order to make them more passable for coaches.[1] London could be reached from Oxford on horseback in a day, and by coach in two days, and so its inhabitants were well informed of events in the capital.

Oxford had always had close links with royalty. Woodstock, a few miles west of the city, had been the site of a royal residence and hunting lodge for centuries, and the Manor was described in 1634 as "ancient, large, strong and magnificent, so it was sweet, delightful and sumptuous, and situated on a fair hill." James I however, had found it cramped, damp and over-rural.[2]

Oxford was regularly visited by English monarchs, most recently in August 1636, when King Charles and Queen Henrietta Maria visited the town and University. The visit was described by George Garrard, chaplain to the Earl of Northumberland, in a letter to Viscount Conway.[3] The royal party lodged in Christ Church College, with the main entertainment taking place in the newly constructed long gallery of St John's College, where a banquet was held. A play was presented in Christ Church Hall, described rather sniffily by Garrard as "Fitter for scholars than a court. My Lord Carnarvon flew out against it, said that it was the worst that ever he saw, but One he saw at Cambridge." A convocation was held at which the young Elector Palatine and his brother, Prince Rupert, were admitted as MAs. The King then inspected the gallery at Christ Church "and was loath

---

1   *V.C.H.*, p.75.
2   David Eddershaw, *The Civil War in Oxfordshire* (Stroud, 1995), p.2.
3   A. J. Taylor, 'The Royal Visit to Oxford in 1636' in: *Oxonensia*, Volume I, 1936, pp.151-158.

Woodstock. The manor was fortified as an outlying garrison of Oxford during the war. (Author's collection)

to leave the place" before going on to St John's for another "mighty feast." "I do wonder" observed Garrard "where there could be found mouths to eat it." The food provided included oxen, and 20 "fat sheep, brace of stags, brace of buck," the latter being presented by William Laud, Archbishop of Canterbury, who was Chancellor of the University. Lord Bristol provided the "20 fat sheep" and 20 brace of partridge. Sir Thomas Morven gave "such a Present of fowl as Pay the clerk of the Kitchen told me, he never saw presented to a Prince by any Subject. But the Bishop of Winchester exceeded all, for Venison, fish and fowl, 18 dozen of fat capons." Then there was another play *Love's Hospital* by George Wilde, a Fellow of St John's, though Garrard complained that "The Dialogue is too long."

The royal audience may have been glad to return to Christ Church, for supper, and perhaps less enthusiastically, to see another play. This seems to have been somewhat racier, entitled *The Royal Slave* with the players in Persian dress, and "acted to admiration and generally liked by all the Court." There were hopes that the play would be performed again next day, but unfortunately "there was no audience to be got."[4]

The townspeople have generally been viewed as anti-Royalist during the Civil War, although this attitude has probably been exaggerated. Like the rest of the Kingdom, the majority of the citizens no doubt hoped in the summer of 1642 that the scourge of war would leave them unscathed.

4   Ibid., p.157.

King Charles I
(1600-1649). (Author's collection)

The university was overwhelmingly Royalist in sentiment, though with some reservations. As early as July 1642 the King was requesting money from it. Doctor John Prideaux, the Vice Chancellor, at a convocation persuaded the university to give the King £160 from the University Chest and £500 from the Bodleian Chest. On 24 July Prideaux was replaced as Vice Chancellor by Doctor Robert Pinke, Warden of New College,[5] an enthusiastic Royalist, who, on receipt of the King's declaration of 9 August calling for the suppression of rebellion, began military preparations. This was partly inspired by reports of Parliamentarian troops on their way to secure Banbury and Warwick.

Dr Pinke called a muster of 350 privileged men, their servants and scholars in New College Quadrangle. They were to bring with them any arms and equipment they possessed. Anthony Wood's father had "armour or furniture for one man, viz., a helmet, a back and breast piece a pike, and a musket, and other appurtenances,

---

5   Robert Pinke (1573-1647) – Warden of New College and Vice Chancellor; a supporter of Archbishop Laud.

and the eldest of his menservants ... named Thomas Burnham did appear in those arms, when the scholars and privileged men trained, and when he could not train, as being took up with business the next servant did train, and much ado there was to keep Thomas Wood, the eldest son, then a student at Christ Church, and a youth of about 18 years of age, from putting on the said armour and to train among the scholars."[6]

There was a great deal of fairly disorganised enthusiasm to take up arms amongst the younger members of the University. Dr Pinke himself, despite having no military experience, personally directed drilling in New College Quadrangle. "And it being a novel matter, there was no holding of the school boys in their school, and Mr Wood remembered well that some of them were so besotted with the training and activity and guilty therein of some young scholars, as being in a longing condition to be one of the train, that they could never be brought to their books again ... Mr Wood removed his pupils from the temptations of Oxford, otherwise 'they would be spoiled.'"[7]

On the afternoon of Thursday 18 August, Pinke's motley band was mustered, and marched along High Street to Christ Church College, where they drilled, watched by the King's recently appointed Commissioners of Array, responsible for military recruitment for the Royalist forces. However, between 4:00 p.m. and 5:00 p.m. it began to rain, and enthusiasm dampened, the recruits marched back to the Schools and dispersed.[8] Two days later they mustered again, and marched through the town to New Parks, "where by their commanders, they were divided into four squadrons, whereof two of them were musketeers, the third was a squadron of pikes, the fourth of halberds. And after they had been reasonably instructed in the words of command and their parts, they were put into battle array, and skirmished together in a very decent manner." Training continued until about 2:00 p.m., when the recruits were marched back along the High Street to the Schools and stood down.[9]

At the same time Pinke's followers began to prepare improvised defences. At the East Bridge near Magdalen College a road block of long timber logs was prepared to keep out horsemen, with a wooden gate which could be opened to allow carts and carriages through. Three or four loads of large stones were taken to the top of Magdalen College to be hurled down at any attackers who tried to force the barricade. A hornwork fortification was constructed on the road from New Park near St John's College. Guards were stationed at both places, at night. Two wooden posts were set in the ground at the South Gate for chain to be attached to block the road, and guards were stationed here also.[10]

---

6   Anthony à Wood (ed. Andrew Clark), *The life and times of Anthony Wood, antiquary, of Oxford, 1632-1695, described by himself* (Oxford, 1891), Volume I, pp.52-53.

7   Ibid., p.53.

8   Ibid., pp.54-55.

9   Ibid.

10   Ibid.

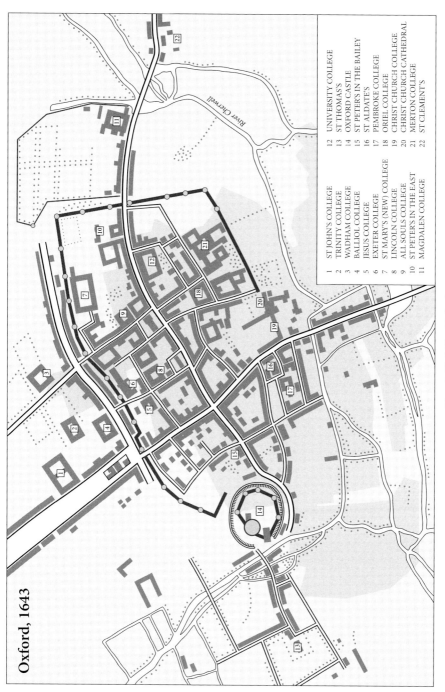

Oxford, 1643

River Cherwell

12	UNIVERSITY COLLEGE
13	ST THOMAS'S
14	OXFORD CASTLE
15	ST PETER'S IN THE BAILEY
16	ST ALDATE'S
17	PEMBROKE COLLEGE
18	ORIEL COLLEGE
19	CHRIST CHURCH COLLEGE
20	CHRIST CHURCH CATHEDRAL
21	MERTON COLLEGE
22	ST CLEMENT'S

1	ST JOHN'S COLLEGE
2	TRINITY COLLEGE
3	WADHAM COLLEGE
4	BALLIOL COLLEGE
5	JESUS COLLEGE
6	EXETER COLLEGE
7	ST MARY'S (NEW) COLLEGE
8	LINCOLN COLLEGE
9	ALL SOULS COLLEGE
10	ST PETER'S IN THE EAST
11	MAGDALEN COLLEGE

Map 1 Civil War Oxford.

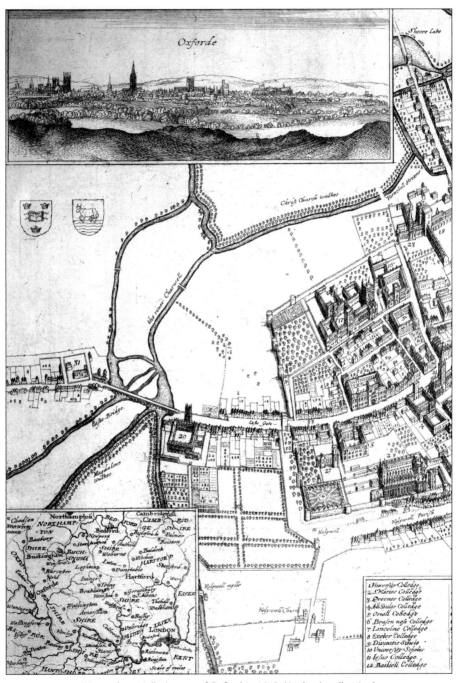

Wenceslaus Hollar's map of Oxford in 1643. (Author's collection)

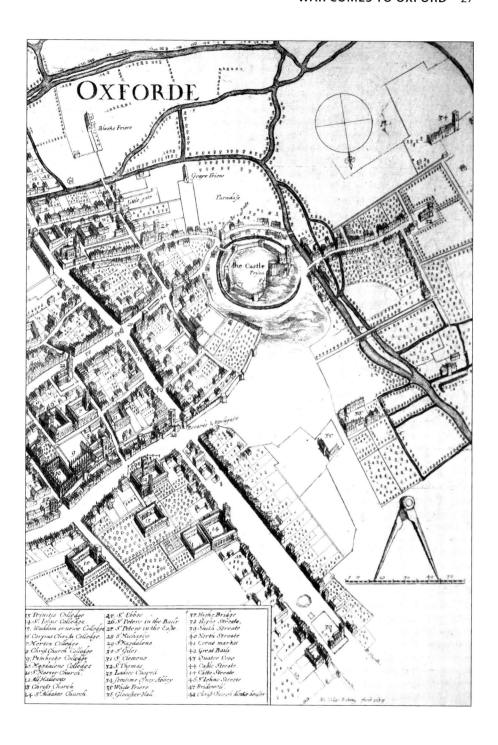

The townspeople were playing little part in all these martial preparations. Wood said that many felt that the town Trained Band should have paraded at the same time as the university force, to demonstrate that the scholars were not using arms and equipment belonging to the town. But apparently, it was said, the Town Council, clinging to hopes of neutrality, forbade the townspeople from training in case it was thought they were acting in support of the King.

The Oxford MPs, John Whistler and John Smith,[11] withdrew[12] to Abingdon, from where they wrote on 3 September to John Lenthall, Speaker of the House of Commons, with news of what was happening in Oxford. On 10 August there had been a meeting in the Star Inn between the King's Commissioners of Array, headed by the Earl of Berkshire, and the officers of the university and the mayor, at which a letter from the King was produced, calling on town and university to set aside their differences in the face of the threat presented by rebellion. A further meeting was held next day, attended by Sir Richard Cave, who was asked to give advice on possible fortifications.[13] He and Dr Pinke spent half an hour discussing "a line with redoubts and a foot pace, on the north side of the town from the Cherwell to the Thames, for that they would leave out no colleges …"[14]

> Then we asked them in what time that would be done, Sir Richard Cave said presently, for that everyone would work having his portion of ground allotted him. We told him we had not shovels for 40 persons. Then we asked what the charge of such a work would be. Sir Richard he knew not that, but asked the stranger that was brought, who desired time to consider of it. Then we asked them how many men would man this work. Sir Richard Cave said 1,000. We told them, the work being a mile in length at the least, we conceived many 1,000 men would not do it, and that we had not arms for above 100 men, and told them plainly we did not like the business, and thought it would draw enemies upon us, and make it the seat of a war, so nothing at that time was concluded, but that we would join with them for the keeping of a diligent watch both by night and day. That night Mr Whistler's windows were broken, and it was generally given out that he should be mischiefed for speaking against their fortification.[15]

There was a further acrimonious meeting between Dr Pinke and the two MPs on 23 August, in which the MPs demanded to be fully involved in consultations, and complained that the town constables were being "threatened and beaten, and

11   Ibid., p.56.
12   V.C.H., p.177.
13   H.M.C. Portland MSS, I, p.163.
14   Ibid.
15   Ibid.

other civilians abused" by the university levies. They also accused the university authorities of planning to bring in Royalist troops and were further incensed by the rudimentary defences which had been built, they claimed, without the agreement of the city council.[16]

On 28 August there were dramatic new developments when 150-200 cavalry troopers came riding wearily into town along the Brackley road. They were the Royalist regiment of horse of Sir John Byron. Byron, until recently Lieutenant of the Tower of London, was a Nottinghamshire man, eldest of seven brothers, all of whom would fight for the King in the Civil War.[17] His Regiment had been the first cavalry unit to be completed for the King's army, and Byron had been sent to secure financial contributions in the Midlands for the Royalist cause. He had just been worsted in a skirmish with Parliamentarian troops near Brackley, losing several men and the contributions he had so far collected, as some of his men, now prisoners in Northampton gaol, related:

> On the 27th of August last Sir John Byron's troop with two of his brothers' troops marched from Leicester and marched all night and all the next day till 4:00 p.m. without any injury committed to any man by us till we came to Brackley and there we were to be quartered four hours, but before we could get meat for ourselves or our horses, being almost all tired out by the long march, there was of a sudden a sound 'To horse', and our enemies coming so fierce on us before we could get horse [sic] that after a little scrimmage being but three hurt of our side [we] was forced by the command of our captains to fly every man for his safety, and the country had got such force and strength of a sudden that separated us into several parts that before 8 o'clock next morning there was 44 of us taken, our captains and officers being fled towards Oxford, and so taken prisoners, our horses, swords, money and all our arms and other materials taken from us and so brought prisoners pinioned as traitors to the state to this lamentable place of prison. The Committee of Northampton allow us 6d a day, but the gaoler is so hard that he constrains us to pay 4d a day every night for our bed, so that we are almost starved for want of maintenance. We entreat your Lordship to make this our petition known to the King, and to our Colonel Sir John Byron, hoping that we shall have some relief or order taken for our liberty out of this woeful place of prison.[18]

16 Ibid., p.164.
17 Byron was an excellent cavalry commander, though he had mixed success in higher command. See article in D.N.B.
18 Portland MSS I, p.173.

Sir John (later Lord) Byron (c.1599-1652). A capable cavalry commander, Byron would have a chequered career in higher command, though he was scapegoated by Prince Rupert for the Royalist defeat at Marston Moor. (Author's collection)

In these relatively innocent opening days of the war, Byron even wrote indignantly to one of the Northamptonshire Parliamentarian leaders demanding the return of his belongings and money! He hoped to compensate for his loss in Oxford. Byron's approaching horsemen caused initial alarm in the town:

> ... being discovered by the watch or sentinel of scholars that lay abroad that night, and their sudden coming at that time of night, put both the University and Town in great fright, until it was known whose part they came in.[19]

The immediate consequence was that a number of suspected Parliamentarian sympathisers, including Alderman John Nixon[20] and the two town MPs, decamped hastily to Aylesbury. On the following afternoon, Dr Pinke with some

19   Wood, pp. 56-57.
20   *V.C.H.*, p.177.

other Royalist supporters held a meeting to confer with Byron at the Schools, and that night both troopers and scholars shared guard duties.

Whistler and Smith gave distinctly unfavourable accounts of the impact of Byron and his men:

> On Sunday last about 12:00 a.m. at this redoubt they [the guards] let in a troop of horse and at Smithgate the entrance into Cat Street they came suddenly upon the Watch, which, albeit were not very strong, it stayed them for a good space, until some part of the City were armed, but having so great a number before them, and the Vice Chancellor and his company being ready behind them, the Vice Chancellor commanded the watch to let them in, and bid the Cavaliers 'Welcome Gentlemen', and said they were their friends and he, with Doctor Bailey and others, did conduct them to their inns, and caused the inns to open their gates and entertained them. How they have broken up houses and pillaged citizens and others we doubt not you have sufficiently heard already.[21]

The MPs claimed that if a report of Byron's approach to Oxford had not been kept from them, they might:

> have prevented the disaster, for that the number was not – or we conceive – 200 whereof not above 160 some soldiers and the rest grooms and guides, and the most of those ragged starved companions, having lost their arms in their flight from Brackley, and their horses tired and spent with hunger and travel. Their behaviour hath been so injurious that many that stood indifferent before or were seduced by the persuasion of some scholars do now detest them, in so much as some of them attempting to pull down the bridge going to Botley called Bullstake bridge, the citizens did arm themselves and drove them away, and had the Mayor done his duty by all likelihood they might have driven them out of the town.[22]

According to Anthony Wood, after wet weather had prevented any activity on 30 August on 1 September troopers and scholars attempted to remove an arch on Osney Bridge on the Botley road, intending to replace it with a wooden drawbridge, but the town's Trained Band appeared. About 4-500 of them had mustered that day in Brokenhayes, and some were sent to prevent the demolition "on pretence that would hinder the passage of supplies." The work was abandoned after a stand-off.[23]

---

21   Portland MSS I, p.175.
22   Ibid.
23   Wood, pp.57-58.

In the afternoon two letters from the King were read to the University Convocation, in which he thanked the university for the loan of money, and stated that Byron had been sent to defend the town. A council of war was set up to oversee the defence of Oxford, and Byron's officers reviewed the scholars in New Park. Next day, in a rather desperate move, the scholars were issued with 100 bows and "barbed arrows to shoot against the [Parliamentarian] troops if they should come."[24]

On 5 September, writing from Abingdon, Whistler and Smith informed the Speaker that:

> Many motions have been made and earnestly pressed for training the citizens with the scholars which as yet hath not been agreed on. Yesterday there came in a load of arms unto the Cross Inn; some say from my Lord of Darby, some say from Sir William Waller, the truth whereof we yet know not. The scholars generally feed themselves an expectation of Prince Rupert's coming to their aid with a great army. Our Mayor's weakness we can neither defend nor excuse, which is a great part of our present misery. One of our Bailiffs – the honester man- is much distempered.[25]

The Mayor, Leonard Bowman, was, of course, in an impossible position. His aim was to minimise the impact of the looming war on Oxford, and any attempt to disarm the scholars and Byron's men would plunge the town into open conflict. By now the tide of events was turning against the Royalist faction in Oxford. On 9 September the University was informed that the town council had told Parliament that its sympathies lay with them, and that Parliament was proposing to send troops to Oxford. The university authorities, seeing themselves to be increasingly isolated, sought ways to persuade Byron and his men to leave, and sent representatives including Dr Pinke to Aylesbury to see the Oxford MPs. Pinke was promptly detained as a "delinquent" (a supporter of the King) and sent under guard to London.

On the afternoon of 10 September, realising that his position in Oxford was untenable, Sir John Byron and his men took the road west out of Oxford, heading for the Welsh border to join the King. With them went a number of scholars, including Doctor Peter Turner of Merton, Doctor John Nurse of Magdalen and Doctor Thomas Rede of New College. Doctor Nurse was killed in October at the Battle of Edgehill. Also accompanying Byron was a large consignment of university plate.

Byron had a difficult journey across the Cotswolds. At Stow-on-the-Wold he was attacked by Parliamentarian supporters, and Doctor Turner's brief military career ended with his capture and despatch to join Byron's other men in Northampton gaol. Eventually Byron reached Worcester where he was reinforced by Prince Rupert. After defeating a Parliamentarian force outside the town on 23 September

24   Ibid., p.58.
25   Portland MSS I, p.185.

at Powicke Bridge, Rupert conducted Byron and his convoy to join the King at Shrewsbury.

Meanwhile Oxford apprehensively awaited the advent of Parliament's forces. At 10:00 a.m. on 12 September, Colonel Arthur Goodwin, at the head of a large force of Parliamentarian troopers from Aylesbury, arrived. Goodwin took up his quarters in Merton College, with his men billeted in the town and the surrounding villages. On the following afternoon Goodwin mustered his soldiers in Christ Church Meadow, and turned their horses loose to graze there. "Many of [the troopers] came into Christ Church to view the church and painted windows much admiring of the idolatry thereof, and a certain Scot being amongst them, said that "he marvelled how the scholars could go to their books for these painted idolatrous windows," but surprisingly, no damage was done, possibly because many of the Parliamentarian soldiers came from neighbouring areas.[26]

Between 4:00 p.m. and 5:00 p.m. more troops escorted into town Lord Saye,[27] riding in his coach and six. Saye was Parliament's newly-appointed Lord Lieutenant of Oxfordshire, and an energetic opponent of the King. He ordered the scanty Royalist-built defences to be demolished, and late in the night he and his guards, with the light of burning torches, began searching the colleges for arms. A quantity were found over the next two days, and taken by wagon under armed guard to Saye's lodgings at the Star. On the same night a quantity of concealed college plate was discovered at Christ Church, hidden behind some wainscoting. It was confiscated and taken away to the Star in a large wooden tub carried on a pole. The homes of a number of prominent Royalists were also searched.

On Friday 16 September presumably to overawe potential opponents, the troops were mustered again in Brokenhayes. Mr Humphrey Lloyd, a Fellow of Oriel, was imprisoned for a time in the Star for uttering words to the effect that "if he were able, he would rather lend the King a thousand pounds than one penny to Parliament." Three members of Christ Church were arrested for similar comments and for taking part in the training of the scholars.[28] Next day there was a potentially ugly incident when a musket shot fired from a baker's shop hit a woman in the leg. Three scholars were imprisoned on suspicion of trying to shoot a Parliamentarian captain who was lodging nearby.[29]

Saye was still trying to impose his puritan views, and on 19 September he ordered the burning outside the Star of "divers Popish books and pictures" he had found.[30] There were also attempts made to establish Parliamentarian control of the town council, although the councillors, jealous of their privileges, proved

26 Wood, p.60.
27 William Fiennes, 1st Lord Saye and Sele (1582-1662) – Puritan and leading opponent in Parliament of King Charles during the "Personal Rule".
28 Wood, p.62.
29 Ibid.
30 Ibid., p.63.

William Fiennes, 1st Lord Saye (1582-1662), a leading opponent of Charles I during the years of 'Personal Rule', and a Puritan, nicknamed 'old Subtlety' in reference to his political manoeuvrings. (Author's collection)

uncooperative. They declined a proposal by Saye that MP John Nixon should be elected Mayor, on the grounds that he had abandoned the town and gone to Abingdon during the Royalist occupation, and instead chose Thomas Dennis, a mercer, as "they would have a mayor that should not fly out of the town if occasion served."[31]

Some of the Parliamentarian troops in Oxford were from London, and more politically and religiously radical than the local men apparently were. On 20 September, despite, or perhaps because of, being presented with wine by the outgoing mayor, Leonard Bowman, they declared themselves discontented with the reception they had received in Oxford, and one of them fired a brace of pistols at the image of the Virgin Mary over the porch of St Mary's Church, striking off the heads of her and her child. Another soldier fired at Christ's image over the gate of All Souls College, but was persuaded to desist by John Nixon and some of the townspeople.[32]

On Thursday 22 September, a regiment of Bluecoats, around 450-strong, from London and its surrounding area arrived, "commanders most of them very likely

31   Ibid.
32   Ibid.

and proper men, but most of the company very young and but meanly apparelled and very unexpert in their arms." They were paraded in New Park "where they appeared very intractable and undocile and mutinous, demanding 5/- a month in addition to daily pay and would do no more" until Saye was able to pacify them and imprisoned some.[33]

Saye took a party of troops to search Dr Pinke's study for evidence of his Royalist sympathies, and one of the soldiers smashed a portrait of the King "for which my lord was much displeased."[34] Next day (24 September), Lord Saye called a meeting of the heads of colleges, reprimanding them for taking up arms and "unless they could assure him of the quiet and peace of the university for the time to come he was minded to place a garrison of soldiers here to [overawe] both the university and the town." A long argumentative discussion followed without a decision being reached. Saye was in fact in no position to do very much, because he was fast losing control over the mutinous troops, and retired to his own home at Broughton Castle, near Banbury, to consider the situation.[35]

On 26 September the Bluecoats "very unwillingly it seems" were persuaded to return to duty. Troops were continuing to march into Oxford as part of the army being formed under the Earl of Essex. On 27 September Lord Brooke's and Lord Grantham's regiments arrived: "there were eight or 10 ancients [flags] of them of a purple colour and seven stars in the field." By nightfall there were about 3,000 troops in the town, and next day, apparently amidst the rising discontent of the inhabitants, more soldiers marched through Oxford.[36]

There were more incidents of indiscipline. On the afternoon of 30 September some "of the soldiers fell out amongst themselves, and fought with their naked swords, one with another in the High Street at Carfax and about the Star, some their thumbs cut off and some their fingers. The quarrel arose amongst some of them being in drink, and calling out words to this purpose that when they came to fight, if it were against the King, they would take his part rather than fight against him. The quarrel was between the blue coats and russet coats and their captains."[37] Next day the Bluecoats marched out towards Woodstock, but the Russet coats stayed in Oxford until the next day to avoid further fighting.[38]

At about noon on the 30th the Russet coats also left "but many both of the blue and russet coats were missing at the time of their departure, the captains and constables going up and down the town to seek them, many of them having flung away their arms, and run away."[39]

---

33 Ibid., p.64.
34 Ibid.
35 Ibid., pp.64-65.
36 Ibid., p.66.
37 Ibid., p.67.
38 Ibid.
39 Ibid.

Other detachments of troops passed through the town during the next few days, but the bulk of Essex's forces were now concentrated in the Worcester area.

With the departure of the Parliamentarian troops, and the University disarmed, or at any rate keeping a low profile, the townsmen now began fortifying the entrances to Oxford with posts and chains, supposedly to keep out the Royalists.

But the opposing armies were now in the field, and on 23 October met in battle at Edgehill in Warwickshire. It was not the decisive battle which many on both sides had expected and hoped for. The Royalists had the best of an indecisive though bloody engagement, and Essex withdrew to Warwick, leaving the road to London via Oxford temporarily open to the King. Sending a detachment of troops to take Banbury, from whence Lord Saye had departed, King Charles himself, accompanied by his sons, entered Oxford on horseback by the North Gate on 29 October. They lodged at Christ Church, and 60 or 70 colours allegedly captured at Edgehill were paraded through the streets to impress the townspeople. The Royalist artillery train was parked in Magdalen Grove. The King was entertained by Doctor Richard Gardiner, the prebend of Christ Church.[40]

Oxford was only a staging post in the advance on London, but from early November some of the King's courtiers and officials began to move and take up what they expected to be temporary lodgings. Lord Colepeper, Master of the Rolls, took over Anthony Wood's house opposite Merton College, and the Wood family had to move to a smaller house behind it.[41]

On 1 November as University Convocation was held at which Charles, Prince of Wales and James, Duke of York were awarded honorary MAs.

The royal stay in Oxford was brief. Two days later the King and his army marched out on the next stage of their advance on London. Left behind was a small force of horse and dragoons, (possibly Lord Andover's or Lord Digby's Regiments). As a precaution the Trained Band munitions, a cartload of gunpowder and another of match, were lodged in the top floor room of the Schools Tower.[42]

On 5 November the Oxfordshire County Trained Bands paraded on Bullingdon Green before the Commissioners of Array and told that either they enlisted with the Royalist forces or be disarmed. Unsurprisingly, they chose the latter option, and their weapons were taken for storage to Christ Church.[43]

Many still believed that the King's advance on London would result in a speedy resolution to the war. Hopes of this were raised by news of Prince Rupert's victory at Brentford which arrived on 13 November. Bells were rung and celebratory bonfires lit. However, the advance on London had ended in stalemate at Turnham Green, on the outskirts of the capital, with the Royalists unwilling and unable to

---

40   Ibid., p.68.
41   Ibid., p.69.
42   Ibid.
43   Ibid., pp.70-71.

Cavalry. (© Estate of Stephen Beck)

risk an attack on Essex's strongly-positioned men. The Royalists gradually pulled back, initially to Windsor, whilst in Oxford on 22 November a herd of "fat great oxen," requisitioned in the Buckinghamshire countryside were driven through the streets by Royalist cavalry, and penned in Christ Church Quadrangle. However they were then discovered to belong to the Royalist Earl of Carnarvon, and had to be rather shamefacedly returned to him, apart from a few which were described as having "strayed"! A few days later another herd of cattle and 300 sheep were brought in.[44]

44   Ibid., p.71.

Work on fortifications had also begun. Young Anthony Wood went to see the laying of the foundations of a new timberwork gate against Magdalen Bridge, and work began on a new earth rampart from the Bridge to the corner of the physic garden, where guns could be mounted to cover the approaches to the bridge.[45]

On 29 November King Charles re-entered Oxford, riding over Magdalen Bridge in a coach with the young Duke of York, newly recovering from an attack of the measles. With them was with Prince Rupert, who with his brother Prince Maurice took up quarters in the house of Timothy Carter, the Town Clerk. The King and Prince lodged at Christ Church College.[46]

Oxford's role as "Royalist capital" had begun.

45   Ibid., p.72.
46   Ibid.

3

Royalist Capital

For the inhabitants of Oxford, Christmastide 1642 was the climax of a tumultuous year. The establishment of Oxford as the King's headquarters and *de facto* capital brought with it an influx of more than 3,000 newcomers of all kinds.[1] There were soldiers, of course, swaggering and brawling in the taverns and streets, but also a varied array of civilians of many kinds. Courtiers, officials, wives and children, ladies of more dubious trades, craftsmen, musicians, clergy and artists, and all the numerous servants of the royal household were arriving in Oxford, and had to be found accommodation. Among them were many families of Royalist supporters, fleeing from Parliamentarian territory. One of them was a London girl, Lady Anne Fanshawe, who left a vivid account of her experiences:

> 1642 my father was taken prisoner at his house, called Montague House, in Bishopgate Street, and threatened to be sent on board a ship with many more of his quality, and then they plundered his house, but he getting loose, under pretence to fetch some writings they demanded in his hands concerning the public revenue, he went to Oxford in 1643, and thereupon the Long Parliament, of which he was a member for the town of Lancaster, plundered him out of what remained, and sequestered his whole estate, which continued out of his possession until the happy restoration of the King.
>
> My father commanded my sister and myself to come to him to Oxford where the Court then was, but we, that had till that hour lived in great plenty and great order, found ourselves like fishes out of the water, and the scene was so changed, that we knew not at all how to act any part but obedience, for, from as good a house as any gentleman of England had, we came to a baker's house in an obscure street, and from rooms well furnished, to lie in a very bad bed in a garret, to one dish of meat, and that not the best ordered, no money, for we were as poor as Job,

1   *V.C.H.*, p.181.

nor clothes more than a man or two brought in their cloak bags: we had the perpetual discourse of losing and gaining towns and men; at the windows the sad spectacle of war, sometimes plague, sometimes sicknesses of other kind, by reason of so many people being packed together, as, I believe, there never was before of that quality; always in want, yet I must needs say that most bore it with a martyr-like cheerfulness. For my own part, I began to think we should all, like Abraham, live in tents all the days of our lives. The King sent my father a warrant for a baronet, but he returned it with thanks, saying he had too much honour of his knighthood which his Majesty had honoured him with some years before, for the fortune he now possessed: but as in a rock the turbulence of the waves disperses the splinters of the rock, so it was my lot, for having buried my dear brother, William Harrison, in Exeter College Chapel, I then married your dear father in 1644 in Wolvercote Church, two miles from Oxford, upon the 18th day of May. None was at our wedding but my dear father, who, at my mother's desire, gave me her wedding-ring, with which I was married, and my sister Margaret, and my brother and sister Boteler, Sir Edward Hyde, afterwards Lord Chancellor, and Sir Geoffrey Palmer, the King's Attorney. Before I was married, my husband was sworn Secretary of War to the Prince, now our King, with a promise from Charles I to be preferred as soon as occasion offered it, but both his fortune and my promised portion, which was made 10,000 pounds, were both at that time in expectation, and we might truly be called merchant adventurers, for the stock we set up our trading with did not amount to 20 pounds betwixt us; but, however, it was to us as a little piece of armour is against a bullet, which if it be right placed, though no bigger than a shilling, serves as well as a whole suit of armour; so our stock bought pen, ink and paper, which was your father's trade, and by it, I assure you, we lived better than those that were born to 2,000 pounds a year as long as he had his liberty. Here stay till I have told you your father's life until I married him.

Now we appear on the stage, to act what part God designed us; and as faith is the evidence of things not seen, so we, upon so righteous a cause, cheerfully resolved to suffer what that would drive us to, which afflictions were neither few nor small, as you will find. This year the Prince had an established Council, which were the Earl of Berkshire, Earl of Bradford, Lord Capel, Lord Colepeper, Lord Hopton, and Sir Edward Hyde, Chancellor of the Exchequer. My husband was then, as I said, newly entered into his office of secretary of the Council of War, and the King would have had him then to have been sworn his Highness's Secretary, but the Queen, who was then no friend to my husband, because he had formerly made Secretary Windebank appear in his colours, who was one of her Majesty's favourites, wholly obstructed that then, and, placed with

Lady Anne Fanshawe (1625-80), later noted as a traveller
and writer. (Author's collection)

the Prince, Sir Robert Long, for whom she had a great kindness; but the
consequence will show the man.

The beginning of March 1645, your father went to Bristol with his
new master, and this was his first journey: I then lying-in of my first son,
Harrison Fanshawe, who was born on the 22nd of February, he left me
behind him. As for that, it was the first time we had parted a day since
we married; he was extremely afflicted, even to tears, though passion
was against his nature; but the sense of leaving me with a dying child,
which did die two days after, in a garrison town, extremely weak, and
very poor, were such circumstances as he could not bear with, only the
argument of necessity; and, for my own part, it cost me so dear, that I
was ten weeks before I could go alone; but he, by all opportunities, wrote
to me to fortify myself, and to comfort me in the company of my father
and sister, who were both with me, and that as soon as the Lords of the
Council had their wives come to them I should come to him, and that I
should receive the first money he got, and hoped it would be suddenly. By
the help of God, with these cordials I recovered my former strength by
little and little, nor did I in my distressed condition lack the conversation

of many of my relations then in Oxford, and kindnesses of very many of the nobility and gentry, both for goodness sake, and because your father being there in good employment, they found him serviceable to themselves or friends, which friendships none better distinguished between his place and person than your father.

It was in May 1645, the first time I went out of my chamber and to church, where, after service, Sir William Parkhurst, a very honest gentleman, came to me, and said he had a letter for me from your father and 50 pieces of gold, and was coming to bring them to me. I opened first my letter, and read those inexpressible joys that almost overcame me, for he told me I should the Thursday following come to him, and to that purpose he had sent me that money, and would send two of his men with horses, and all accommodation both for myself, my father, and sister, and that Lady Capell and Lady Bradford would meet me on the way; but that gold your father sent me when I was ready to perish, did not so much revive me as his summons. I went immediately to walk, or at least to sit in the air, being very weak, in the garden of St. John's College, and there, with my good father, communicated my joy, who took great pleasure to hear of my husband's good success and likewise of his journey to him. We, all of my household being present, heard drums beat in the highway, under the garden wall. My father asked me if I would go up upon the mount to see the soldiers march, for it was Sir Charles Lee's company of foot, an acquaintance of ours; I said yes, and went up, leaning my back to a tree that grew on the mount. The commander seeing us there, in compliment gave us a volley of shot, and one of their muskets being loaded, shot a brace of bullets not two inches above my head as I leaned to the tree, for which mercy and deliverance I praise God. And next week we were all on our journey for Bristol very merry, and thought that now all things would mend, and the worst of my misfortunes past, but little thought I to leap into the sea that would toss me until it had racked me; but we were to ride all night by agreement, for fear of the enemy surprising us as they passed, they quartering in the way. About nightfall having travelled about 20 miles, we discovered a troop of horse coming towards us, which proved to be Sir Marmaduke Rawdon, a worthy commander and my countryman: he told me, that hearing I was to pass by his garrison, he was come out to conduct me, he hoped as far as was danger, which was about 12 miles: with many thanks we parted, and having refreshed ourselves and horses, we set forth for Bristol, where we arrived on the 20th of May.[2]

2   Lady Anne Fanshawe, *Memoirs of Lady Fanshawe, wife of Sir Richard Fanshawe, Bart., Ambassador* (London: Forgotten Books, 2012), pp.12-18.

Lady Anne, with many of the courtiers, met and flirted in New College Grove, to the considerable annoyance of Dr Ralph Fell, President of Trinity College, and Anne, with her friend, Lady Isabella Thynne, would attend chapel there, "half-dressed like angels." On another occasion, the two ladies began to tease Dr Fell, who remarked caustically to Anne Fanshawe "Madam, your husband and father I bred up here, and I knew your grandfather; I know you to be a gentlewoman, I will not say you are a whore, but got you gone for a very woman!"

On 4 December 1642 all the horses in Oxford, apart from those belonging to cavalry troopers in the town, were ordered to be taken to St Giles field "there to be taken view of" and 300 were requisitioned for the use of the cavalry and dragoons. Next day, in what was to become a familiar sight to those in Oxford, Prince Rupert rode out with a large party of horse and dragoons in a probe towards Thame.[3]

The immediate concern of the Royalist authorities was to re-fortify Oxford, and on 5 December the bellman of the university was sent out to summon the "privileged" and their families to work next day on the New Park defences. The King rode out in the afternoon to inspect the progress of the work. It had been ordered that 122 of the townsmen should work on the section of the planned defences north of St Giles, but to his annoyance Charles found only 12 men present.[1]

On 9 December there was great excitement, when, following the capture of Marlborough by Lord Wilmot on the previous day, the Parliamentarians taken prisoner there were marched into Oxford "bound and led with matches, whereat there was much hooting."[5] Some of the prisoners were put to work on the defences, or incarcerated in Oxford Castle. Troops came and went constantly. Even on Christmas Day, Anthony Wood noted: "more dragoons despatched out of Oxford, but whither I cannot yet learn."[6]

There were less martial activities also. On the 29th the King and Prince Rupert were playing tennis "at Mr Edwards' tennis court" when Parliamentarian trumpeters arrived asking for a safe-conduct for envoys from Parliament.[7] On Monday 2 January two coaches arrived from London carrying six commissioners from Parliament. There was concern that they might be attacked by enthusiastic Royalist supporters among the scholars, so for security the commissioners were lodged at the Fleurs de Lys Inn, where they could be guarded. It was recounted with relish that as their coaches approached Magdalen Bridge, one of the commissioners threw a coin to the sentries there, "who flung it back to them into the Coach again, saying that their master the King paid them their wages, and that

3   Wood, op. cit, p.75.
4   Ibid., p.72.
5   Ibid., p.73.
6   Ibid., p.72.
7   Ibid., p.75.

they scorned their money, calling them Roundheads, for which (as they say) the King sent them five piece."[8]

Parliamentarian accounts complained of the generally hostile reception the Commissioners received, with stones and dirt thrown at their carriages as they passed and Bulstrode Whitelocke describes their accommodation as being "little above an ale house" where their servants were not even allowed near the inn fire. However the commissioners seem to have been treated correctly in official circles. Wood alleged that the commissioners believed that there were severe food shortages in Oxford, and so brought with them their own supplies of food such as poultry and wine. Finding that provisions were actually plentiful, the commissioners' servants sold their emergency rations![9] This was the first of a regular succession of delegations and foreign envoys to arrive in Oxford, and like virtually all of them without any result other than to provide a diversion for the inhabitants.

Royalist victories, real and sometimes imaginary or premature (as was the case with the first reports of Rupert's success at Marston Moor in July 1644) were celebrated with the ringing of church and college bells bonfires and the discharge of cannon. One such occasion was on 3 February 1643 following news of Prince Rupert's capture of Cirencester. The prisoners taken at Cirencester arrived in Oxford at around 11:00 a.m. on 6 February, and with about a dozen captured colours were marched into the town through St Giles:

> His majesty having been abroad all that afternoon as far as Wolvercote, viewed them as they came in, most of them being able and lusty fellows. For the night most of them were lodged in St Giles' Church and Magdalen parish church, from whence they were afterwards dispersed some to the Castle, some to other places etc. And then some of the properist fellows of them, after they had taken the new protestation appointed for his Majesty were new apparelled and took into service for His Majesty and most of them dispersed up and down into other regiments, as occasion served.[10]

Joining the Royalist army was certainly a tempting alternative to remaining a prisoner. Those incarcerated in Oxford Castle were allegedly treated particularly badly. This was reported to be especially the case under the custody of the first Royalist Provost-Marshal, Captain William Smith, and during their visit early in 1643, the Parliamentarian commissioners were permitted to visit the Castle and speak to some of the prisoners, although only in the presence of Captain Smith. The complaints of the prisoners were considered by the House of Commons on 13 May 1643. The main allegations made concerned violence, extortion, shortage of

8   Ibid., pp.79-80.
9   Ibid.
10   Ibid., p.88.

Oxford Castle. (Author's collection)

food and drink and surgeons for the sick and wounded. Shortages of beds meant that many prisoners were "lodged in heaps not only upon the ground, upon bare boards, but in loathsome and filthy dungeons."[11]

Parliament threatened retaliation against Royalist prisoners in their hands. In fact it seems likely that most of the failings were the result of shortages and administrative inefficiency rather than deliberate acts of cruelty. Captain Smith himself presented a petition to the King, complaining of neglect. He was not given the necessary guards and gaolers, he had to work single-handed without a deputy, and had himself received no pay for eight months. It does appear that conditions for the prisoners gradually improved, although resources for their upkeep was supplemented on at least one occasion (18 April 1644) by a special collection in London churches for the "poor soldiers imprisoned in Oxford."[12] Some Parliamentarian officers, such as Edmund Ludlow, were allowed to lodge in the town on giving their parole. Oxford Castle was also the place where Royalists convicted of a crime or sentenced to death by court martial, were incarcerated prior to their execution.

As it became evident that Oxford would be the King's headquarters for some time to come, the whole range of court and administrative functions began to be

11   Quoted in F.J. Varley, *The Siege of Oxford: An account of Oxford during the Civil War, 1642-1646* (Oxford, 1932), p.90.
12   Ibid., p.91.

set up. The main advantage of Oxford was that the colleges and halls of the university provided lodgings for the influx of courtiers and officials. But so many arrived, in some cases refugees from Parliamentarian-held areas, that already by early 1643 shortages of accommodation were becoming acute. On 20 January the King issued a proclamation ordering that:

> … all persons having rooms to report number – beds- and persons entertained – their names and qualities.
> All so lodged to report their names and business.
> Refusal to answer to be punished.
> Persons without justification for staying to be driven out in 24 hours.
> Women and children to be especially considered.
> Those with houses in the country to go to them.
> Visitors to report to the Governor.[13]

In practice such restrictions proved almost impossible to enforce. Further proclamations ordering the departure of unauthorised persons were issued in October 1643, and before the first session of the Oxford Parliament in January 1644.

Although the King's court was considerably reduced in size and splendour from its pre-war days, Charles maintained a good deal of the ceremonial. He still dined in state in the Hall of Christ Church College, attended services in the cathedral, and on one occasion at least, in March 1643, distributed the Maundy Money to the poor. The need for the King to be frequently visible to his subjects, and accessible to some, led to concerns about his personal security and early in 1643 to measures being taken to safeguard his person, as described in the issue of *Mercurius Aulicus* of 26 January fearing that "some desperate design might be in hand against his Majesty's person" the Privy Council issued orders to prevent "mean and unknown persons" having access to the King. It was commanded that:

1. Two of the Yeomen of the Guard should be perpetually attending at the bottom of the stairs, going up into the Presence and Privy Chamber, and suffer no unknown or mean person to pass by them.
2. That one of the Gentlemen Ushers quarter waiters, should be continually attending at the door of the presence and Privy Chamber, to keep out all such mean and unknown persons, as possibly might pass by the Guard without observation.
3. That one of the Gentlemen Ushers daily waiters should attend always at the door of the Presence and privy Chamber, going into the withdrawing room, and suffer none to go into the same but the Nobility,

---

13   Ibid., p.57.

Privy Councillors, Bishops, Judges, and the Commissioners for the Council of war.

4.   That two of the Pages of the Bed-Chamber should always wait at the bottom of the back-stairs, and permit none but those before remembered, and the Bed-Chamber men, to go that way.

5.   That four of the Gentlemen of His Majesty's Troop, appointed by their Captain, should be continually near His Majesty's person in the Presence and Privy Chamber, to keep all unknown and mean persons from approaching too nigh his Sacred Majesty.

6.   That as often as His Majesty did ride abroad, the Captain of His Majesty's Guard, and the Lieutenant of his Pensioners, with four of the Gentlemen Pensioners, should ride continually near His Majesty's Person, and suffer none of mean condition, or unknown to them, to come near His Majesty.

7.   That when His Majesty was pleased to walk in his Privy Gardens, two of the Yeomen of the Guard should keep the doors, and suffer none to come to it, but men of quality, and such as were well known to them.[14]

The surviving lists of those resident in St Aldate's parish, where many of the royal household servants lodged, gives a good idea of the variety of roles to be found. Among them were bakers, the King's surgeon, Michael Andrewes, his tailor, his barber, his apothecary, Johann Wolfgang Rumler a German from Augsberg, a coal carrier and a poultrer.[15]

The love of culture and the arts which had been a feature of the peacetime court were much diminished, though not entirely abandoned. Present in Oxford throughout the war was William Dobson, "the most excellent painter that England hath yet seen."[16] Born in Holburn, London, in 1611, Dobson's father was possibly a minor legal official. William Dobson began his career as an apprentice to William Peake, a dealer in pictures, and later studied under the German artist Francis Cleyn in Covent Garden. Dobson set up independently around 1640, and, not having enjoyed much success chose to follow the royal Court to Oxford. Here he found ready recipients for his work, and may have been appointed Sergeant Painter and a Groom of the Privy Chamber. He was working in Oxford by March 1643 at the latest, and made an immediate impression in court circles with his dramatic portrait of Sir John Byron, complete with the scar on his cheek obtained at his victory at Burford of 1 January, a skirmish made much of in the first issue of *Mercurius Aulicus*.

---

14   F.J. Varley, *Mercurius Aulicus* (Oxford, 1930), pp.50-51.
15   Margaret Toynbee & Peter Young, *Strangers in Oxford* (Chichester, 1973), pp.265-267.
16   D.N.B.

Christ Church Hall. (Author's collection)

Dobson's studio may have been in a house in the High Street almost opposite St Mary's Church. During the next three years he produced a series of portraits of Royalist notables, particularly military commanders. Among them were several portraits of the King, one in campaign dress with Sir Edward Walker, Princes Rupert and Maurice, the Marquis of Montrose, Sir William Russell, and Sir Charles Lucas.

Dobson evidently worked at speed, portraying subjects who were often in Oxford only for brief periods. It has been said that his work was unimaginative in its approach, and it may be that Dobson was at times ill, or short of artistic materials. His portrait of Prince Rupert, possibly begun in the winter of 1644-45, was never completed, though it captures perceptively the haunted aspect of a man still suffering from the effects of his defeat at Marston Moor. After the fall of Oxford, Dobson returned to London, where he died "very Poor" in October 1646.[17]

17   Ibid.

William Dobson (1611-1646). (Author's collection)

Also present in Oxford was the composer William Lawes. Lawes spent all his adult life in Charles's employ. He composed secular music and songs for court masques (and doubtless played in them), as well as sacred anthems and motets for Charles's private worship. He is most remembered today for his viol consort suites for between three and six players and his lyra viol music. Lawes joined the Royalist army, and was for a time a commissary. In 1645 he rode with the King's Lifeguard of Horse at the Battle of Rowton Heath (23 September) near Chester and was shot dead. Hs body was never recovered.[18]

The Court in Oxford might have been expected to have been enlivened by the arrival of Queen Henrietta Maria from the North of England in July 1643. She was to reside in Merton College, adjacent to the King in Christ Church, and a private passage was constructed between them for the King and Queen to use. Henrietta's arrival in Oxford on 14 July was greeted, it was claimed by streets thronged with cheering spectators, among them Anthony Wood, who witnessed the Queen's reception at Carfax with "loud acclamation … the Mayor and his brethren

18   Ibid.

entertained her Majesty with an English Speech, delivered by Master Carter, the Town Clerk, and presented her with a purse of gold." Wood added that: "On Friday in the evening the King and Queen with all their train came into Oxford. They rode into Christ Church in a coach … there was a speech made to the Queen for her entertainment and welcome; books of verses and gloves presented to her by the University and Mr Denys, the mayor of the town, accompanied only with his mace bearer on horseback, brought his Majesty into Christ Church, the mayor in scarlet bearing the mace upon his own shoulder, riding with Garter in chief of the heralds … but no other of the town came with him."[19]

The Council spent £3 8s 2d on wine, and 6s 6d for flowers with which to strew the streets. The Queen was also presented with a volume of poems compiled by members of the university, with a fulsome Latin dedication.[20]

Henrietta Maria disliked the damp air of Oxford, and apparently had no great impact on the town during her stay. Debate still continues on how much influence she had on politics and Royalist strategy, but in all probability it was less than has sometimes been suggested. She was also apparently ill for part of her time in Oxford. It was in Oxford that the Queen's last child, Princess Henrietta, was conceived, though some, then and later, suggested that the father was actually the Queen's favourite, Henry Jermyn.

If the Queen, as suggested, wished to influence Royalist strategy and politics, she was ideally situated, for Oxford was not only the seat of the Court but also the centre of the King's administration. The King's Privy Council met in Christ Church, and administrative matters were directed by the King's Secretaries of State. Sir Edward Nicholas served in this capacity throughout the war, and also apparently had a role in directing intelligence operations.[21] The Earl of Falkland was second Secretary of State until his death at the First Battle of Newbury, his successor was George, Lord Digby.[22] Also based in the colleges were the Lord Treasurer, John Ashburnham,[23] and the legal functionaries, headed by the Lord Keeper, Sir Edward Littleton[24] and, in so far as they operated, the Courts of Law.

King Charles viewed the Parliament in Westminster as an illegal body, and on 20 June 1643 issued a proclamation calling all members of Parliament to meet at

---

19   Wood, p.103.
20   Ibid.
21   Sir Edward Nicholas (1593-1669) – A pre-war government official and clerk to the Council; became a Secretary of State in 1641.
22   George, Lord Digby (1612-77) – An ambitious and erratically brilliant Royalist and intriguer, Digby is best known for his intermittent enmity with Prince Rupert and his sometimes over-optimistic advice to King Charles.
23   John Ashburnham (1603-71) – A dedicated Royalist who accompanied the King on his flight from Oxford in 1646.
24   Edward, Lord Littleton (1589-1645) – A lawyer and moderate supporter of the King; appointed Lord Keeper of the Privy Seal in 1641.

Oxford. In December this order was renewed, with members to assemble in Oxford on 22 January 1644. The records of the "Oxford Parliament" were destroyed before the surrender of the city in 1646, but it seems that around 83 members of the House of Lords and 75 MPs took part in 1644.The opening session, held in Christ Church Hall, was attended by 44 Lords and 118 of the Commons, and was addressed by the King. Many of the members were also army officers, and frequently absent on campaign.

The Oxford Parliament would be something of a disappointment for King Charles. It pressed, without success for a peaceful settlement with Westminster, and was not as ready to vote taxation and recruitment measures as the King would have wished. In fact, the Parliament probably had relatively little real influence on Royalist policy and the war effort. It was prorogued on 16 April 1644 until the following October, although because of the military situation, it did not actually assemble until 9 November. On 10 March 1645 the Parliament was adjourned until 10 October, and it is unclear whether it ever assembled again in any numbers. King Charles had little time for his Oxford Parliament, writing to Henrietta Maria on 13 March 1645 "I being now freed from the place of base and mutinous Motions (that is to say, our Mongrel Parliament here)."[25]

A key role in military decision-making was played by the Council of War. It was usual for any general to listen to, though not necessarily to follow, the advice of his council of war. Initially, at least, King Charles followed this practice. Apart from the rough notes made by its Secretary, Sir Edward Walker, the records of the Royalist Council of war were destroyed in 1646, but the broad outline of its organisation and role can be seen. Like the councils of lesser commanders, it had no executive powers and was intended to act as an advisory body to the King, who was invariably present at its meetings. In Oxford the Council customarily met in the King's quarters at Christ Church, and wherever appropriate when on campaign. Membership varied, but normally the Council consisted of high-ranking military officers, the Lord General, General and Lieutenant Generals of Horse and the Major General of Foot, together with civilian officials, such as Secretaries of State, Lord Treasurer and Chancellor of the Exchequer, together with currently favoured courtiers, such as the King's cousin, James, Earl of Richmond, who held no formal position in army or government. Also called in as required for their advice were various "experts," normally lower-ranking military officers.

Much of the Council's work involved logistical and recruitment matters, mainly relating to the Oxford army, as its influence in the more distant parts of Royalist territory tended to be limited, and it had little control over strongly independent commanders such as Prince Rupert. Gradually much of the work of the Council of War seems to have been hived off to separate committees, whose exact roles were sometimes unclear.

25   Varley (1930), pp.47-49.

The Council's influence was also limited by the attitude of King Charles himself. All major decision-making revolved around him. Without his approval no major order could take effect, and decisions were increasingly made by the King without reference to most, or even any, of his councillors. In the intrigue-ridden Royalist court the opportunities for 'special interest' groups to put their case directly to the royal ear were endless. Charles's well-known tendency to be unduly influenced by his current favourite, and his preference for subterfuge and behind-the-scenes dealing, led to a dangerous lack of continuity and clear decision-making. As a result, open discussion was increasingly replaced by intrigue.[26]

By now a mint had been established in Oxford. It was organised by the Royalist entrepreneur Thomas Bushell, who had been in charge of the pre-war mint at Aberystwyth, moved to Shrewsbury in the summer of 1642 and then transferred to Oxford. On 10 January the colleges were sent letters by the King asking them to donate their remaining plate for the use of the mint, with the promise of a later refund of its value. These appeals had previously met with a mixed response. In many cases the colleges hung on to their plate, instead borrowing money claimed to be its equivalent in value which was sent instead. The mint equipment arrived from Shrewsbury on 3 January, and was set up in New Inn Hall.

The response to the latest appeal from the King was more positive, although Exeter and St John's Colleges continued to delay. Balliol College sent 41 lb of plate, Magdalen 296 lb. After prevaricating, St John's again sent what they claimed to be the equivalent in money, but this time the King demanded the plate as well, at which point St John's provided 224lb 4 oz in weight. Exeter College put up a stubborn resistance but eventually parted with all except its communion plate. They were also allowed to keep an ostrich egg mounted in silver!

By early February 1643 plate to the value of £8,500 had reached the mint, together with £100 or so of Welsh silver which arrived at weekly intervals until the summer. Between November 1642 and October 1643 a total of £13,188 14s 6d was recorded as being received from the mint by the Treasurer of War, William Ashburnham, but the actual total was probably higher.

In the late summer of 1643 Thomas Bushell, who had hitherto directed operations at the Oxford mint, left to establish a mint at newly-captured Bristol. He was succeeded at Oxford by Sir William Park with two assistants, Richard Nichols from Shrewsbury and who had been at Aberystwyth. Also at the Oxford mint was Nicholas Briot, who in 1643 was appointed Graver of Seals, Stamps and Medals. Oxford was the only Royalist mint to coin significant amounts of gold, mainly obtained from jewellery donated from supporters or confiscated from alleged Parliamentarian supporters.

---

26   Ian Roy, 'The Royalist Council of War 1642-46' in: *Bulletin of the Institute of Historical Research*, Volume 35, Issue 92, November 1962, pp.150-168.

Thomas Bushell (1594-1674). (Author's collection)

Briot designed several medals for the Royalists. In May 1643 the mint began to produce badges for soldiers "who have done us faithful service in the Forlorn Hope." This was probably the idea of Thomas Bushell, who also made a gold medal for Sir Robert Welsh, who was said to have been one of those involved in the rescue of the captured Royal Standard at the Battle of Edgehill. There were also a few other medals produced for specific events, such as the capture of Bristol in July 1643, and for the meeting of the King and Queen Henrietta Maria at Kineton in the same month.

The Oxford mint remained in operation until the end of the war. Thomas Bushell had been an extremely wealthy businessman at the start of the war, but a good deal of his fortune was expended in the Royalist cause. He claimed later to have spent £36,000, but to have only received £1,000 in compensation. He died, apparently living in fairly straitened circumstances, in a grace and favour apartment in the Palace of Whitehall.[27]

27   Edward Besly, *Coins and Medals of the English Civil War* (London, 1990), pp.33-44.

A mint in operation. (Author's collection)

Coins produced by the Oxford mint. (Author's collection)

The impact of war was brought home in Oxford, especially to the Royal court, on 13 January 1643 with the funeral of Lord D'Aubigny, who had died at Edgehill. The funeral was conducted with great ceremony, as witnessed by Anthony Wood:

> The body was brought up from Magdalen College and so brought and attended all the way through the street to Christ Church the cathedral and there interred. The footmen soldiers came first with their muskets under their arms, the noses of the muskets being behind them; the pikemen trailed their pikes on the ground; the horsemen followed with their pistols in their hands the handles being upwards, the tops of the ancients [standards] also was borne behind. A chariot covered with black velvet, where the body was, drawn by six horses and the man that drove the chariot strewed money about the streets as he passed. Three great volleys of shot at the entering of the body, and lastly a herald of arms proclaimed his titles etc.[28]

D'Aubigny was one of the first of many Royalist notables to be buried in Christ Church cathedral.

Mercurius Aulicus

The Civil War saw an explosion in the publication of newspapers, or "news-books," to use the contemporary term. Because of it possession of London, with its printing presses and advantages in distribution, Parliament initially had a distinct advantage in the propaganda use of these sources. It was clearly important for the Royalists to counteract their opponents' propaganda, and so on 1 January 1643 was born *Mercurius Aulicus*, "communicating the intelligence and affairs of the court to the rest of the Kingdom."[29]

The first editor of *Aulicus*, as it was popularly known, was an Oxford scholar, Doctor Peter Heylin. He would continue to write for the newspaper throughout its existence, as did Lord George Digby from time to time. But the principal contributor to *Aulicus*, and its longest-serving editor, was Dr John Berkenhead. Born in Cheshire of fairly humble origins, Berkenhead was admitted as a "servitor" of Oriel College, and distinguished himself as a scholar, entering the service of Archbishop Laud. In 1639, with Laud's support, he was elected as a fellow of All Souls.[30]

By 1642 Berkenhead, an unprepossessing figure physically, had a reputation as "exceeding bold, confident and witty," a poet and active in Royalist circles.

---

28 Wood, p.82.
29 Title page of *Mercurius Aulicus*, 1 January 1643.
30 D.N.B.

P.P. Oxford.

(1)   X.

30

MERCVRIVS AVLICVS,

Communicating the intelligence,
and affaires of the Court, to the
reft of the KINGDOME.

The firſt Weeke.

THe world hath long enough beene abuſed with falſhoods : And there's a weekly cheat put out to nouriſh the abuſe amongſt the people, and make them pay for their ſeducement . And that the world may ſee that the Court is neither ſo barren of intelligence, as it is conceived , nor the affaires thereof in ſo unproſperous a condition, as theſe Pamphlets make them: it is thought fit to let them truly underſtand the eſtate of things that ſo they may no longer pretend igno-rance, or be deceived with untruthes: which being premiſed once for all, we now go on unto the buſineſſe ; wherein we ſhall proceed with all truth and candor.

SUNDAY. *Jan.* 1.

New-yeares-day ſhall give entrance to this new deſigne. And that which was the greateſt buſineſſe and diſcourſe thereof, was the report which came from *Burford* in the morning of Sir *John Byrons* carriage and behaviour there. At firſt reported variouſly (as in ſuch actions commonly it doth uſe to be) according as men feared or hoped: but afterwards before night, a more exact and punctuall relation of it was brought from thence, which in briefe was thus. On Friday being the 30. day of *December*, Sir *John* had order to march with his whole Regiment to *Burford* (a towne about twelve miles from *Oxford*) to convey thither two cart loads of ammunition for the Lord Marqueſſe of *Hartford*, who was expected the next day at *Stow*, with all his forces . Being arrived at his quarter, his firſt enqui-ry was what forces the Rebels had at *Cyrenceſter*, or any other place adjoyning. In which when as he could receive no ſatiſfaction from the Towneſmen there, hee ſent a party of horſe that night towards *Cyrenceſter*, who went within a mile & an halfe of the towne, and brought word, that there were not above 500 dragoons there quartered, the horſe which had bin there being marched to *Tedbury*. The next day being Saturday there was litle newes, more then the day before had yeelded. But about ſeaven of the clocke at night, a party that had beene ſent forth towards the enemies, brought word , that about two miles from the towne in the way to *Cyrenceſter* they had diſcovered foure Dragoons with light matches, who ſo ſoone as they made towards them, rid backe ſo faſt that they could by no meanes overtake them. Sir *John* imagining by this diſcovery that there might be ſome de-ſigne that night upon his Quarter, commanded Captaine St *John* to ride towards *Cyrenceſter* with forty horſe; and that the whole Regiment ſhould be in a readi-neſſe

January . iſt 1640 oxon A

Title page of *Mercurius Aulicus*. (Author's collection)

He was a natural choice as a member of the team which would produce *Aulicus*, a skilful propagandist, who used sarcasm, literary skill, wit and access to Royalist ruling circles to produce what would soon be regarded as the most successful newsbook of either side in the war. *Aulicus* was printed in Oxford, probably by Leonard Lichfield and certainly by Henry Hall, Printers to the University. Hall would later complain that he had printed *Aulicus* for two years "for which I was never paid farthing, though it amounted to above £90 … by my book."

Aulicus rapidly gained widespread popularity in ruling and influential circles on both sides, at whom it was aimed, rather than seeking more general circulation. Witty, informative, and, making due allowance for its propaganda role, more reliable than most of its Parliamentarian counterparts, *Aulicus* was eagerly read by Parliamentarians as well as Royalists and, though officially banned, was smuggled into London – on one occasion 16 copies by a servant of the French Ambassador who had visited Oxford. It was also from time to time printed in London, and its popularity was attested by its sale price of between 3d and 18d, compared with an average price of 1d for its Parliamentarian counterparts.

The great days of *Aulicus* were in 1643, with the string of Royalist successes that year providing fertile copy for Berkenhead and his team, and ample opportunity to satirise their opponents. With the change of fortunes in 1644, particularly after Marston Moor, times became harder for *Aulicus*. Issues became smaller, with gaps in publication, notably in the autumn of 1644, and with a nine-week silence following the Royalist disaster at Naseby in June 1645. Increasing prominence was given to local successes in the vicinity of Oxford, and to usually imaginary victories elsewhere.

The last issue of *Aulicus* appeared on 7 September 1645, reporting Will Legge's successful attack on Thame. There would be other short-lived, Royalist newsbooks, but nothing with the same success. John Berkenhead would go into exile in 1648, but was rewarded with a knighthood after the Restoration, and regained his Oxford fellowship. His role as a Royalist propagandist was outstanding, for it was said that "*Aulicus* hath done the Parliament more hurt than 2,000 of the King's soldiers."[31]

---

31   *Mercurius Aulicus*, p.6.; quoted ibid., p.8.

4

Oxford: The Garrison

Day-to-day control of the garrison was exercised by the governor or his lieu-tenant. The role of governor of a town was an important one which, in theory at least, required both military ability and administrative skills and diplomatic tact. A governor was responsible for the defences and troops in the garrison. He also had to liaise with the civilian authorities regarding a variety of matters, including financial contributions, billeting, labour for work on the defences, supplies and the discipline and behaviour of the garrison and sometimes their civilian compan-ions. A wise governor attempted to stay on good terms with the citizens, although this was not always possible, particularly in times of military emergency or siege, when the interests of civilian and soldiers might be sharply at odds with each other over issues such as the destruction of property or the rationing of food. In Oxford relations were further complicated by the presence of the King and in his absence his Lords Commissioners, the terms of whose authority over the governor, partic-ularly in the latter stages of the war, became a source of conflict.

The first Royalist Governor of Oxford, appointed in December 1642, was Sir Jacob Astley, who was also Major General of Foot in the Oxford Army. Born in 1579, Astley, a Norfolk man, was a highly competent professional soldier of vast European experience. A man of few words, and no courtier, Astley was ideally suited for the job of establishing Oxford as a military base and garrison town. His appointment was only intended to be temporary however, as with the start of the 1643 campaigning season, he resumed his command in the field army.[1] It seems likely that Astley was followed briefly, in a stop-gap appointment, by Lewis Kirk, another professional soldier, who had been deputy governor of Cirencester from February 1643, until his appointment at Oxford in April, when he was knighted. Kirk was, judging by his later time as Governor of Bridgnorth, another military man first and foremost.[2]

---

1   D.N.B.
2   Peter R. Newman, *Royalist Officers of England and Wales* (New York, 1981), item 833.

Kirk was quickly replaced as Governor by Sir William Pennyman. A Yorkshire Royalist, Pennyman had raised a regiment of foot at the beginning of the war, and served with the Oxford Army throughout the 1642 campaign. Pennyman was more closely linked to court circles than his predecessors as governor, and had been an MP in the Long Parliament. However Pennyman, other than directing the first major work on the Oxford defences, had little time to make an impression, dying in August of one or other of the diseases which were raging in Oxford.[3]

Pennyman's successor, Sir Arthur Aston, was Oxford's longest-serving and most controversial Governor. Born in around 1590, with Middlesex and Cheshire connections, Aston, as a younger son of a younger son, took military service abroad, and in 1614 he was serving the Tsar of Russia against the Poles. Four years later, in true mercenary fashion, Aston was fighting for the Poles against the Turks! Soon afterwards he was fighting for the Poles against the Swedes, and then for King Gustavus Adolphus of Sweden in Germany, receiving plaudits for his courage and leadership skills. Returned to England, Aston was with the English forces in the Bishops' Wars, and was knighted in 1640. Nevertheless in 1642 it was not at first clear which side he would support in the Civil War. Initially rebuffed by King Charles because he was a Catholic, Aston was making approaches to Lord Fairfax, commanding Parliamentarian forces in Yorkshire, when he was recruited by Prince Rupert to be Major General of Dragoons in the Oxford Army.

Aston fought at Edgehill and was then made Governor of Reading. He proved unpopular with both townspeople and soldiers as a result of his strongly disciplinarian approach better suited to "ordering a loose Army in the Field, than in awing a regular Garrison in a Town."[4] During the siege of April and May Aston played a somewhat equivocal role. Struck on the head by a roof tile dislodged by Parliamentarian bombardment, Aston supposedly lost the power of speech, and was replaced by Richard Feilding. On reaching Oxford, Aston quickly regained his faculties, leading to suspicions that his incapacity had been assumed to avoid responsibility for the loss of Reading.

Aston served under Prince Rupert at the capture of Bristol in July 1643, and was reportedly under consideration to be appointed as its Governor. However, on 23 August he succeeded Sir William Pennyman as Governor of Oxford. It was alleged that the appointment was due to the influence of Queen Henrietta Maria, who favoured Aston because of his Catholicism. Anthony Wood described him as "a testy, froward, imperious and tyrannical person, hated in Oxon and elsewhere by God and man."[5]

On 22 December Aston was wounded in the side in a nocturnal street scuffle (see below). His relations with the civilian population and the Oxford Council

3   D.N.B.
4   Quoted Newman, item 41.
5   Wood, p.110.

were generally abysmal. In February 1644 he was reportedly confined to his chamber for beating the mayor. The garrison certainly resented the severity of his discipline, and a Parliamentarian scout reported on 11 April that his relations with the citizens over completion of the fortifications were so bad that he begged the King to evacuate the whole civilian population.

On 1 May the university, somewhat inappropriately, awarded Aston a doctorate in medicine. Ironically on 19 September he had the misfortune to break his leg in a riding accident, which his enemies ascribed to "kervetting on horseback on Bullingdon Green before certaine ladies."[6] Gangrene set in, the leg was amputated (on 7 December), and Aston was replaced as governor on 25 December by his deputy, Sir Henry Gage, a fellow Catholic. He was given a pension by the King of £1,000 per annum. Aston disliked Gage, especially after his successful relief of Basing House, a mission Aston had earlier declined. Aston bitterly resented his replacement by Gage, protesting that he was fit to resume the command himself, and arguing that his own low-key practice of Catholicism gave no scandal to Protestants, he launched a bizarre verbal assault on Gage, accusing him of being a Jesuit stooge who attended Catholic sermons (a more serious offence than merely attending mass). Gage's telling riposte alleged that he had merely been entrapped into being present at a single such sermon, at the house of Aston's own daughter, Elizabeth (who had been born in Russia).

On Gage's death in January 1645, Aston had hoped to be reappointed, and was furious when Will Legge was made Governor. He seems to have left Oxford soon afterwards, and took service with the Marquis of Ormonde in Ireland. In 1649, whilst Governor of Drogheda, Aston was killed when the town was stormed by Cromwell's troops, allegedly beaten to death with his wooden leg by soldiers who believed he had money hidden in it![7]

Henry Gage was born in 1597 to a Catholic family from Surrey. He was educated at the English colleges in St Omer and Rome and in 1620 joined the Spanish Army of Flanders, and was present at the sieges of Bergen op Zoom and Breda. In 1627 Gage published a translation of Herman Hugo's account of Breda. In Flanders at the outbreak of the Civil War, Gage worked actively to supply the Royalists with munitions, and in February 1644 was given leave to join the King at Oxford. Appointed a member of the military council in Oxford, Gage made his name with a number of exploits during the summer and autumn of 1644, notably his capture in June of Boarstall House, and his relief of Basing in September and Banbury Castle a month later. Gage's appointment as Governor of Oxford on December 25 was greeted with satisfaction by almost everyone except Sir Arthur Aston, and he worked with determination to reorganise the garrison. On 10 January 1645 Gage was mortally wounded in a skirmish near Culham Bridge, and buried two days later

6   Ibid.
7   D.N.B.

in Christ Church Cathedral, Oxford. Several years later Clarendon, in his *History of the Rebellion*, described Gage as a "man of extraordinary parts." He recalled that he was "a large and very graceful person, of an honourable extraction" and "a great master in the Spanish and Italian tongues, besides the French and the Dutch, which he spoke in great perfection." Gage had been welcomed for many years at Brussels "which was a great and very regular court at that time." Later at Oxford "the lords of the council had a singular esteem" of him and "consulted frequently with him, whilst they looked to be besieged." He was, concluded Clarendon, "a man of great wisdom and temper, and among the very few soldiers, who made himself to be universally loved and esteemed."[8]

In a reflection of Prince Rupert's current influence with the King, the next Governor of Oxford was one of the Prince's closest followers, Colonel William Legge. Born in 1607-8, to a minor English gentry family settled in Munster, Legge followed the example of many other younger sons in taking up a military career. After serving with the Dutch and Swedes, Legge returned to England to command the English artillery during the Bishops' wars. He was Governor of Hull in January 1642. In June he was condemned as a delinquent by Parliament.

Legge was among the first to join the King at Nottingham in August. He was a notable cavalry commanding, serving with Prince Rupert, with whom he developed a close friendship, throughout the campaigns of 1643. At the Battle of Newbury in October, Legge's bravery brought the offer of a knighthood. He declined it.

As we will see, Legge had an important role in Oxford as Master of the Armoury. Legge was with Rupert in 1644 at the Relief of Newark, and was then made Governor of Chester "a person every way qualified for so great and important a trust." He was very unpopular with local Royalist commanders such as Lord Byron, who saw him as a "creature" of Prince Rupert's.

Legge was recalled from Chester to succeed Gage as Governor of Oxford and received the honours customary for holders of the post. He was elected a freeman and alderman of the city (18 March), made a groom of the bedchamber (12 April), and created DCL by the university (16 April). Rupert further commissioned him, on 7 May 1645, to take charge of the ring of strongholds protecting Oxford. In contrast with his time at Chester, Legge seems to have been generally popular with the city, court, and army, a remarkable feat in the increasingly divided counsels of the King. He was often spoken of as "honest Will" Legge.

After the Royalist defeat at Naseby, Legge was caught up in the power struggle between George Digby, and Prince Rupert and shared the latter's disgrace after the fall of Bristol, being dismissed as Governor and briefly placed under house arrest.

8   D.N.B.

But the failure of Digby to produce any evidence of treachery—"more particular proofs"— and a period of reflection by the King, led to Legge's partial reinstatement. Thereafter he worked tirelessly, when Charles returned to Oxford, to effect a reconciliation between sovereign and prince. Rupert was allowed to remain in the royal headquarters. At the fall of the city to Fairfax on 22 June 1646 Legge was listed among the prince's followers, given a pass, and allowed the benefit of the surrender terms. In due course he compounded for his estate, and was fined at a tenth, £40.

Clarendon wrote of Legge:

> He was a very punctual and steady observer of the orders he received, but no contriver of them; his modesty and diffidence of himself never suffered him to contrive bold counsels.[9]

Oxford's final Royalist governor was Sir Thomas Glemham, born in 1595, into a Suffolk family, and, according to Clarendon "a gentleman of noble extraction and a fair fortune." After matriculating at Trinity College, Oxford, in 1610, he became a professional soldier and was knighted by James I on 10 September 1617. Glemham later served as a JP and deputy lieutenant for Suffolk, and was said to have been "a fierce presser of the recusancy laws from which he hoped to profit," yet he was also noted as a supporter of common rights against enclosure in Suffolk. Glemham commanded a regiment of foot in the Second Bishops' War, and in 1642 became Governor of York, where he held out with success until 16 July 1644, following the defeat at Marston Moor. Glemham reassembled 3,000 men in Cumberland in August 1644, and defended Carlisle from the Scots, where "he was the first man that taught soldiers to eat cats and dogs." After enduring much extremity he surrendered the town on honourable terms on 25 June 1645, and was escorted by the Scots to Hereford. With his 200 survivors he joined the King at Cardiff in August. Glemham's regiment briefly formed the King's lifeguard before he was appointed governor of Oxford on 2 October 1645.[10]

The strength and composition of the garrison of Royalist Oxford varied considerably at different periods. Until the spring of 1643, when the auxiliary regiments of the University and Town were formed, the garrison was drawn entirely from the regiments of the Oxford Army, and fluctuated both in numbers and composition. In general terms, there seem usually to have been three or four regiments of foot, and at least one regiment of horse in the garrison, together with some independent troops of horse.

9   D.N.B.
10 D.N.B.

The earliest regular units in the garrison from the winter of 1642 until the opening of the spring campaigning season of 1643 were the King's Lifeguard of Foot, Charles Gerard's Regiment, Sir William Pennyman's Regiment and Sir Ralph Dutton's Regiment. All had been at Edgehill and in the subsequent advance on London, and were probably somewhat understrength. On 18 February 1643, the Lifeguard mustered about 400 men, and was ill-armed, as Sir Jacob Astley wrote to the Ordnance Office:

> Sir John Heydon may be pleased to take notice that the regiment of the King's guards being very weakly Armed, as the last time his Majesty saw this garrison in Arms, where they appeared 190 armed and 210 unarmed whereof I pray as any arms shall be brought into the Magazine let some especial care be taken first to furnish the King's guards before any other regiments, with the number of 110 Arms or some such sufficient supply and for so doing this shall be your warrant.[11]

By 18 February the Regiment had 512 rank and file – 322 still unarmed. Adding to this total NCOs, drummers and officers, the Lifeguard probably had a strength of around 600.[12]

It is unlikely that any of the other regiments in the garrison were in any better case, which highlights the parlous state of the Oxford Army's arms and ammunition supplies prior to the arrival of the first munitions convoy from the North of England.

Throughout the war, detachments from the field army regiments in the garrison would be employed in particular operations. A contingent, including some of the Lifeguard, were with Prince Rupert at the storming of Cirencester on 2 February 1643; a detachment of the Queen's Regiment of Foot joined Colonel Henry Gage in his relief of Basing House in October 1644 and full regiments would be drawn out to join the field army for major campaigns. The Lifeguard and Gerard's men for example were with the Oxford Army during the First Newbury campaign of October 1643. Units might also be redeployed elsewhere; Sir Ralph Dutton's Foot left Oxford in the spring of 1643, but returned in 1644, after, Dutton's successor as colonel, Stephen Hawkins, stubbornly defended Greenland House near Henley with it. The Regiment was based in Oxford for the remainder of the war, with detachments taking part in Gage's operations in the autumn of 1644. Hawkins was knighted thanks to the influence of the Earl of Dover, and was appointed as Deputy Governor of Oxford on 31 January 1645. Charles Gerard's Regiment went to South Wales early in 1644.

---

11   Ian Roy (ed.), *The Royalist Ordnance Papers Part I* (Oxford, 1964), p.195.
12   Ibid., p.199.

Some units seem to have had a particular association with the garrison. The Queen's Regiment of Foot, for example, seems to have mostly been based in Oxford from the summer of 1643, when it was raised, until the end of the war. The Lord General's Regiment also seems to have been based in Oxford or its surrounding garrisons for much of the war.

At a muster in New Parks on 13 February 1644, the following regiments were present:

> King's Life Guard: red coats
> Queen's Regiment: red coats
> Lord Percy's Regiment: white coats (a unit formed from the "commanded" detachments from several units of the Earl of Newcastle's Northern Royalist army which had escorted the first munitions convoy from York to Oxford in May 1643)
> Charles Gerard's Regiment
> Colonel Lunsford's Regiment
> "Sir Arthur Aston's Regiment now raising, sans arms."[13]

Aston evidently began raising his regiment after he was appointed Governor in September 1643. Little is known of its history, although 11 indigent officers are listed. It seems that the regiment remained in Oxford for the remainder of the war, and at the time of the surrender was probably commanded by its major, Hannibal Bagnell.

Other units became part of the garrison in the later stages of the war as troops from surrendered garrisons arrived at Oxford. Among them were about 2,000 foot from the garrison of Bristol, probably mainly Welsh, under Colonel Henry Tillier

In April 1646 the last major reinforcements arrived in the shape of 700 of Sir John Berkeley's foot from Exeter, who probably included men of his own regiment and William Ashburnham's and William Godolphin's regiments raised in Devon and Cornwall.[14]

From the spring of 1644 onwards, the intended mainstay of Oxford's garrison were the three auxiliary regiments of foot. The Earl of Dover's Regiment was raised by a proclamation of 28 April 1644. It recruited among the scholars and "strangers" in Oxford, and is noted as exercising in Magdalen College Grove on 14 May and again as being mustered on Bullingdon Green on the 21st. On 24 May all strangers then in Oxford were ordered by proclamation either to enlist in the regiment or leave town by the 27th.[15]

---

13   Toynbee and Young, pp.24-30.
14   William Hamper (ed.), *The Life, Diary and Correspondence of Sir William Dugdale* (London, 1827), p.67.
15   Toynbee and Young, p.27.

The second regiment, also formed on 28 April 1644, was under the nominal command of Lord Keeper Littleton, and seems to have included a larger proportion of courtiers and their servants. Like Dover's it remained in existence until the end of the siege and seems to have been employed entirely in the defence of Oxford.[16]

Sir Edward Walker explained that the units were formed with the primary aim of freeing up other troops for service with the field army, they "were raised and completed to considerable numbers, and have done duty ever since, to their great honour, and the manifest preservation of this city."[17] Though probably never approaching full regulation strength, and so continuing to need reinforcement from army units, the regiments saw service in the sieges of 1645 and 1646.

The third auxiliary regiment, the so-called City Regiment, was formed from townsmen, and had a more chequered career. As we have seen, there were continuing doubts regarding the loyalty of many of Oxford's citizens, and the regiment, raised at the same time as the other auxiliaries, and again in theory consisting of volunteers, was never accounted entirely reliable. It was raised on 17 or 25 June 1643, and placed under the command of Colonel Sir Nicholas Selwyn, from Sussex, a Gentleman Pensioner who was also apparently a professional soldier.[18] It seems likely that the "parachuting" in of an "outsider" to command the regiment, probably with the aim of ensuring its reliability, was never popular. In December 1643, the officers of the Regiment were:

Colonel Sir Nicholas Selwyn
Lieutenant-Colonel Thomas Smyth, a brewer and Mayor in 1643
Major Mr Hall
1st Captain Leonard Bowman, mercer and Alderman
2nd Captain Peter Langston, barrister at law, attorney etc.
3rd Captain Henry Stephens, citizen of High Street and Wagon Master General to the King's Army.[19]

It is unlikely that this is a complete listing of the Regiment's officers, which otherwise would have been badly understrength.

It seems that discontent with Selwyn continued to simmer among the town councillors, and reached a head on 21 October 1644, when the Council formally protested to the King that Selwyn, "a stranger", had not been appointed by them or approved as Colonel of the City Regiment by them, despite the King having supposedly given them free choice of its commander.

16   Ibid.
17   Sir Edward Walker, *Historical Discourses* (London, 1707), p.6.
18   Newman, item 1294.
19   Richard Symonds, *Diary* (London, 1859), p.26.

Memorial to Sir Edward Littleton in the Lucy Chapel. (Author's collection)

Neither doth this housed conceive him to be a man that hath either will or power to do this city any good office but only aimeth at his own ends and to enrich himself by the City … Besides he hath affronted the late Mayor [Leonard Bowman] by assaulting and striking him in his place and seat in the City office, a thing not to be forgotten by this house.

The Councillors said that they would continue to raise contributions to pay the other officers of the Regiment, but not Selwyn. This was just the beginning of a catalogue of financial complaints revolving around the upkeep costs of the garrison. The councillors claimed that that they had been told that in consideration of the sums of money already given to the King that they should be free of all other charges relating to the upkeep of the garrison. But they had already had contributions demanded towards the pay of the governor of £21 a week. They had been required to contribute £2,000 towards the cost of the fortifications and the labour required for them, amounting to "a good value and 220 labourers per day for the last five weeks." Supplying fire and candles for the Courts of Guard was costing them £10 10s a week in the summer, and at least £14 since Michaelmas as the colder weather and longer nights began.[20]

The general demand of the Excise tax – "a great weekly sum" – which had been imposed throughout Royalist-controlled territory earlier in the year was a major grievance in Oxford as elsewhere. And more money was demanded for "relief of common soldiers without which it is conceived they could not subsist." The need for billets for "officers and soldiers with their wives and children [meant] that room cannot be obtained for the poor distressed Inhabitants whose houses are burnt."[21]

The general hardship resulting from the disruption of town life for military demands, and the continuing effects of disease meant that many citizens were unable to pay the amounts demanded of them, and

that most of these payments arising forth of the soldiers of the City Regiment, whose sad condition cannot less than cause them to believe themselves to be the most miserable of all of His Majesty's soldiers, other foreign officers and soldiers having conveniences in their houses to their great prejudice, so that their wives and families are distressed and themselves discontented.[22]

The King's response was uncompromising. Aldermen Wright, Whistler and Dennis, evidently viewed as the principal malcontents, were imprisoned, until the

20   M.G. Hobson & H.E. Salter (eds.), *Oxford Council Acts Volume II: 1626-1665* (Oxford, 1933), pp.123-126.
21   Ibid.
22   Ibid., pp.126-127.

council backed down, and on 6 November agreed to levy a tax to pay Selwyn for a month. It petitioned for the release of the imprisoned members and agreed to raise an additional tax of £50 "for the provision of bread for His Majesty's army." The Aldermen were to be reimbursed for any money which they had been forced to pay for their upkeep during their imprisonment.[23]

In the event, possibly in a conciliatory move by the King, Selwyn was replaced as Colonel of the City Regiment by Will Legge after his appointment as Governor in 1645, but it is perhaps an indication of tightening military control that, despite the fact that the regiment was theoretically intended only for the defence of Oxford, a detachment of 60 musketeers under Captain Burgh took part in the raid on Thame on 5 September.

Various cavalry units served in Oxford during the war. The King's Lifeguard of Horse was often present in the city, but was not regarded as part of the garrison.

After he became Governor, Sir Arthur Aston's Regiment of Horse was evidently part of the garrison, although part least of it was frequently detached to serve with the field army.[24]

In 1644, an auxiliary unit, the Lord Treasurer's Regiment of Horse, was formed from gentlemen volunteers and their servants and placed under the command of Colonel Webb, a professional soldier "dear to Prince Rupert." This unit was probably always quite small, possibly no more than a couple of troops, and also served further afield on occasion, notably with Henry Gage at his relief of Basing in October 1644.[25]

The last major cavalry unit in the Oxford garrison was probably Colonel Will Legge's Regiment, formed in January 1645 around two troops from Prince Rupert's Regiment, Legge's own and that of Captain Thomas Gardner.[26] Latterly remnants of a number of units evidently formed the "Oxford Horse" under Sir John Cansfield, former colonel of the Queen's Regiment, which had been destroyed at Shelford House in October 1645.[27]

The impact of being a garrison town on civilian life in Oxford was dramatic and far-reaching. The townspeople were most immediately affected by having soldiers billeted on them. The system of billeting was used widely by both sides in the Civil War. In broad terms, a civilian household, depending on the size of the family and its premises would have one or more soldiers lodged with them, and would have to feed them, being paid a stipulated amount to cover the cost on presentation to the civil or military authorities of a receipt or "billet." Sometimes the system worked reasonably smoothly, with billets promptly paid, but there were also frequent

---

23   Toynbee and Young, p.30.
24   Ibid.
25   Ibid.
26   Ibid.
27   Newman, item 240.

abuses. Civilians would be left unrecompensed, whilst soldiers would forcibly extort more than the agreed food and drink from their "hosts." They could also frequently be overcrowding. In 1644 there were instances of five soldiers being quartered in a house.[28]

Accommodation for officers varied according to their rank and personal circumstances, but it was usual for senior officers, such as the Earl of Forth, the Lord General of the Oxford Army, to be lodged with a prominent citizen. Others, like the civilians of the Royalist court and administration, lodged in civilian homes, inns and colleges. Lodgings also often had to be found for the dependents of soldiers, women and children, for example the "Irish wives" of some of the King's Lifeguard of Foot.[29]

There were often of course, quite frequent changes in the lodgers of a particular household. Regiments were transferred or departed on campaign, or soldiers and their dependents died. These changes must have been viewed with either hope or anxiety, depending on the natures of the previous lodgers. There were problems with officers taking up unauthorised quarters, especially when the meeting of the Oxford Parliament led to additional demands and on 3 February 1644, an official Proclamation was issued:

> Whereas divers officers of horse and foot of our Army that are not of this Garrison do not only absent themselves from there several commands, but likewise possess themselves of lodgings and stable room in several Colleges and Halls in the University and in other parts of this City whereby the Members at both House [of the Oxford Parliament, then in session] by our proclamation here assembled want that fitting accommodation for themselves, servants and horses as is necessary and as we have assured them by our said proclamation. We do therefore hereby strictly charge and command all and singular officers and soldiers of our Army (not being Officers … of this Garrison) forthwith to depart this City and University and repair to their respective garrisons and quarters and leave behind them lists of the respective Chambers and stables and those who have been lodged in Colleges or halls to leave their Keys with the Governor whereby the Members of the houses here assembled, may be accommodated with lodgings and stables to their satisfaction.[30]

28 Hobson and Salter, p.125.
29 British Library, Harleian MSS 6851, f.95.
30 *Mercurius Aulicus*, p.897.

Discipline was an ever-present problem in garrisons. From the time that Royalist troops first arrived in Oxford, there were frequent cases of soldiers selling clothing and equipment, including weapons, for beer money.

In March 1643 a gibbet was erected at Carfax, and on the 18th "a common soldier was at the market place in Oxford for killing in a desperate passion, a poor woman dwelling in the town."[31]

The Royalist articles of war tended to be applied somewhat erratically, particularly where the ever endemic problem of desertion was concerned, but on 30 March "three soldiers were brought to the gibbet at Carfax, to be hanged for running away from their colours, but that word came from the court that but one of the three was to suffer for all the rest, and that due shots be cast to try who that one should be; but when all came to all, other word was brought, that the prince [of Wales] had begged all their lives this time, and so they were all pardoned and set free."[32] For lesser offences, soldiers were made to ride the wooden horse near the Guildhall.

Disorder, though not, it seems, very often actual killing, was a common feature of Oxford as a garrison town, with brawls in the streets and taverns, and theft. On one occasion a soldier, possibly drunk, ran into Trinity College and broke Doctor Kettle's hour glass.[33]

More of an endemic problem was duelling among the officers. On one occasion Prince Rupert forcibly parted with his poleaxe two officers about to fight a duel about a horse.[34] The "further end of Christ Church meadows" was a favourite spot for duels, which were, of course, officially forbidden. The majority did not end fatally. On 15 March, Lord John Stuart, a cousin to the King, and William Ashburnham, Paymaster to the army met to settle their differences, but no hurt was done on either side.[35]

Captain Richard Atkyns recounts a similar bloodless outcome:

> In Oxford a knight provoked me with so ill language that I could not forbear striking of him; and being very angry, I took his periwig off from his head and trampled it under my feet. The next morning he sent me a challenge by his second, a person of quality, who found me in bed. I desired him to stay a little, and I would send for my second, to go along with him to his friend, which he did; when I sent my servant for my second, I also commanded him to secure a good charging horse by the way (intending to fight him on horseback). In less than half an hour, my second and servant came to me, and then (having the privilege to chose

31 Wood, p.91.
32 Ibid., p.93.
33 John Aubrey, *Brief Lives* (London, 1949), p.98.
34 John Barratt, *Cavaliers* (Stroud, 2000), p.91.
35 Wood, p.93.

Richard Atkyns (1615-1677), later a writer on typography who died in a debtors' prison. (Author's collection)

time, place and weapon) I told him I would meet his second and himself, with this gentleman my second, on horseback in Bullingdon Green, between 2:00 p.m. and 3:00 p.m., with sword and pistols, and without arms [armour] and showed him my sword and pistols, saying withal, I would not except against any his friend should bring, which he desired me to send in writing, and I did it by mine own second, who brought me word back, that all was well accepted. We all dined together with other company (as we used to do) without any suspicion of a quarrel, that I know of; after dinner, my second and I mounted, and as we passed by Magdalen College (which was the way to the place appointed) the second on the other side called to my second desiring to speak with him; his business was to persuade me to alight and treat of the matter in his chamber there; they both entreated me to alight, assuring me 'twas not dishonourable … but I not convinced by their arguments, utterly refused, unless the principal himself would come and desire it, and absolve me from my promise of meeting him at the place appointed; which he did, and then we went up together to his second's chamber, where we found an earl (whose sister the knight had married) who also pretended friendship to me; he

Christ Church and Merton Colleges viewed from Christ Church Meadow. (Author's collection)

urged how much I was beforehand with his brother, and proposed … that I should declare that I was sorry for it, which I desired to be excused in. At last he offered that if I should say I was sorry for what I had done, he should say he was sorry for giving the occasion, which was acknowledged on both sides, and so we were made friends.[36]

All did not always end so bloodlessly, however, although it seems that duels were more often carried to a conclusion in areas more distant from the Oxford Provost Marshal. More common were murderous brawls and assaults. On 9 December 1642, Sir Thomas Byron, Lieutenant Colonel in the Prince of Wales' Regiment of Horse, was shot, possibly accidentally, or possibly as a result of a grudge, by a Captain Hurst. Byron was mortally wounded, and Hurst condemned to death by a court martial and executed in Oxford Castle.[37]

An incident which evidently caused a good deal of satisfaction to many in Oxford was an attack on Sir Arthur Aston, the hugely unpopular Governor. On the night of 22 December 1643 he was involved in a scuffle in the street. Versions of the event differ, but Sir Samuel Luke's informants told him that Aston had told his servant to push out of the way a gentleman who was in his path, and the gentleman drew his sword and struck Aston, wounding him, evidently slightly, in the side.

36   Richard Atkyns, 'Vindication', in Peter Young (ed.) *Military Memoirs: the Civil War* (London, 1967), pp.34-36.
37   Hamper (ed.), p.68.

On Thursday last the governor of Oxford was riding in the streets, his footman running by him who jostled a gentleman. The governor bid his footman cut the gentleman. Then the gentleman struck the teeth out of his [the footman's] head and ran a tilt at the governor and ran his sword against one of his ribs … its likely to prove mortal, which the generality of the city pray for.[38]

Unfortunately for Oxfordian hopes, Aston was evidently only scratched, but thereafter he was "dayly attended by a guard consisting of four men in long red coats and halberds."[39] Undeterred by his scuffle, two days later Aston was put briefly under house arrest for striking the Mayor![40]

38   D.N.B.
39   D.N.B.
40   D.N.B.

5

Oxford: The Fortifications

It was immediately clear to the Royalists that the existing medieval walls of Oxford would not be adequate for its protection. Most of the suburbs, where much economic and military activity took place, and many of the inhabitants lived, lay outside of them.

The town had considerable natural defensive advantages. It was located on a spit of land between the rivers Isis and Cherwell. These could easily be dammed to create inundations, which, together with the rivers themselves, would provide Oxford with protection on three sides, leaving only the northern side of the town requiring the construction of major defences.

As early as 1642, during the initial brief Royalist occupation, work had begun on "a line of redoubts and a foot place" running from the Cherwell to the Isis, and basic defences of barricades and turnpikes were set up. These defences were suggested by Royalist Sir Richard Cave at a meeting of representatives of the city and university on 11 August. It was proposed that a defence line, with redoubts and "a foot pace" be constructed on the north side of the town between the Cherwell and Isis. This was agreed, despite the opposition of Oxford's two MPs, John Whistler and John Smith, who argued that it would result in Oxford becoming "the seat of war."[1]

Work had begun in early September, when Whistler wrote "the scholars night and day gall their hands with mattocks and spades." It is unclear how far the work had progressed before the Parliamentarians, in their brief occupation demolished the outworks. Work was resumed by the Royalists on 22 November, initially with an earthen wall between Magdalen College to the Botanical Gardens.

The defences were always earth field works, not masonry, consisting of earthen banks and ramparts fitted with palisades, storm poles and gun platforms, with a ditch or moat in front.

There are considerable differences between the contemporary plans of the defences. The often reproduced plan of Anthony Wood, allegedly showing the defences in 1644, is stylistic and not at all accurate, and that in the same writer's

---

1   H.M.C. Portland MS, I, p.59.

Work on defences. Both soldiers and civilians, male and female, could be required to work on their construction, or in the case of civilians to pay for substitutes. (© Estate of Stephen Beck)

history of the University published in 1674 purports to show the defences in 1648, when however the great majority had been slighted.[2] The plan has been attributed to Henry Shirburne, who may have been an engineer under Sir Thomas Glemham until the surrender of Oxford in 1646. The plan of the defences has also been credited to Richard Rallingson, a student at Queen's College, but this is highly unlikely. What is depicted is more a work of the imagination than reality. Based partly on the actual defences, the plan shows them as far more complex than was actually the case. Such an elaborate system could never have been adequately manned by the troops available, nor were there ever sufficient cannon for it. There were only 39 guns in Oxford at the time of the surrender.[3]

A more accurate plan is that credited to Bernard de Gomme (or de Gomez). Born in Lille in 1620, de Gomme was a Walloon who after serving under Prince Frederick Henry of Orange came to England in 1642 with Prince Rupert. Despite

2   Anthony Kemp, 'The Fortification of Oxford during the Civil War' in: *Oxoniensia*, Volume XLII, 1977, pp.239-240.
3   Ibid., p.239.

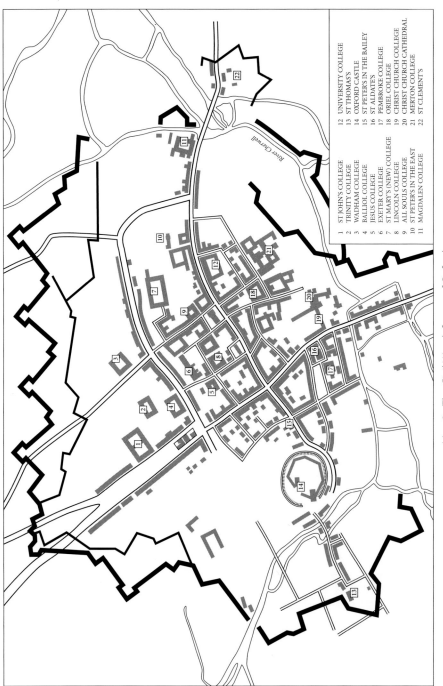

River Cherwell

Map 2 The Civil War defences of Oxford.

Map 3 The Civil War defences of Oxford traced against the present day city.

what is sometimes claimed, there is no evidence that de Gomme was engineer or quartermaster general at this stage. More probably he was employed as mapmaker to Prince Rupert, although his knowledge of military engineering was acknowledged by an advisory role at several siege operations, notably at Lichfield in 1643 and Brampton Bryan in the following year.

De Gomme was in fact more prominent in Restoration England after 1660 than he was during the Civil War, though he may have been responsible in 1644 for the drawing up of a proposed plan for the refortification of Liverpool by the Royalists, which was probably never carried out. His plan of the Oxford defences is in the form of an engineer's working drawing, with very few landmarks added. It may well be that de Gomme and the Swedish engineer Henrick Beckman were responsible for some of the later additions to the fortifications. The details of the defences shown in Jan de Wyck's well-known painting of the siege of Oxford in 1646 are copied from de Gomme. In reality the work of constructing Oxford's defences was both lengthy and beset with difficulties.

The first defence line, probably completed by August 1643, ran from Gloucester Hall (now Worcester College) through St Giles and the garden of Wadham College to Holywell. The bridgehead work at St Clements was begun in April 1643, when work was also going on in the meadows and at South (folly) Bridge. It is most likely that the plans for this defence line were laid out by Colonel Sir Charles Lloyd. He also laid out the defences of Chester, and was chief engineer to the Oxford Army in 1643. Other input may have come from Sir Jacob Astley, as first governor of the city.

The remaining medieval walls were utilised to some extent. One of the towers near to Merton College was cut down to form a gun platform, and gun ports were also made in the tower behind the chapel at New College. The stretch of medieval wall to the south of Merton College and north of New College was incorporated into the defences. The result was that by the end of 1643 these defences were in place behind the fortifications shown by de Gomme, and depicted on his plan as a thin line. This line still probably formed the basis of the defences in the summer of 1644 when, on 25 July, Sir William Waller wrote that "I find Oxford much stronger fortified than it was when I was here last, the new works being finished and the whole north side pallisadoed."[4]

On 16 March 1643 Sir Samuel Luke recorded in his Journal:

> The works about the town against New College are finished and made wonderful strong. There is a mount made in the College, about six score within the works. Against Wadham College there is a mount cast up

---

4   C.S.P.D. 1644, p.363.

Christ Church Meadow. (Author's collection)

where there is two pieces of ordnance but the works are not finished, and there is very easy entrance.[5]

During the summer of 1644 there seems to have been work on a number of outlying redoubts, particular in the vicinity of Magdalen Grove.

De Gomme's plan was probably produced in November 1645, and reflected a speeding up of work on the defences after the Royalist defeat at Naseby meant that a siege was inevitable. His plan shows two bastions on the western side of the city, together with two more which were possibly never completed. On the south side of the city, in Christ Church Meadow, were two simple lines, one of them rather oddly situated in front of an arm of the river, not behind it, as might have been expected. There was a fort at Magdalen Bridge, and also clearly shown is the large hornwork at St Clements to protect the bridgehead there.

Certainly by the end of the war the defences of Oxford were sufficiently formidable to deter any thoughts of taking the town by assault when the New Model Army mounted the final siege.

5   I.G. Phillip (ed.), *The Journal of Sir Samuel Luke Part I* (Oxford, 1947), pp.34-35.

6

Town and Council

Most contemporaries were agreed that the attitude of the townspeople and the city council towards the Royalist occupation of Oxford was much more ambivalent than that of the University. Whilst it was indeed the case that many of the inhabitants, particularly those of the Puritan persuasion and with strong trading connections in London, now severed by the war, favoured Parliament, many others actually profited financially from the newcomers.

It is sometimes suggested that the reluctance of the townspeople to turn out to work on building the fortifications ordered by the Royalists reflected their opposition, but it is more likely to have been caused by the fact that they were expected to provide a day's unpaid labour, at the expense of their own business.

The City Council in some ways reflected the attitude of those it claimed to represent. In part its lack of enthusiasm was rooted in long standing rivalries with the University, which much more enthusiastically espoused the King's cause. Thirteen of the Council's members, including Alderman John Nixon, a strong supporter of Parliament, left Oxford before the King arrived.

In the summer and autumn of 1642, the councillors had agreed that it was desirable "in these tumultuous times" that there should be a stock of arms for the defence of the town, against whom not being specifically stated. In the autumn it was resolved that iron chains be bought to be placed on the gates and at other places where needed, and supplies of powder and match were also to be purchased.[1]

On 29 October, in what was to be the first of a series of similar demands, the council accepted that £250 be borrowed to be presented to the King "to supply his present wants" and the city was to purchase three pairs of gloves as presents for Prince Rupert, Prince Charles and James, Duke of York.[2]

On 17 January, in recognition that Oxford might soon find itself under siege, it was agreed that a magazine of wheat and maslin [mixed grain] should be bought

---

1   Hobson & Salter, p.107.
2   Ibid., p.111.

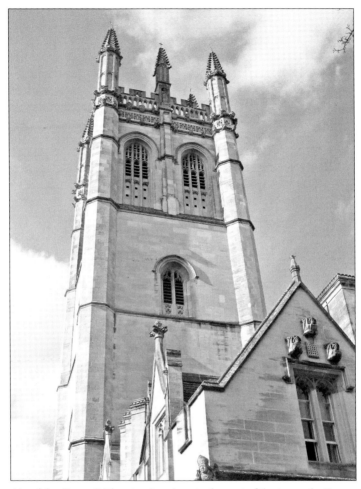

Magdalen Tower. With extensive views to the east of the town, the Tower
served as a look-out point in times of attack. (Author's collection)

and stored at the expense of the citizens, with each of "The Thirteen," the aldermen, contributing £5 towards the cost.[3]

The Council minute books, contain, however, relatively few direct references to the effects of the war. They portray a council, and perhaps town, which so far as possible were endeavouring to continue life as normal.

Charles, determined to root out potential opposition in the Council, told its members on 10 September 1643:

3   Ibid.

> We understand that there are diverse as well aldermen as Common Councilmen of our City of Oxford who many months since have gone from thence into rebellion or have adhered unto them, whereby that town must needs be the worse governed, such ill members possessing these places. We have therefore thought it necessary to recommend it to your special care forthwith to disfranchise and remove such as have deserved it by this their absence and make choice of other able and fit men to supply their places.[4]

The Council somewhat reluctantly complied.

Financial demands continued to be made. In June 1643, the King demanded a loan of £2,500, which the Council had little option but to borrow, lacking sufficient funds themselves to meet the request. These financial demands, including contributions towards the upkeep of the garrison and fortifications, became a major source of grievance as the war went on. These became more acute after the Council was also expected to support the City Regiment. In January 1644, the councillors refused a request from the privy council for £200 a week towards the fortifications. The City Regiment, they pointed out, was already costing them £120 a week. They did somewhat half-heartedly, offer labour for work on the defences, though they added that "they are much weakened in this service since the Governor's soldiers and the soldiers of the City Regiment, owing to their other duties, are freed of this service."[5] A week or so later further discontent was aroused when the governor, the much-hated Sir Arthur Aston, who had recently physically attacked the Mayor, demanded a payment of £10 a week for his major to open and close the town gates each day. This was seen as a demand too far:

> Mr Mayor desired the advice of the house who all with one mind did say that they are unable to pay taxes already imposed upon them much more [than] to pay the said weekly payment. And therefore this house desire Mr Mayor … to offer him that this duty shall be performed by some of the captains of this City or by some others whom Mr Mayor and his brethren will undertake for.[6]

Given his well-attested mistrust of the townspeople, it is unlikely that Aston will have received this proposal favourably.

As well as periodic food shortages, the influx of over 3,000 newcomers on top of Oxford's existing population of around 10,000, resulted in major problems of hygiene and public health. In March 1643 the Council noted that "great complaint

---

4   Ibid., p.114.
5   Ibid., p.117.
6   Ibid.

The Lucy Chapel, Christ Church Cathedral. A number of leading Royalists were buried here in the course of the war, and the memorials to several of them can still be seen.
(Author's collection)

is made to his Majesty for the not cleansing the streets of this city, but suffering the filth and dirt to lie in the same not only to the scandal of the government of this place but also to the great danger of the breeding an infection amongst us." Indeed, this would happen a few months later. It was agreed that two men should be nominated in each parish to cleanse the streets.[7]

In August the King sent an order to the mayor and bailiffs ordering that the streets be cleaned. There are several references in the town records to this work.

7   Ibid., p.112.

In October for carrying away "29 loads of durt" a payment of 19s 4d was made, in November £1 1s for 26 loads. In comparison in 1642-43 a man had been paid £1 for cleaning the streets for a full year.[8]

It is difficult to estimate just how great the burden of increased taxation was on Oxford, given that there are no comprehensive records of pre-war taxation. In the years before the war an annual Ship Money payment of £150 was demanded. This was divided up among the parishes in varying amounts: St Mary the Virgin, as the wealthiest area of the city, paid £12 10s, St John's only £1 2s. But in December 1642 alone, the Council was required to raise £150 for "the better ordering this city, University and county of Oxon as well as for providing for maimed soldiers and fuel for soldiers that keep the watches and wards as also for the building of the sheds for the defence of the same soldiers from the weather." Again the amounts required from each parish varied. St Aldate's had to raise £17, St John's £2.[9]

The maintenance of the City Regiment imposed a much heavier and regular burden of taxation. In October 1643, when the city had to raise £1,500 for its upkeep, St Mary the Virgin parish had to contribute £170, and St John's £18. This of course was in addition to the regular demands for payments for the fortifications. It seems that the wealthier Council members continued to make personal contributions. In 1642, on the King's arrival in Oxford after the Battle of Edgehill, the Mayor and several aldermen made significant payments towards the £520 presented to him.[10] The Council of course in theory received taxes from the inhabitants and rents from properties, but the disruption caused by the war made both of these difficult to obtain.

Another source of grievance was the annual demand from the King for the first hay crop of the year from Port Meadow to provide fodder for his cavalry. As the war went on, the Council became more grudging in their approval. In 1644 the King was told:

> It is unanimously consented unto that his majesty shall have the first crop of the said Meadow this present ensuing year provided that … the citizens be not compelled to help make the hay thereof or to make any allowance of money towards the making thereof.[11]

By 1646, as we shall see, permission was yet more conditional.

The financial demands made on the Council worsened relations with the University whose "privileged" members were exempt from taxation by the Council.

---

8   Ibid., p.119.
9   Eddershaw, p.66.
10   Ibid.
11   Hobson & Salter, p.118.

In June 1643, however the King, when asking the Council to raise £2,000, stipulated that the "privileged", though not the heads of Colleges or scholars, should also be liable for taxation. However on receiving a petition of protest from the university, the King backed down, handing over responsibility for deciding how the money should be raised to three commissioners, headed by the Earl of Bristol. Further argument followed, with both University and Council pressing their respective cases. On 15 August the commissioners effectively gave up on the issue, saying that the vice-chancellor and mayor should meet to settle the matter. It is unclear from surviving records what the final outcome was. But the whole affair did little to endear either the University or the Royalist cause to the councillors.[12]

12   Eddershaw, p.68.

7

The University

The scholars of the University were predominantly Royalist in sympathy, as witnessed by the large numbers of them who took up arms on the outbreak of war, and the relative readiness of some at least of the colleges to send part of their plate to bolster the King's war effort.

However after Oxford became the King's *de facto* capital, the impact of the war on the University became increasingly evident. College life was in most cases totally disrupted. Christ Church and Merton became effectively royal residences. New College became a military magazine and workshops.

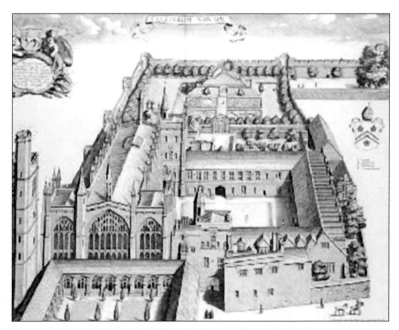

New College. (Author's collection)

By 1644 the number of scholars matriculating had dwindled almost to nothing, most having either enlisted or left the city. The majority of degrees conferred were honorary ones, bestowed on royalty or leading Royalist supporters On 21 February 1643 the university petitioned the King to protest against this practice, which saw 140 honorary MAs granted between November 1642 and February 1643, not only involved significant expense for the University, for which they received no compensation, but also diminished the status of the degrees themselves. The practice, however, was continued, as a cheap way for the King to honour his supporters.[1]

As well as the periodic demands for financial contributions, the colleges, particularly after the Oxford Parliament was convened, were required to provide accommodation for strangers, officers, civilians, and, probably a matter of horror to many of the fellows, their wives! Most of the remaining scholars were sent away in order to find space for these "lodgers."

The "strangers" were enrolled on the college books, and partook of college provisions, for which they evidently frequently failed to pay. Anthony Wood wrote that by the end of the war "Colleges and Halls were much out of repair through the negligence of courtiers, soldiers and others" who had been lodged in them. Such scholars as remained, Wood tells us were "much debauched and became idle by bearing arms and keeping company with rude soldiers," and spent much of the time in the more dubious taverns of the town, such as the Holly Bush and the Angel Inn.[2]

1   Varley (1932), p.43.
2   Wood, p.58.

8

Munitions

The increasing likelihood of prolonged war left the Royalists with the task of creating a munitions industry virtually from scratch, and as King Charles's capital, and headquarters of what is known to modern writers, though rarely at the time, as the "Oxford Army," the King's main field force, Oxford found itself at the forefront of these efforts.

Before the war, the Ordnance Office, based in the Tower of London, had regulated all munitions supplies in England. Its officials negotiated with manufacturers and suppliers and the material purchased was stored by the Ordnance Office in the Tower and a small number of other magazines such as those at Hull and Portsmouth. They issued or re-sold munitions to county militias and Trained Bands and to the Navy.

The Ordnance Office was governed by the Master of the Ordnance, his Lieutenant and four other principal officers. It was a notoriously inefficient and corrupt organisation, involved in frequent disputes with those with whom it dealt.

On the outbreak of the war the Ordnance Office officials had to choose sides. The Lieutenant, Sir John Heydon,[1] and two of his principal officers, Richard March and Edward Sherburne, elected to join the King. Six of the other senior Ordnance Office officials also stayed loyal to the crown. But many of the lesser officers, partly for financial reasons and because their homes and families were in London, chose Parliament. As a result the Royalist artillery train was at first seriously undermanned. But Edward Stephens, Heydon's clerk, and some of the gun founders went with their employer to join the King at York in the early summer of 1642, although they had to leave behind their workshops and much of their equipment. As a result the Royalist army initially depended mainly on cannon imported from abroad, with gun carriages made in York.

From the beginning of hostilities Heydon proved to be an efficient and generally well-regarded officer. He was a professional soldier of great experience, who had

---

1   D.N.B.

been in post since 1627. His chief assistant was Captain Henry Younger, another professional soldier. A small team of Artillery Commissioners were appointed in the summer of 1642, of whom the most notable, steadily increasing in influence throughout the war, were John Wandesford and George Strode. Strode was a London businessman and strongly Royalist supporter. Wandesford was of Yorkshire gentry background, who had been a pre-war MP and diplomat. Both would go into exile at the end of the Civil War as a result of their Royalist activities.

At first their work was largely confined to maintaining and expanding the artillery train, although Strode was wounded in action at the Battle of Edgehill.

Anthony Wood described the first impact of the Ordnance Office and need for munitions on Oxford. "The ordnance and great guns were driven into Magdalen College grove, about 26 or 27 pieces, with all their carriages."[2] Magdalen College Grove would be the Oxford Army's main artillery park throughout the war, and many of the workshops and forges for repairing equipment were set up there.

Strode and Wandesford were appointed Keepers for the supplies of arms and equipment – muskets, powder and shot – which were removed in November 1642 from the town magazine in the Guildhall and taken to the Schools Tower. The Schools became both the main Oxford armoury and an important workshop for the assembly and repair of weapons.

The central magazine, the equivalent of the Ordnance Office in the Tower of London, was established in New College, in its tower and cloisters, with the remaining scholars ejected and moved to a "dark nasty place."[3] Richard Sherburne and Edward March were Keeper and Clerk of the Stores, responsible for maintaining its records.

As well as the train of artillery, the Ordnance Office would also take charge of the manufacture, supply and transportation of munitions to all Royalist forces south of the Trent, only the Earl of Newcastle's Northern army having a separate administration.

In May 1643, following his arrival from the North of England with the first convoy of munitions sent by the Queen, Lord Henry Percy was appointed General of the Ordnance. Percy was the younger brother of the Earl of Northumberland, who was a Parliamentarian supporter.[4] Percy owed his appointment to being a favourite of Queen Henrietta Maria, though even she admitted that he had "his weak points." The Earl of Clarendon was more uncompromising, commenting that Percy was "generally unloved, as a proud and supercilious person." Certainly Percy never displayed any particularly active role, leaving most of the work to Heydon and the other officials. He was dismissed with Lord Wilmot in August 1644, for suspected disloyalty, and replaced by Ralph, Lord Hopton, who would

2   Wood, p.68.
3   Ibid., p.69.
4   D.N.B.

Magdalen College Grove, the principal artillery park for the Oxford Army throughout the war. (Author's collection)

Lord Henry Percy (c.1604-1659). Dismissed as General of the Ordnance in 1644 for alleged involvement in plot to force the King to make peace, he went to France and joined the Queen. (National Trust Images)

probably have been more effective if he had not been absent on other duties in the West Country most of the time. Heydon continued to exercise overall control.

By early 1644 the Ordnance Office personnel included 17 Gentlemen of the Ordnance who were in charge of individual artillery batteries or magazines. There were several engineers and battery masters, and rank and file including conductors, gunners and mattrosses, as well as hundreds of pioneers and carters, mostly concerned with maintenance and the transport of munitions. There were also large numbers of craftsmen, wheelwrights, carpenters and gun founders, responsible for maintaining wagons and gun carriages and repairs to the guns. Overall, the Ordnance Office had a total strength roughly equal to that of a regiment of foot, and had on its establishment a chaplain, surgeon, secretary and provost marshal.[5]

Transport was always a major headache for both the Ordnance Office and the army as a whole. Carts and equipment were under the overall control of the Wagon Master General of the Army. Winter Gaunt was the first holder of the post, followed by Henry Stevens. A permanent pool of wagons and carts of the Ordnance Office were held at Magdalen College Grove and New College, and were supplemented when required by calling on the Wagon Master General. He in turn had a permanent establishment of wagons and horses and oxen, which were added to as required by hirings and requisitions from the surrounding countryside. In 1643-44 civilians were in theory paid at a rate of 6d a mile per cart supplied.[6]

The Ordnance Office supplied outlying garrisons in the network around Oxford either by means of wagons, or when possibly by barges along the Thames. An ordnance officer had to calculate the number of personnel, quantity of transport etc required for each artillery train required for a specific operation or campaign. The train had its own stock of horses and at the end of 1643 about 400 oxen. Some were kept in Oxford, probably in Magdalen College Grove, and others out at Iffley. Any surplus or unfit beasts were sometimes sold off in Christ Church Meadow, but more usually there was a shortage. Many horses for the train seem to have been obtained from the Kidlington area north of Oxford, which also provided winter quarters for many of the rank and file of the artillery train.

There was a considerable difference in the rates of pay of the personnel of the Ordnance Office. Lord Percy received £4 a day, a pioneer 1/-. In practice pay was frequently in arrears, resulting in considerable hardship. Heydon and the Ordnance Commissioners on occasion attempted to settle the most pressing needs from their own pockets. In theory all financial payments for the Ordnance Office came via the Treasury, administered by John Ashburnham. The Treasury also had to pay the Master Fireworker and the powder makers.

---

5   Roy (ed.), *The Royalist Ordnance Papers Part I* (Oxford, 1964) p.21.
6   Ibid., p.22.

Captain Will Legge, was appointed Master of the Armoury at the end of 1642, with responsibility for arms supplies. With Oxford established as the headquarters of the King and his principal field army, it was inevitable that it also became an increasingly important centre for arms manufacture. This was mainly organised by Strode and Wandesford, and commenced in December 1642 when the Council of War ordered them to co-operate with Heydon regarding the repair and supply of firearms. Especially they were to organise the employment of gunsmith and metal workers, many of whom worked in the Schools Tower. There were also independent craftsman within the city contracted to supply arms.

In January 1643, in preparation for the coming campaigning season, the Council of War ordered the Ordnance Office to ready an artillery train of 40 guns.[7] By now the Oxford munitions industry was becoming clearly organised. A number of workshops, foundries and mills were established, run by artificers from the Tower with a locally enlisted labour force. The King's Master Smith, Michael Bastian, was supplied with a forge and tools by a local blacksmith, Thomas Adams. Craftsmen from villages around Oxford were also involved in producing and repairing weapons and in supplying other munitions. Some foreign workers were also based in Oxford, for example a German armourer who would voice the common complaint among those who worked for the Royalist war effort that he had not been paid. The Oxford workforce was a mixture of English families with a long-established connection with the arms industry, local craftsmen who adapted their premises and equipment to the needs of the Royalist war effort, and a variety of foreign workers. Many of these came from France and the Low Countries, including Monsieur Fluery, the Chief Engineer to the Artillery Train, and Monsieur Montgarnier, a controller in 1643. There was also the engineer Bernard de Gomme, and the fireworker Bartholomew La Roche. Another prominent figure was the Dutch or Swedish engineer Doderick or Henrick Beckman, who may have been involved in the construction of Oxford's fortifications.[8]

The Oxford gunsmiths do not seem to have manufactured very large quantities of firearms. They seem to have concentrated rather more on repairs. However Michael Bastian, the King's master smith, did assemble new muskets, receiving locks and other parts manufactured by smiths in surrounding villages. William Standinought, another leading Oxford smith, spent most of his time repairing weapons. Between 12 January and 23 October 1643 he fixed 505 muskets, but only definitely manufactured four.[9]

7   Ibid., p.26.
8   Ibid.
9   Peter Edwards, *Dealing in Death: The arms trade and the British Civil Wars, 1638-52* (Stroud, 2000), pp.76-77.

In February 1643 140 "broken" muskets belonging to Lord Wentworth's Regiment of Dragoons were distributed for repair among the Oxford gunsmiths. Ten of them were given a deadline of three days to refurbish 80 muskets, whilst three others were given a fortnight to carry out more extensive repairs to another 56, which required new locks and stocks. It is possible that they had been damaged in the hand-to-hand fighting at the capture of Cirencester.[10]

Pikes and bills were assembled at the workshop in the Schools Tower. In April 1644 499 were sent to the magazine, in May 1645 another 900. Many of the pike heads and staffs were manufactured in the neighbouring villages. Thomas Hill, a pikestaff maker from Chieveley, was a major supplier. On 18 June 1643 he provided 202 pikestaffs each 15 feet 6 inches in length, rather than the theoretically preferred length of 18 feet. By the end of July he had sent a further 160 together with 232 and 50 half-pike staffs.[11] Several blacksmiths supplied pike heads. Among them was Robert Frise from Blewbury, a village which seems to have been a location for several weapons manufacturers. In February 1645 1,000 pikeheads were ordered from there. Others were sent from Shropshire and the West Midlands.[12]

Poleaxes were said to have been popular amongst the Royalist horse, at least in the earlier stages of the war, and John Buller, an Oxford locksmith, produced 916 during the first half of 1643. David Wood produced halberds, and, rather puzzlingly, the occasional javelin.[13]

Some workers were issued with components from the stores to assemble. Among them, on 23 February 1643, was Martin Goldbourne of Cat Street who was given parts for 40 muskets and a fortnight in which to assemble them. Having finished the job in nine days, he was given two more batches to complete in March.[14] A cannon foundry was established in Christ Church, and workshops and forges in Magdalen Grove, where supplies of timber and sea coal were also stored.

From early in the Royalist occupation of Oxford the Ordnance Commissioners had authority to requisition supplies of metal wherever they could. Lead and iron were taken from private individuals, and the inhabitants of Oxford were encouraged to bring in kettles, pots, pans etc to be melted down. Old cannon and others which for various reasons were found to be unsuitable for military use were also melted down. Contractors supplied iron shot, and implements, baskets, spades, picks and mills were established for the production of munitions at Holywell, Folly Bridge and Osney. The cannon were probably bored at one of these after being cast at Christ Church.

10   Ibid., p.77.
11   Ibid.
12   Ibid.
13   Ibid.
14   Ibid., pp.77-78.

Cannon making. (Author's collection)

The chief Oxford gunfounder was a "Mr Lanyon" – possibly John Lanyon, who had been a proof master in his earlier years. He does not seem to have been particularly skilled. There were two small brass guns manufactured by him in the armoury in May 1643, but both were melted down later. However the standard of Lanyon's work evidently improved, and by February 1644 new contracts had been made with him. These included both brass and iron guns. The iron sakers were intended for the Oxford defences, and the brass guns were held to be more suited for the field army. However the bulk of Royalist ordnance came from elsewhere, notably the Shropshire and Worcestershire foundries. Nevertheless, the gun foundry in Oxford continued to operate throughout the Royalist occupation.[15]

In the summer of 1643 the cannon foundry was also equipped with tools to grind sword blades. Eventually Will Legge was given the task of establishing and running a separate sword mill at Wolvercote, and Legge also forged blades at Gloucester Hall. Various Oxford cutlers also forged blades. On 11 February 1643 Jeremy Poole sent 14 swords to the New College magazine. As more were needed on 20 June the Council of War authorised Strode and Wandesford to fit grindstones and wheels to cannon boring equipment in Christ Church to enable it to grind sword blades. Around 400 swords were sent to the stores from the Schools Tower. On 20 November Will Legge was granted £100 to build forges and a grinding mill and equip it. Blades were forged at Gloucester Hall and edged at a new mill on the Thames at Wolvercote. It may well be that Benjamin Stone, the King's pre-war sword maker, was responsible for organising the work.[16]

---

15 Roy, p.28.
16 Edwards, p.78.

There were reports of more esoteric weapon production. In September 1643 the Parliamentarian newspaper *Mercurius Civicus* said that the Royalists were manufacturing bows and arrows in a room above the North Gate.[17]

The commissioners supervised the production of powder and match. Match was in production from early in 1643, and new mills were built and older ones adapted for the production of gunpowder on the banks of the Isis and the Cherwell. The defences on the south side of the city had to be adapted to include them within its circuit. Sir Charles Lloyd, the Chief Engineer, dug wider channels from the rivers to the mills in order to increase the water power, with local labour used to build and repair the mills. A converted fulling mill at Osney was also used to manufacture powder. Although in 1646 only two powder mills were in operation in Oxford, it seems likely that there were more in earlier years.[18]

Powder making was organised initially by William Baber, a Bristol powdermaker. He and his uncle, a Mr Thrupp of Bristol, had begun production by June 1643, and Thrupp's works was taken over by the Ordnance Commissioners. In February 1644 Baber said construction work had cost him £3,000 but he only received a tenth of that in compensation. Soon afterwards Baber seems to have returned to Bristol, where he continued to produce powder.

Shot was cast by James Fletcher, a plumber, and Charles Greene, a conductor of the artillery train. In June 1643 Fletcher cast two-and-three-quarter tons and Greene two cwt. Both continued production for some time. Fletcher was still operating in April 1644, by which time he had cast over 20 tons. Both he and Greene evidently continued work until the end of the war.[19] They received their supplies of lead from the royal stores, who in turn obtained it from various sources. In some cases, particularly early in the war, it was stripped from the roofs of buildings. On 13 April 1644 a consignment arrived from Bristol which had probably been mined in the Mendip Hills.

Some armour was made in Oxford. John Nicholas had been a master armourer in the royal service before the war, and before his death in August 1643 he had set up the means to manufacture armour in Oxford, though he was initially mainly engaged in refurbishing the armour which had been brought in as result of the appeals made in Oxford and its surroundings.

Strode and Wandesford contracted for munitions with private manufacturers and frequently paid them themselves, so that the Royalist command found itself increasingly indebted to them. With few resources to settle these debts, the King instead compensated the commissioners with an extension of their powers and privileges.[20]

---

17   Ibid., p.94.
18   Roy, pp.29-32.
19   Edwards, pp.104-105.
20   Roy, p.32.

By early 1644 the sweeping powers granted to Strode and Wandesford were causing considerable resentment in Oxford. Arthur Trevor, Prince Rupert's agent in Oxford, told his master that the original Oxford powder makers had refused to hand over their equipment to the commissioners and as a result had been imprisoned. On the day after the patent transferring powder manufacture to the commissioners was sealed "the drying house and some six men blew up" in an incident alleged to be sabotage.[21]

Although it seems that the Commissioners were never awarded a complete monopoly, by early 1644 their magazine at the Schools was the main manufacturing centre in Oxford, with most of the munitions made there despatched to the magazine at New College. The Commissioners planned to produce 50 barrels of powder a week, although it is unlikely that this target was ever achieved.

After the war Wandesford claimed that he and Strode had spent £18,000 in the Royalist cause, of which £5,000 was still outstanding.[22]

Bartholomew La Roche, a Walloon, was one of the military professionals who accompanied Prince Rupert from the Continent in the summer of 1642. He was appointed "fireworker" to the Oxford Army, and established his premises in "some little houses" by Magdalen Bridge. La Roche produced a variety of incendiary and explosive devices for the army, including mortar shells, granadoes, fire pikes, petards and various similar items. The records of the Ordnance Office list payments for various often exotic ingredients supplied to La Roche. For example, on 25 April 1643 he was supplied with 3 lb 13 oz of Camphor, three quarts of linseed oil 2 lb of "peter oil" old linen, and two bottles. Also listed on other occasions were items such as bees wax, resin, frankincense and turpentine, as well as various pieces of equipment, such as ladles and kettles. Mortars were ordered to fire his products, and shell cases ordered from the Shropshire iron forges to contain his mixtures.[23]

La Roche and his assistants sometimes accompanied the army on campaign. He was in charge of a mortar at the capture of Cirencester in February 1643, and his assistants, Fawcett and Hendricks, if not La Roche himself, were at the sieges of Lichfield and Bristol in 1643. In July La Roche was appointed Captain General of all masters of artificial fires and fireworkers. In December La Roche's fee of £600 a year was made an annuity for life.[24] La Roche's devices were costly to produce and required often difficult to obtain materials, so it is not surprising that payments, sometimes totalling over £70 a week, were frequently in arrears. In early 1644 La Roche quarrelled with Lord Percy over the issue of payments, and Prince Rupert, preparing for his campaign in Lancashire, was left waiting

21   Ibid., p.30.
22   Ibid.
23   Roy, pp.32-33.
24   Ibid.

A petard – a device almost as dangerous to the user as to his intended target. (Author's collection)

for supplies. Arthur Trevor visited La Roche in his little house in an attempt to resolve the problem, but the Frenchman "swore, stared, cried: 'No money, no money' … Without money he has no more motion than a stone … "[25]

In 1645 the discontented La Roche asked that what was owing to him to be paid, and for permission to leave the King's employment. Instead, in April, he was apparently mollified with a knighthood, and, despite Parliamentarian attempts to subvert him, La Roche remained in Royalist service until he departed with Prince Rupert for the Continent in 1646.

25   Ibid.

Some Royalist troops were poorly or unarmed at the close of the 1642 campaign, and, as a stop-gap until new supplies were obtained, the inhabitants of Oxford were asked to bring any arms or armour in their possession to be stored in the Schools. From April 1643 it was ordered that all arms, except those necessary for private use, were to be deposited, with penalties for defaulters. The results were distinctly mixed. Many of the weapons delivered were obsolete or in poor condition. Among the donations were on 23 January from Thomas Clerk, an innkeeper "one back, two breasts, one headpiece, one carbine firelock, and one sword." Or on 12 March "from Mr ffoubeard living at the East gate one Caliver, two Bandoliers, one helmet. From Thomas Bennet of St Peters in the Body one Binding Piece and a sword without a scabbard."[26]

Although the calls for arms were in part for propaganda purposes, and to disarm potentially troublesome elements within the town, they also produced some useful acquisitions, including 100 muskets.

From the spring of 1643 onwards the magazines and armouries at Oxford began to receive supplies of munitions via the Cotswolds from Worcestershire, the Forest of Dean and Shropshire, with supplies from the latter area often brought down the River Severn to Worcester aboard barges and flat boats. Later, as the Oxford arms industry developed, the same trans-Cotswold route would be employed to transport arms and powder to the West Midlands. Convoys would be reasonably safe until they reached the vicinity of the Parliamentarian garrison at Gloucester, where they would need a heavy escort. Convoys moving in the opposite direction would have to be heavily guarded from the time they left Worcester. They would be escorted by Worcester troops as far as Chipping Campden or Stow-on-the-Wold, where troops from Oxford would take over. This route would be virtually closed in May 1645, when the Parliamentarians captured Evesham.

The Ordnance Office had the responsibility for the organisation of the distribution of munitions supplies, and keeping a record of these. As in other respects, there were various difficulties in the opening months of the war, when soldiers frequently sold arms and horses for money. There was also later a Town Armoury in Oxford to arm and supply the regiments raised for town defence. This was set up in 1644, on the urgings of the Oxford Parliament which provided funding.

Other deliveries for the defence of the city were supervised by the Ordnance Office. The Oxford garrison regiments received a weekly supply of powder and match and for the ordnance positioned on the defences. There were several artillery batteries, including a small iron gun at the East Gate, a battery at the Physic Garden, St Clements, South Bridge and St Giles in North Gate. Each was under the command of a Gentleman of the Ordnance.

One of the more unusual undertakings by the Ordnance Office was the production of pontoon bridges for the Oxford Army for the 1645 campaign. It had

---

26   Roy, pp. 63-95 lists a large number of these receipts.

originally been intended that 12 large leather boats be obtained from the governor of Shrewsbury, but Shrewsbury fell before the work was completed and construction was transferred to Oxford. The King "caused 14 boats to be made for transporting his artillery over any river, and one day makes trial upon the river against Oxford to find how these boats would carry these guns causing two of the biggest to be drawn over by them." Only eight pontoons were included in the train when the King left Oxford in May. In June supplies to complete the others were still being received. The smith, Michael Bastian, supplied iron stakes, and a large quantity of tools to Thomas Wells, bridge maker, on 14 April, including 12 boat poles shod with iron. John Ham, ropemaker of Oxford, supplied tarred and white rope on 28 April. But the carriages were still being constructed on 12 June.[27]

The Schools magazine issued munitions to the Oxford army and its detachments for use on campaign. On 29 April 1645, for example, 80 barrels of powder, 50 cwt of match and 25 cwt of musket shot were issued at the start of the Naseby campaign. Further supplies were sent as required. For example there were urgent requests for additional powder and shot on the evening of 20 September 1643, after heavy fighting at the First Battle of Newbury.

The effective destruction of the Oxford Army as a viable fighting force at the Battle of Naseby (14 June 1645) meant that the work of the Ordnance Office was greatly reduced in the closing months of the war. Some of its personnel were formed into a troop of horse under Sherburne, and acted as part of the Oxford garrison in the closing months of the war, although New College workshops and the Schools magazine continued to operate until the end of the siege. It may have been in these less busy times that one of the clerks scribbled on the journal of receipts a wistful verse:

"What thing
is love is love,
How sure I am
It is King …
It is a …
Pretty thing …"[28]

---

27   Ibid., pp.195, 428.
28   Ibid., p.58.

9

The Thames Valley Campaign 1643

As the arrival of winter brought major campaigning to an end, the Royalists established a circle of garrisons and quarters for their troops around Oxford, intended to secure both the town itself and an area to supply its and the army's needs. Major garrisons were established at Reading, Banbury, Abingdon, Faringdon and Wallingford, together with a string of lesser outposts at locations such as Woodstock and Brill on the Hill.

Minor skirmishing took place at intervals. On 1 January 1643 Sir John Byron won a spirited little encounter at Burford with Parliamentarian troops from Cirencester, providing excellent copy for the first issue of the new Royalist newspaper *Mercurius Aulicus*. Royalist troops took both Marlborough and Cirencester, opening up communications with the West of England.

By far the most important of the outlying Royalist garrisons was that at Reading, held by Sir Arthur Aston with six regiments of foot and two of horse, perhaps totalling at this point about 3,000 men. It was clear that the capture of Reading must be the first stage in any Parliamentarian advance on Oxford, and Aston, who according to his own account, faced problems with mutinous soldiery and uncooperative townspeople, made some effort during the winter to strengthen the defences. It was not until April that the Earl of Essex's Parliamentarian forces were ready to take the field, with around 12,000 foot and 3,000 horse, with at least 16 guns. They arrived before Reading on 15 April, and over the next few days invested the town. A fairly intensive bombardment began, and it was soon clear that Aston was in difficulties. On 20 April Sir Arthur was struck on the head by a roof tile dislodged by the bombardment, and, by his own later account at least, rendered speechless and incapable of exercising command. Colonel Richard Feilding took over. Prince Rupert had been absent operating in the Midlands, but on 16 April he was summoned by the King to return to Oxford as soon as possible to assist in the attempt to relieve Reading. Understrength and short of munitions, the Oxford Army possibly totalled no more than 6,000 men. It is therefore not surprising that relief attempts quickly foundered in skirmishing at Caversham Bridge, Nevertheless the Royalists were able to slip some additional supplies of ammunition in Reading.[1] It was too late – on 26 April, Feilding had agreed surrender terms with Essex. The Royalists, retaining most of their weapons, marched out next day, *en route* for Oxford. Feilding could argue that he had saved some 3,000 invaluable foot to add to the Oxford Army, but the loss of Reading caused near-panic in the Royalist capital. Clarendon captured the sense of dismay. He admitted that Oxford was "not tolerably fortified," and that the large number of courtiers and other Royalist refugees in the town "bore any kind of alarum very ill."[2] As we have seen it is likely that the fortifications were already rather stronger than Clarendon admitted, but there were certainly frantic efforts to prepare to meet an imminent attack. "They take the bells from Churches, formerly counted sacrilege, and all other metals, as Brass Kettles, pots and the like," gloated the Parliamentarian newsletter *The Kingdom's Weekly Intelligencer*.[3] Further efforts were made to round up all weapons in the area, this time from the surrounding countryside. One of Samuel Luke's spies reported "there are warrants come forth from his Majesty ... to search all the houses in the country thereabouts for all manner of arms, pikes, halberds, muskets, birding pieces, etc, and for the arms collected to be delivered to Wallingford Castle."[4] In Oxford itself, at least one loyal supporter of King Charles, Richard Billingsley, the cook at Wadham College, handed over breast and back plates and a sword without a scabbard.[5]

On 28 April, King Charles, accompanied by the Prince of Wales and Princes Rupert and Maurice, re-entered Oxford after the failed Reading expedition. With him came the rest of his army, including the defenders of Reading. The outlook was worrying. Not only the Royalist courtiers and their followers were apprehensive; the King himself "was so far from believing the condition he was in to be tolerable, that upon the news of the Earl of Essex his advance towards Oxford within three or four days after the loss of Reading, he once resolved ... to march away towards the North, to join with the Earl of Newcastle."[6] It is possible that an immediate advance by the Earl of Essex might have resulted in the evacuation of Oxford but the failure or inability of Essex immediately to follow up his success gave the Royalists a breathing space. Morale in Oxford remained low.

Recriminations came to a head in the court martial proceedings against Richard Feilding. As soon as Feilding reached Oxford there grew a whisper that there had not been fair carriage, and that Reading had been betrayed. The rumour quickly "made a noise through Oxford" especially among the troops, with "divers

1   See M.C. Barres-Baker, *The Siege of Reading April 1643* (N.p., n.d.), pp.104-146.
2   Clarendon, *History of the Rebellion and Civil Wars in England begun in the year 1641* (Oxford, 1888, Volume) Book VII, p.38.
3   Quoted Barres-Baker, p.158.
4   Ibid.
5   Clarendon, op. cit.
6   Ibid., pp.40-45.

King Charles reviews Sir John Owen's Regiment, c. 1643.
(Drawing by Peter Dennis © Helion & Company)

of the officers and common soldiers crying out for justice."[7] Feilding immediately "came to the King to desire that an account might be taken of the whole business at a council of war, for his vindication." Charles was "marvellously incensed" and according to a Parliamentarian account, struck Feilding across the face with his cane. Around the same time a deputation of common soldiers from the Reading garrison approached the King "in a disorderly manner" calling for their former commander to be court-martialled.[8]

Given the feverish state of morale in Oxford, and the desire to find a scapegoat for the loss of reading, the King probably had no choice but to put Feilding on trial. Indeed there was good reason to believe that he strongly supported the action.

The Council of War met on 2 May to hear the case, and unsurprisingly Feilding was found guilty "upon an article of not obeying orders" though not of treason. In theory this made little difference to Feilding's fate as the penalty for both was death. Perhaps significantly, though, the execution was not to be immediate. Instead the "the time and place of execution were referred unto his Majesty." By now the trial and verdict were "the great business and discourse of the present day in Oxford," and led to increasing divisions. "Great animosities grew between the officers of the army, some being thought to have been too passionate and solicitous in the prosecution of the colonel, and too much to have countenanced the rage and fury of common soldiers. Of both these some were more violent than they should have been."[9]

On Saturday 13 May Feilding was led to the block in the yard of Oxford Castle, and had to mount the scaffold twice, before, on the urgings of Prince Rupert, the young Prince of Wales came forward to move the King to clemency. It was a face-saving deal intended to reconcile the opposing factions, but although pardoned, Feilding was not forgiven. "Though he had been always before of an unblemished reputation for honesty and courage and had heartily been engaged from the beginning of the troubles, and been hurt in the service … he never recovered the misfortune and blemish of this reputation." He also lost his regiment of foot, which was given to Sir Jacob Astley.[10]

Whilst the fate of Feilding was being resolved, the immediate perceived military threat to Oxford seemed to diminish. Within days of the army's return from Reading work began on a fortified camp "beyond Culham bridge by Abingdon." The bulk of the Royalist cavalry were already stationed in the Abingdon area, and the intention was to construct a fortified camp for the foot which would block any Parliamentarian advance on Oxford. The site of the camp was in a bend of the Thames which provided protection on three sides. It also blocked any advance

7   Ibid.
8   Ibid.
9   Ibid.
10   Ibid.

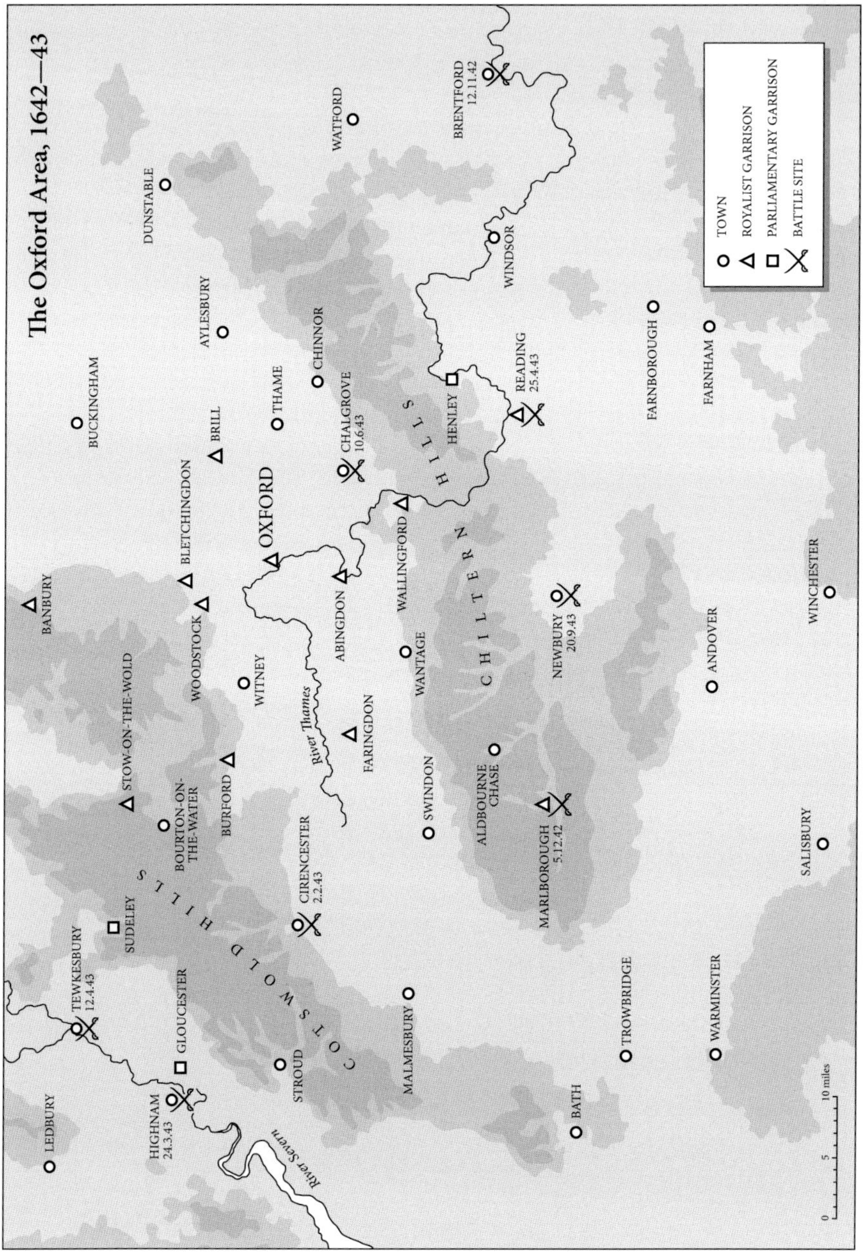

The Oxford Area, 1642—43

LEDBURY O

TEWKESBURY
12.4.43 ✗

HIGHNAM
24.3.43 ✗

GLOUCESTER □

SUDELEY □

STROUD O

MALMESBURY O

BATH O

TROWBRIDGE O

WARMINSTER O

SALISBURY O

WINCHESTER O

ANDOVER O

FARNHAM O

FARNBOROUGH O

WINDSOR O

WATFORD O

DUNSTABLE O

BUCKINGHAM O

AYLESBURY O

CHINNOR O

THAME O

OXFORD ◁

BRILL ◁

BLETCHINGDON ◁

WOODSTOCK ◁

BANBURY ◁

STOW-ON-THE-WOLD ◁

BOURTON-ON-
THE-WATER ◁

BURFORD ◁

WITNEY O

ABINGDON ◁

FARINGDON ◁

WANTAGE O

SWINDON O

CIRENCESTER
2.2.43 ✗

River Severn

River Thames

C O T S W O L D   H I L L S

C H I L T E R N   H I L L S

WALLINGFORD ◁

CHALGROVE
10.6.43 ✗

HENLEY □

READING
25.4.43 ✗

BRENTFORD
12.11.42 ✗

ALDBOURNE
CHASE O

MARLBOROUGH
5.12.42 ✗

NEWBURY
20.9.43 ✗

	TOWN	ROYALIST GARRISON	PARLIAMENTARY GARRISON	BATTLE SITE
	O	◁	□	✗

0   5   10 miles

Map 4 The Oxford area 1642-43.

south of the Thames, which would leave the way open for the King either to cross the Thames and take Essex in the rear or thrust into Buckinghamshire and Berkshire.

Although no evidence of Culham Camp now survives, it was evidently substantial, with fairly basic houses built with "turf, timber and board," along streets with names like "London," and 500 tents. Culham Camp was protected by trenches and also by a complex of pits or "foxholes," which Luke's scouts described as "caves."

Work was also underway strengthening the defences of the garrisons of Wallingford and Abingdon, and in Oxford the defences were strengthened by demolishing houses in St Clement's parish to clear the line of fire for the battery erected at the end of Magdalen Bridge. However, there were growing problems in Culham Camp. Accidental fires destroying huts and tents were common. Keeping the camp provisioned was challenging, and men began to desert. Disease was a growing problem. And several colonels of the 15 regiments in the camp prepared a list of nine "Humble desires" addressed to the Council of War.[11] They were:

1. That every regiment should have waggons to carry ammunition, sick men and their arms.
2. That the sutlers of every regiment have £15 to procure a sutler's cart and a stock of provision 'proportionable to the strength of the regiment'.
3. That all musketeers be supplied with bandoliers or bags to carry their charges.
4. That a physician or apothecary may continually attend the Leaguer and that some village near the Leaguer may be appointed in regards that the soldiers which have gone to Oxford are neglected, and seldom or never return to their colours.
5. That the soldiers may be furnished with shoes and stockings.
6. That the officers be prevented from leaving their regiments and obtaining commands in other units, and that those guilty of this be punished.
7. That the quartermasters and baggage masters of every regiment be paid part of their arrears, in regards they have had no pay since they came from Nottingham.
8. That cavalry not be allowed recruit men from infantry units.
9. That his Majesty would be pleased to remember the officers who have long subsisted without pay.
10. That existing regiments be brought up to strength before new units were formed.

11 Barres-Baker, pp.165-166.

These demands illustrated the poor condition of the King's army that spring. Not all of them were met, but the Council of War agreed to the requests relating to pay, equipment, transport and a military hospital. In theory, at least!

By the end of the first week in May the Royalists were growing more confident that the immediate threat from Essex was passing. On Sunday the 7th, a collection for wounded soldiers was held in the churches and colleges of Oxford. The King contributed "in a very bountiful manner" along with his sons and leading nobility.[12]

Another cause of satisfaction for the Royalists came with the arrival at Woodstock on 13 May of the munitions convoy under Lord Henry Percy sent from the North of England by Queen Henrietta Maria. This removed the most pressing problem of lack of powder for the Oxford Army. According to *Mercurius Aulicus*, the consignment included 300 barrels of powder, 1,500 muskets 1,500 bandoliers and "proportionate quantity of match, and some store of corselets, helmets and other Arms."[13]

Many Parliamentarian supporters had anticipated a speedy advance on Oxford after the fall of Reading. But soon The *Kingdom's Weekly Intelligencer* was having to explain, somewhat defensively, that the advance had been delayed by the need to rest and resupply the troops "after 14 days and nights unaccustomed lying in the fields" and also by lack of pay for the troops.[14]

Speciall Passages explained:

> many amongst us expected his excellency's advance from Reading before this, they considering that nothing rideth on swifter wings that opportunity ... these forget that an Army, though consisting of valiant men, and furnished with warlike abilities, yet is but lame and useless, and unable to move itself, without money, the sinews of war, for pay is the poor Soldiers' Aqua vita, but want is such an aqua fortis, as it eats through the iron doors of discipline.[15]

Suitably eloquent words, but they did little to stifle the growing criticism in London of Essex's apparent inactivity. Clarendon claimed that the City was "very angry that he had not marched to Oxford when he first sat down before Reading ... and thought they were betrayed."[16] Awareness of this criticism, together with the failure of Parliament's commanders in the Midlands to intercept Percy and his

12   Ibid.
13   *Mercurius Aulicus*, p.154.
14   *Kingdom's Weekly Intelligencer* 21-28 May 1643, p.242 (E242 (2)).
15   *Special Passages* 21-28 May 1643 (E249 (3)), quoted in Barres-Baker, p.85.
16   Clarendon, p.46.

Robert Devereux, 3rd Earl of Essex
(1591-1646), Parliament's Captain
General from 1642 to 1645. A
uninspired commander, whose
relief of Gloucester and avoidance of
defeat at the First Battle of Newbury
in 1643 may well have saved
Parliament from being forced to a
compromise peace.
(Author's collection)

convoy, did nothing to improve Essex's mood. He headed back to London to complain in person to Parliament.

Efforts were meanwhile being made by the Mayor, corporation and city of London to raise funds for the army. Reports of their success were mixed, and it seems that willingness, if not resources, were running low. Essex told the House of Lords of his "great want of Provision of Money, which is the reason why the army cannot march, and take the advantages which occur to them." Parliament was evidently convinced, or at any rate chose not to push the issue, and "resolved that Public Thanks be given to my Lord General, for his great Pains and fidelity in the service of the state in general, and in particular, in that great service of Reading." He was also granted an annuity of £10,000 in recognition of the personal losses he had incurred in the service of Parliament.[17] Essex also apparently received part of the promised £40,000 towards the upkeep of his army, though possibly no more

17 *House of Commons Journal*, III, pp.74, 82, 95.

than a quarter of the agreed amount. No more was despatched until the middle of June. Essex was now faced by the additional problem of a growing epidemic of sickness among his troops, quartered in crowded conditions in Reading, and there were reports that such limited supplies of provisions which reached the army from London were seized upon by the officers for their own use at the expense of the common soldiers.

Whilst Essex, citing various reasons, continued to remain inactive at Reading, Rupert's cavalry were raiding far and wide, driving large numbers of plundered sheep and cattle back into Oxford, and plundering the surrounding country-side. It was not until 26 May that Essex at last got underway, and then only with the limited objective of crossing the Thames and occupying the higher ground around Caversham, hoping that this would reduce the impact of disease. The army remained here for 10 days, and evidently the rate of disease was reduced, and the ranks filled out to some extent by some new recruits. A renewed advance was about to begin.

Rupert and his cavalry were by now harassing their opponents at every opportunity. On the night of 2 June the prince with a large force of horse, captured a convoy of wagons loaded with corn and cheese at Pangbourne on its way to Essex's army, and beat up a party of dragoons before returning.[18]

On 6 June Sir Lewis Dyve, Governor of Abingdon, reported that Essex was advancing from Reading towards Henley, but that barge loads of sick were being taken along the Thames to London, "and a great number remain behind unable to stir, and many who have the use of their legs employ them in running away from the misery that follows their army. They are certainly in great confusion, and are possessed with marvellous fears ... "[19]

On the 8th the Parliamentarians pushed on through the Chilterns from Nettlebed to Stokenchurch next day, appealing for help from the county of Essex, John Hampden wrote, "Our army wants both men and money."[20]

On the 10th Essex's already dispirited men reached Thame, where the earl established his headquarters. Their misery was increased by a downpour of rain which began, and which continued for the next fortnight, complete with thunder hail and a severe gale, which blew down masonry on Christ Church Cathedral steeple in Oxford.[21] A good deal of damage was done in Thame church, with the organ pulled down and tombs defaced, whilst the town's maypole was also destroyed "whereof the Townsmen were extremely enraged." It seems that Hampden's green-coated

---

18   C.H. Firth (ed.), 'The Journal of Prince Rupert's Marches, 5 Sept. 1642 to 4 July 1646' in: *English Historical Review*, Volume 13 Number 52 (October 1898), p.733.

19   Eliot Warburton, *Memoirs of Prince Rupert and the Cavaliers Volume II* (London, 1849), p.202.

20   Quoted John Adair, *A Life of John Hampden* (London, 1976), p.227.

21   Barres-Baker, p.184.

Artillery. (Author's collection)

regiment of foot was mainly responsible, and a guard from Essex's own regiment was placed in the churchyard in an attempt to prevent further damage.[22]

Essex pushed forward outposts to Wheatley, which was only a mile from the Royalists' own forward post at Shotover Hill. Further cavalry skirmishing took place over the next few days, and concern was increasing again in Oxford. More houses were demolished in St Clement's parish to clear a line of fire for the guns of the defenders positioned in a sconce near Magdalen Bridge. The foot were withdrawn from Culham Camp to a new position on Bullingdon Green. There were reports among the Parliamentarians that the King intended to abandon Oxford, but, as Queen Henrietta Maria, currently at Newark on Trent with her great munitions convoy on its way to join the King, wrote to the Earl of Newcastle:

"The King is still expecting to be besieged in Oxford, and is resolved not to leave it, the Lords being unwilling to give their consent, saying they

22   Ibid.

will all leave, unless the King shuts himself up with them. This makes the King press me again to come to him."[23]

Some of Essex's officers, including Hampden, were pressing their commander to lay siege to the Royalist capital. Essex, however, knew that Oxford would be a much tougher nut to crack than Reading had been. The defenders were more numerous and more determined, and the defences, natural and man-made, considerably stronger. The Lord General also knew that with the numbers of troops at his disposal, he would be unable even to blockade Oxford fully. Hopes that he might be reinforced by the army of Sir William Waller faded after the latter was diverted to deal with the threat of the Cornish Royalists under Sir Ralph Hopton. Essex therefore could not realistically hope to capture Oxford, but at the same time he had few other options open to him. He could only hope to intercept or drive back the Queen and her great munitions convoy, and tie down the Oxford Army.

On 17 June he sent a detachment of 2,500 horse and foot to attack the Royalist outpost at Islip. It was held by a body of horse and dragoons under Sir Arthur Aston including his own regiment, that of the Prince of Wales, Lord Henry Percy's and 150 of Wentworth's dragoons, who were reinforced by Wilmot's horse from Bletchingdon, three miles away. Faced by equal, if not superior, numbers, the Parliamentarians retreated again.

Now it was Rupert's turn to strike back. A few days earlier, Colonel John Urry, a Scottish professional soldier who had been serving with Essex's forces, had deserted during the advance to Thame, and had made his way to Oxford along with 12 of his troopers. Urry had become disenchanted with the Parliamentarians after a dispute between English and Scots officers, and he may have made prior contact with Lord Ruthven (the Earl of Forth), who had been a comrade in arms on the continent. Urry will have given Rupert up-to-date intelligence on the condition of Essex's army and the disposition of its troops. It is usually said that he also brought news of the imminent arrival of a bullion convoy, carrying £21,000 from London. This is probably correct. But, although the convoy took refuge in the Chiltern woods, there is actually no evidence that Rupert was looking for it. His objective seems actually to have been a reprisal for the enemy raid on Islip, and to beat up some of the Parliamentarian outposts and quarters.

On the afternoon of 17 June, Rupert, at the head of just under 2,000 horse, foot and dragoons, consisting of his own Lifeguard and Regiment, Lord Percy and the Prince of Wales's Regiments of Horse, 350 selected dragoons under Lord Wentworth, and 4-500 "commanded" musketeers under Colonel Henry Lunsford, who were also evidently mounted, rode out of Oxford at about 4:00 p.m. The Royalists crossed Magdalen Bridge and went on to Chislehampton, crossing the

23   M.A.E. Green (ed.), *Letters of Queen Henrietta Maria* (London, 1886), p.208.

Thames. He then moved north to Stadhampton and Milton Common, where, probably as darkness was falling, the Royalists turned east.

Rupert and his men headed for Chinnor, four miles beyond Thame. Here they were likely only to encounter small Parliamentarian detachments as Essex's attention was focussed further north, in the direction of the Queen's likely approach, and also on protecting the pay wagons.

That same evening Colonel John Hampden had ridden out to inspect the Parliamentarian outposts, and was very concerned about how scattered they were, leaving them vulnerable to being picked off individually. He had pressed Essex to have them more concentrated, with better communications, but little had been done. Hampden quartered for the night at Watlington, at the foot of the Chilterns.

By 1:00 a.m. on 18 June the Royalists were moving through the village street at Tetworth on the London road. Despite their stealth, they were heard by the Parliamentarians, and a sentry opened fire, but Rupert ordered his men to press on into the darkness without replying. At Postcombe they surprised the quarters of a small cavalry detachment, capturing arms, a cornet and other prisoners. As dawn broke they surrounded the village of Chinnor where some of Essex's men were still peacefully sleeping. Rupert's Forlorn Hope took the enemy by surprise. The Parliamentarians "were all weary and new come into the quarters [and] were taken sleepers in the barns and Houses, Divers were killed as they bustled up, and others, that upon the Alarm, had already gotten themselves to Arms. Some Captains and Officers (as we were told) getting into a house at the town's end, would needs stand there upon their guard, shooting at the Prince and his company out of the windows. Upon which the house being fired by a Soldier, divers of them running out at the backside, were there shot by our Foot and Dragoons."[24]

About 50 of the Parliamentarians were killed and 120 taken prisoner, along with their horses and arms, along with three guidons depicting buff bibles on a black background, identifying them as men of Sir Samuel Luke's Regiment of Dragoons.

The alarm was now thoroughly raised, and the bullion convoy took refuge in the woods. If Rupert had ever intended to surprise it, the opportunity was now gone, and the Royalists turned for home. News of the Royalist raid reached Hampden at Watlington, and he sent to Essex for reinforcements, preparing to try to delay Rupert with what troops he could muster.

> The alarm came where Major Gunter lay with three troops viz. his own, Captain Sheffield's, and Captain Cross's, whom he presently drew out and marched towards the enemy: Colonel Hampden being abroad with Sir Samuel Luke and only one man, and seeing Major Gunter's Forces, they did go along with them, Colonel Dalbier the Quarter-master General did

24 Anon., *His Highness Prince Rupert's late beating up of the Rebels' quarters at Postcomb and Chinnor*, Oxford 1643.

likewise come to them: with these they drew near the Enemy, and finding them marching away, kept still upon the rear for almost five miles. In this time there joined with them Captain Sander's troop, and Captain Buller, with 50 commanded men, which were sent to Chinnor by Sir Philip Stapleton, who had the Watch here that night at Thame, when he discovered the fire there, to know the occasion of it, he likewise sent one Troop of Dragoons under the command of Captain Dundas, who came up to them. There were likewise some few of Colonel Melves Dragoons that came up to them … [25]

The Parliamentarians harassed the Royalists' rear, and there was a clash near Watlington with Percy's Regiment and Rupert's under Daniel O'Neale, in which the Parliamentarians were beaten back.

The Royalist detachment rejoined Rupert, who at about 3:00 a.m. had halted his main force in a large cornfield, known as Chalgrove field, four miles from Chislehampton. Here he planned to fight a delaying action whilst Lunsford and the foot, with some of the Prince of Wales's Regiment went ahead to secure the bridge and Chislehampton and line the hedges in the lanes leading to it with dragoons to cover the withdrawal, and to ambush any Parliamentarian horse which followed their own retreating cavalry. The Prince of Wales's Regiment and Lord Percy's were to move off first, with Rupert's Regiment and Lifeguard forming the rearguard. As daylight increased, the Royalists sighted bodies of approaching Parliamentarian horse.

The "official" Royalist account is the fullest description of what followed:

His Highness was now making halt in Chalgrove cornfield, about a mile and a half [actually four] short of Chislehampton bridge. Just at this time (being now about 9:00 a.m.) we discerned several great Bodies of the Rebels' Horse and dragooners, coming down Golder hill towards us from Easington and Thame. Who (together with those that had before skirmished with our rear) drew down to the bottom of a great Close, or Pasture, ordering themselves there among the trees beyond a great hedge, which parted that close from our field. The better to entice them on, the Prince with his Horse made show of a Retreat: whereupon the Rebels advanced cheerfully, doubling their march for eagerness, and coming up close to us. Then we discerned them to be eight Cornets of Horse, besides about 100 commanded Horse, and as many Dragooners of Colonel Mills his regiment, now led by Captain Middleton. We were now parted by a

25   Adair (1976), p.128; see also J. Stevenson & A. Carter, 'The Raid on Chinnor and the Fight at Chalgrove Field, June 17th and 18th, 1643' in: *Oxoniensia*, Volume XXXVIII, 1973, pp.346-355.

hedge, close to the midst whereof the Rebels brought on their Dragooners; and to the end of it came their Forlorn Hope of horse.

Their whole body of eight Cornets faced the Prince's Regiment and troop of Lifeguards, and made a Front so much too large for the Prince's Regiment that two Troops were fain to be drawn out of the Prince of Wales regiment to make our front even with them. And this was their Order. Besides which, they had left a Reserve of three Cornets in the Close aforesaid among the trees, by Wapsgrove House, and two troops more higher up the hill, they were in sight of one another by 9:00 a.m.

The prince's battalions were thus ordered. His highness's own regiment, with the Lifeguards, on the right hand of it, had the middle ward. The Prince of Wales his Regiment making the Left wing, and Mr Percy's having the Right. Both these Regiments were at first intended for reserves, though presently they engaged themselves in the encounter. 'Twas divers of the commanders' councils, that the Prince should continue on the retreat, and so draw the Rebels into the Ambush, but his Highness's judgement over swayed that. For that (saith he) the rebels being so near us, may bring our rear into confusion, before we can recover to our ambush. Yes (saith he) their insolency is not to be endured. This said, His highness facing all about set spurs to his horse, and first of all (in the very face of the Dragooners) leapt the hedge that parted us from the Rebels. The Captain and the rest of his Troop of Lifeguards (every man as they could) jumbled over after him: and as [soon as] about 15 were gotten over, the Prince presently drew them into a Front, till the rest could recover up to him. At this the Rebells Dragooners that lined the Hedge fled having hurt and slain some of ours with their first volley. Meantime Lieutenant-Colonel O'Neal having passed with the Prince's Regiment beyond the end of the hedge on the left hand, had begun the encounter with eight Troops of Rebels. These having before seen ours facing about, took themselves of their speed presently, and made a fair stand till ours advanced up to Charge them. So that they being first in order, gave us their first Volley of Carbines and Pistols at a distance, as ours were advancing: yea they had time for their second Pistols ere ours could charge them. The hottest of their charge fell upon Captain Martin's and Captain Gardiner's Troops, in Prince Rupert's Regiment: and indeed the whole Regiment endured the chief shock of it. To say the truth, they stood our first charge of Pistols and Swords, better than the Rebels have ever yet done, since their first beating at Worcester: especially those of their Right Wing: for their Left gave it over sooner: for the Prince with his Lifeguards, with Sword and Pistol charging them home upon the Flank (not wheeling about upon their Rear, as the London Relation tells it) put them in rout at the first encounter. By this time also was General Percy with some Troops of his Regiment fallen in upon that Flank, and followed upon the Execution. As on the other wing did Major Daniel with the Prince of Wales his Regiment: so that now were the Rebels totally routed. Some of ours affirm, how they heard Dalbier (who brought up some of the Rebels' first horse) upon sight of the Prince's order and dividing of his Wings, to call out to his People to retreat, least they were hemmed in by us.

The rebels now flying to their Reserve of three Colours in the Close by Wapsgrove House, were pursued by ours in execution all the way thither: who now (as they could) there rallying, gave occasion to the defeat of those three Troops also. So that all now being in confusion, were pursued by ours a full mile and quarter (as neighbours say) from the place of the first encounter. These all fled back over Golder Hill to Esington: and so far Sir Philip Stapleton with his Regiment was not yet come. And if he stopped and drew the retreaters up into a body and made a stand for an hour with them (as the London Relation tells us) 'twas surely behind and beyond the great hill where ours could not discern them. Yes plainly our two Prisoners since their return affirm, that 'twas two miles from the place of the fight ere he met them, nor could he stay the Parliamentiers from running. Before this, and in time of the fight, some three of them were observed to wheel about, as if they intended either to get betwixt us and Chislehampton Bridge, or to charge us upon the rear, which being observed by Lieutenant-Colonel O'Neale, he borrowed two troops of General Percy's Regiment, and made out after them, which they perceiving, turned bridles about, and made haste back to their fellows.[26]

Mercurius Aulicus added a few details of the fighting. One Parliamentarian engaged Rupert in personal combat, "and had the honour to die by his pistol." Another was offered quarter by Lieutenant Colonel O'Neale, but when this was rejected O'Neale slew him "in the very act of discourtesy, as well as of rebellion." Major Daniel of the Prince of Wales' Regiment captured an enemy cornet, thus allowing the presentation of a new one to his own Troop which had recently lost one. Major Will Legge, who had commanded the Royalist Forlorn Hope in the expedition, was captured briefly, but escaped. Colonel John Urry, fighting in the ranks of the Prince of Wales' Regiment, had a difficult moment when he was recognised by some of his former Parliamentarian comrades, and surrounded, and offered quarter, but he managed to cut his way out.[27] The main area of fighting was to the south-west of the present day Wapsgrove Manor House Farm, on what on an 1822 map was called Sand Field, now under an airfield.

Although the Parliamentarians disputed some of the details of the fight, they had been comprehensively beaten. The Earl of Essex said that there was a total

---

26 *His Highness Prince Rupert's late beating up of the Rebels' Quarters ...*
27 *Mercurius Aulicus*, p.167.

John Hampden (1594-1643), a leading Parliamentarian and opponent of Charles I in the run-up to Civil War. (Author's collection)

Monument to John Hampden at Chalgrove. (Author's collection)

of 45 dead on both side. The Royalists admitted only to the loss of a dozen men. On the Parliamentarian side, Major Gunter was killed, Captain Butler wounded. Captains Sheffield and Berkeley were wounded and captured, and according to the Royalists later broke their parole after being left to have their wounds dressed, by returning to the enemy quarters.[28]

The greatest loss to the Parliamentarians, and the incident for which the otherwise fairly minor action at Chalgrove would be best remembered, was the fatal wounding of John Hampden. Shot in the shoulder, he rode painfully to Thame, and died six days later.

Rupert and his men were back in Oxford by 2:00 p.m. They had convincingly demonstrated the continuing, albeit narrowing superiority of the Royalist horse over their opponents, and underlined it two nights later when, on 24 June, the newly-knighted Sir John Urry led a spirited raid as far as High Wycombe, dispersing some raw Parliamentarian levies quartered there. It was certainly enough to convince the Earl of Essex of the futility of continuing operations against Oxford, and he withdrew his headquarters beyond Aylesbury. The activity of the Royalist cavalry was not, of course, the only reason for Essex's decision. His lack of success led to recriminations between the earl and the Parliamentarian leadership, with Essex, not for the first or last time, offering to resign. The withdrawal from Thame was also partly occasioned by what would prove to be a totally ineffectual attempt to intercept the Queen and her munitions convoy, *en route* from Newark. But above all, the Parliamentarian army was ravaged by disease. The epidemic, known as "morbus campestris" or "the new disease" was almost certainly typhus. It cut a swathe through Essex's men. The strength of some of his regiments was halved between April and June, and making allowance for casualties in the siege of Reading, the majority of the losses must have resulted from disease and desertion.

The disease spread, of course, among the civilian population in the places where troops were quartered, and also to the Royalists, with perhaps 40 a week dying in some of the Oxford parishes. For much of the summer, the "new disease" was a scourge of soldiers and civilians, Royalist, Parliamentarian and neutral alike.

Major military activity moved westwards, with the Royalist storm of Bristol on 25 July, and their prolonged and unsuccessful siege of Gloucester. The war returned closer to Oxford with the First Battle of Newbury on 20 October, when the King lost his best opportunity of destroying Essex's army and perhaps of winning the war. The Royalists did however regain Reading, abandoned by Essex, and winter arrived with an apparent return to the *status quo* of the start of the year.

---

28   Stevenson & Carter, p.354.

10

Oxford Health

Royalist medical care is often viewed as being somewhat perfunctory, and left largely to regional commanders and local authority. Oxford however found itself thrust into caring for the sick and wounded of the King's army almost from the start of the conflict, when cartloads of wounded from the Battle of Edgehill were brought into the town. They were lodged wherever accommodation could be found, in churches, almshouses, inns and private houses. The city and parish authorities were given the task of providing for them. Many, of course, succumbed to their injuries. The church wardens' accounts for Aldgate's Parish record the expenditure of £4 8s 2d on 31 shrouds. Another £2 8s 4d was spent on the care of wounded in the parish almshouses.[1]

In the spring of 1643, with a permanent Royalist presence in Oxford, a military hospital was set up in the surviving part of St Mary's College in New Inn / Hall Street.[2] The great crisis in health in Oxford during the Civil War came in the spring and summer of 1643 with the outbreak of the epidemic known variously as the "morbus campestris" or the "new disease". This, it is now generally agreed, was almost certainly typhus, with perhaps relapsing fever and malaria also involved. The outbreak, spread by lice and rat fleas, began in the spring, among the Earl of Essex's Parliamentarian forces in the Thames Valley, but spread quickly throughout the surrounding countryside, reaching the Royalist army, and Oxford, soon afterwards.

By late June and early July its effects were ravaging Oxford. The Parliamentarian newspaper *Mercurius Civicus* recounted that in the Royalist capital "great store of them die of several diseases." Sir William Dugdale noted that no social classes were spared, the Countess of Carnarvon among them, though her death was put down to smallpox. However early in July the Parliamentarian newssheets were reporting 1,500 sick from typhus and that 80 to 100 were dying each day, of a "high Fever accompanied with a Frenzy." Samuel Luke's spies told him that when the

---

1   Eric Gruber von Arni, *Justice For the Maimed Soldier* (Aldershot, 2001), p.22.
2   Ibid., p.23.

Sir Samuel Luke (1603-1670), Scoutmaster General to the army of the Earl of Essex, 1643-45. A Presbyterian, he grew increasingly out of sympathy with the Republican regime.
(Moot Hall Museum, Elstow)

King's army lay at Headington Hill many "are very sick, and that there is a contagious disease through the army." Although deaths were not as high as claimed in Parliamentarian propaganda, 875 attributed burials are recorded in the Oxford Parish Registers. Luke's estimate of 40 deaths a week may be approximately correct.[3]

Returns of weapons handed into the stores by Royalist infantry regiments during mid-June, although impossible to quantify accurately indicate those infected, though not necessarily fatally, may have been as high as a third.

There was little effective medical treatment possible. Inducing sweating in victims was believed to help. This could be achieved by means of a cordial. "The poorer sort and Common Soldiers" wrote Sir Edward Greaves, physician to the King, "when they first find the Disease coming upon them, may take a draught of Cordums-Posset- Drink, and with it some Diascordium, Venice, or London Treacle, sweating after it." The better-off might take a posset called an "Electuary", and a "lulep" to follow.[4]

3   Barres-Baker, p.202.
4   Ibid., p.206.

How many sufferers could actually afford these remedies was open to question, as they were to be taken every night until the disease was gone, and preferably every few hours. Greaves also recommended that common soldiers and the poor should take a couple of cloves of garlic each morning, which would help keep infection away. This idea probably had some basis in fact, though his other suggested remedy that firing "a little gunpowder" in a room would also help certainly didn't! Like most contemporary physicians, Greaves advocated the effectiveness of bleeding and said that the sick should avoid eating meat and stick to broth and small beer, and to be "Cheerful and pleasant, as far as the Disease will give leave, avoid all sad thoughts, and sudden passions of the Mind, especially Anger."[5]

The best that can be said for most of these remedies was that they were better intentioned than the multitude of "quack" remedies offered by the unscrupulous at the same time, but the reality was that the epidemic had to be left to run its course. It was not until the autumn that it began to die down, but was quickly followed by a return of the plague.

The abysmal standards of hygiene in Oxford undoubtedly contributed to the problem. Despite spasmodic attempts by the town council to hire men to cleanse the streets of dirt, which was taken away in large quantities, the town remained full of filth, and the rivers were another major source of contagion. John Taylor, the "Water Poet," was Assistant Water Bailiff, and wrote in verse of the condition of the Thames:

> I was commanded with the Water Bailiff
> To see the river cleaned both night and daily
> Dead Horses, Dogs, Cats and well-flayed Carryon Horses,
> Their noisome corpses soiled the water courses
> Both swines and stable dungs, Beasts guts and Garbage
> Street dirt, with Gardeners' weeds and Rotten Herbage
> And from the Water's Filthy Putrefaction,
> Our meat and drink were made, which bred Infection.[6]

The epidemic of sickness undoubtedly made the need for medical provision for the those afflicted, and for the wounded, more acute.

There had already been some attempts to provide pensions for Royalist soldiers unfit for further service because of their injuries, but it quickly proved to be inadequate, as acknowledged in *Mercurius Aulicus* on 7 May, when it was admitted that the promised relief "was only to the future, but not likely to yield help and comfort for the present."[7] Such relief as was available depended upon donations

5   Ibid.
6   Quoted von Arni, p.22.
7   *Mercurius Aulicus*, p.86.

John Taylor (1580-1659), a man of many parts whose exploits included trying to sail in a boat made from brown paper ... it sank. (Author's collection)

raised in each Oxford parish. Alderman Leonard Bowman, the recent Mayor, was appointed Treasurer for Sick and Wounded Soldiers and with the army medical staff was to purchase mainly food from the proceeds. The wounded were still often housed in churches, particularly following the influx after a major engagement. In 1643 St Michael's Church had to be cleansed with pitch and resin fumigation after the wounded soldiers who had been quartered there were moved to a converted old chapel in the grounds.[8]

On 1 June, following the petition of the colonels of the foot regiments stationed at Culham Camp, the Council of War appointed Dr Thomas Goddard as army physician and Thomas Clarges as apothecary. Because of the problems of over-crowding and poor hygiene at Culham, Goddard pressed for the removal of the sick to a healthier environment. The location selected was at Nuneham, five miles south of Oxford, where an emergency hospital was set up in a manor house. The health situation quickly began to improve.[9]

On the same day that Goddard and Clarges were appointed, the Sheriffs of Oxfordshire and Berkshire were ordered to collect from the local inhabitants and deliver to the hospital 60 flock beds with sheets for the use of the sick soldiers. On 2 June the Paymaster General of the Army was instructed to release any back pay due to sick soldiers to pay for their care.[10]

But with the mounting effects of the typhus epidemic, Goddard quickly found himself overwhelmed by the number of sick. He required more beds and also fresh clothing for his patients. By 10 June Parliamentarian sources were claiming over

8   Von Arni, p.25.
9   Ibid., p.26.
10 Ibid.

Peter Heylin (1599-1662), a regular
contributor to *Mercurius Aulicus*.
(Author's collection)

3,000 of the King's men "so sick and weak, that if they were put to march it is thought that half of them were scarce able to march away."[11] The Nuneham facility was now transferred Suningwell, just north of Abingdon, where a hospital was opened in a manor house belonging to the Baskerville family. Goddard and the Wagon Master General were given authority to commandeer wagons and boats to carry sick and wounded, and Goddard also applied successfully for regular pay for himself and his apothecary.[12] A third hospital was opened at Yarnton Manor, four miles north-west of Oxford. The village was fairly remote and this hospital was specifically designated as a medical/isolation unit. As a result, the typhus epidemic hit the villagers as well. During the period from May to August 1643 24 military and 26 civilian burials were recorded in the churchyard.[13] The dead soldiers who were "not of that quality as to be fit to be buried in a shroud, that their body be carried to the churchyard at Osney because the churchyard in this town [Yarnton] being of small extent and be already overfull." Burial services were carried out

11   Ibid.
12   Ibid., p.27.
13   Ibid.

when possible by the chaplain of the regiment to which the dead soldier had belonged, and a detachment of his comrades.[14]

There was a constant shortage of beds, especially during the summer of 1643, which resulted in more demands to the sheriffs. The hospital had a permanent staff of 12 women who were employed as nurses, and who were to be paid 8d a day. There were also three overseers, paid 6d a day, and a commissary, on 5d a day. The physicians had a salary of 2s 6d a day, and the apothecary's servant 2s.[15] All of the hospital staff complained of overwork. On 4 July Thomas Clarges wrote that he had "by some subtle Philosophy become a Doctor of Physick, two apothecaries, three overseers and twelve attendants." He also asked for more surgical assistance "for we bury more toes and fingers than we do men [and] the number of sick are beyond all expectation and too many for the care of one man."[16]

In the middle of June 1643, Doctor Salway, the Dean of Salisbury, and William Gerard were appointed to form an administrative committee to oversee the finances of the hospitals. On 17 July John Bissell was appointed as Commissary for the Sick. Whilst in hospital a sick soldier would be entitled to 3s a week, of which 2s would be for the soldier, in practice largely for his keep, and 1s for the cost of medicines and towards the pay of the doctor. General funding of £10 a week for the food of 100 men was provided, along with £5 for medicines.[17]

On 16 June 1643, Parliamentarian spymaster Sir Samuel Luke reported that 300 sick soldiers in wagons were on their way from Gosford Bridge to Woodstock, where an additional hospital had perhaps been set up.[18] The hospitals also had to handle casualties from further afield. On 12 July 1643, 30 cartloads of injured men from the Battle of Lansdown (4 July) reached Oxford. This resulted in a combing out of the hospitals for men deemed fit for duty in order to release bed space. In September 1,000 wounded from the Battle of Newbury arrived.[19]

The horrific nature of wounds which could be suffered in battle were illustrated in the description by the Parliamentarian chronicler John Vicars of injuries inflicted by Parliamentarian cavalry swords on some unfortunate Royalist infantry: "most woefully cut and mangled, some having their ears cut off, some the flesh of their heads sheared off, some with their very skull hanging down and ready to fall."[20]

Surgeons generally knew how to treat many wounds, with instruments remarkably similar to some in use today, and the main cause of death was from infection leading to gangrene. Cuts, if not infected, usually healed fairly satisfactorily.

---

14   Ibid.
15   Ibid., p.29.
16   Ibid.
17   Ibid., p.30.
18   Ibid.
19   Ibid., p.31.
20   Quoted Charles Carleton, *Going to the Wars* (London, 1992), p.226.

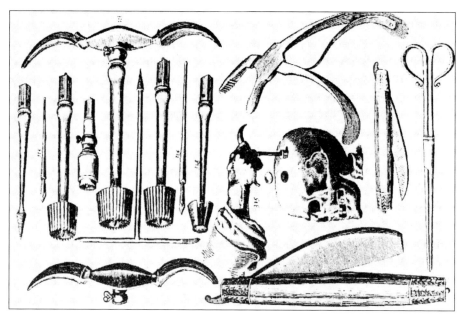

Surgical instruments. (Author's collection)

Gunshot wounds were more problematic. Even with officers, who generally received more prompt and better treatment, the results were frequently fatal as gangrene set in, as in the case of Sir Nicolas Slanning, shot in the thigh at the storming of Bristol in 1643. The wound "swelled, grew black, stank, whereof he died about midnight." Even so, some remarkable recoveries did occur, although more from luck and a strong natural constitution than as a result of medical skill. Colonel Sir John Owen was one example; also wounded at Bristol, he informed his wife: "I was unfortunately shot through the right side of my nose, under the left ear, through all the jugular veins and mouth, and did bleed extremely, but God be praised I am in a pretty good state, if it doth not turn to fever." It did not, and Owen made a full recovery.[21]

Doctors and surgeons were generally fully aware of their limitations. Richard Wiseman, one of the most able of the Royalist physicians, wrote of a Cornish soldier "without Eye, Face, Nose or Mouth", and admitted "I did not know where to begin."[22] Morale among the hospital staff was frequently low, mainly as a result of pay arrears. The hospital at Yarnton closed in the middle of 1644, mainly because

21 Ibid., p.222.
22 *Mercurius Aulicus*, pp.226-227.

the incidence of disease had declined. After a brief move to near Abingdon, the fall of that town to the Parliamentarians in May 1644 caused hospital care to be transferred to Oxford itself. Henceforward the original hospital in New Hall Street and temporary accommodation in the city was used. In late 1644, in what seems to have been the final re-organisation of medical services, Alderman Leonard Bowman was appointed as Governor of the Sick and Wounded. He, so the proclamation published in *Mercurius Aulicus* stated:

> has power both to receive such moneys as were or should be raised for the relief of these soldiers, and to dispose thereof according to their necessities, in paying of Chirgeons, Nurses and other attendants; that as oft as any of the Soldiers were cured of their wounds, and were fit for service, he should return their names unto the Governor of the City of Oxford, by whom they were to be sent to their several Colours; but if unfit for service then to return their names to the chief Justice of the King's bench, who is hereby appointed to commend them to the treasurers for the Counties in which they were born, by them to be relieved with annual pensions, according to their several merits and necessities; and finally that the Vice chancellor should take order to appoint some Minister to visit the sick and wounded Prisoners, and read prayers unto them.[23]

There is no evidence that most of those left unfit for service often received their promised pension. Their home territory might well be under enemy control, assuming they ever reached it, and in any case the local Justices probably had little to offer beyond the uncertain provisions of the parish Poor Law.

When considering the health of the King's soldiers, and the medical provision available, it should be remembered that they lived in a society in which the average life expectancy was no more than 32 years, with 40 percent of the population aged under 20 and about a third dying before the age of 15. Tuberculosis, dysentery and cholera were among a host of diseases which – to modern eyes – took a horrendous toll but led to early death being a more readily accepted fact than is sometimes appreciated.

---

23   Ibid.

11

King Catching:
The Oxford Campaign, spring 1644

In the spring of 1644 the most immediate threat to the Oxford "ring" of defences came from the Parliamentarian forces based at Aylesbury. The failure of Rupert's attempt in the autumn to establish a Royalist base at Newport Pagnell to threaten the Eastern Association was a serious blow for the Royalists, and the situation deteriorated further with Hopton and Forth's defeat at Cheriton in March. Although the Royalists were able to extricate most of their army, Cheriton ended hopes of the King being able to take the offensive in the south, at least until Prince Rupert could bring reinforcements from the North or the Western Army by released by taking Lyme. In the interim the King's forces at Oxford were now likely to have to cope with the Parliamentarian armies of both the Earl of Essex and Sir William Waller.

On 10 April the King held a muster of his army of 6,000 foot and 4,000 horse at Aldbourne, five miles north east of Woodstock. It was a respectably-sized array, probably large enough to take on either Waller or Essex individually, but not both of them together. It was clear that the course and outcome of the imminent campaign was far from certain, and in preparation the King on 11 April prorogued the Oxford Parliament until the autumn. Apart from the risk of its members being captured in their entirety, many of them were, in any case, required for military duties. Partly because of her pregnancy, and also because she did not wish to hinder the King's operations by remaining in a vulnerable situation, on 17 April Queen Henrietta Maria went from Oxford to Abingdon, on the first stage of her journey to the apparent safety of Exeter. The King and Prince of Wales accompanied her on this first day of a journey. King Charles was never to see his wife again.

The Royalist position might have been even more perilous than it was in reality. There had been a plan to assemble both Essex's army and the Army of the Eastern Association at Aylesbury on 19 April, but various factors, including an unwillingness by Essex to co-operate and a perceived Royalist threat to Lincolnshire, caused the scheme to be aborted. But Parliament had now ordered that Waller be

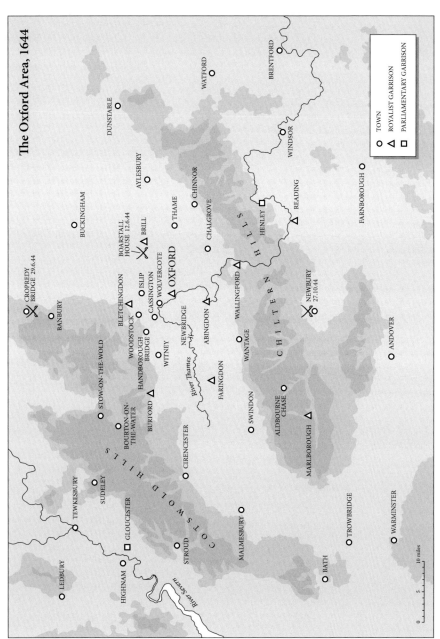

The Oxford Area, 1644

TOWN
ROYALIST GARRISON
PARLIAMENTARY GARRISON

○ TOWN
△ ROYALIST GARRISON
□ PARLIAMENTARY GARRISON

BRENTFORD

WATFORD

DUNSTABLE

WINDSOR

AYLESBURY

FARNBOROUGH

BUCKINGHAM

CHINNOR

READING

THAME

BOARSTALL
HOUSE 12.6.44
BRILL

CHALGROVE

CROPREDY
BRIDGE 29.6.44

HENLEY

BANBURY

BLETCHINGDON

ISLIP

WOLVERCOTE

OXFORD

CASSINGTON

WALLINGFORD

NEWBURY
27.10.44

STOW-ON-THE-WOLD

WOODSTOCK

HANDBOROUGH
BRIDGE

WITNEY

NEWBRIDGE

ABINGDON

WANTAGE

ANDOVER

BOURTON-ON-
THE-WATER

BURFORD

River Thames

FARINGDON

SWINDON

ALDBOURNE
CHASE

CIRENCESTER

MARLBOROUGH

TEWKESBURY

SUDELEY

GLOUCESTER

MALMESBURY

STROUD

TROWBRIDGE

WARMINSTER

LEDBURY

HIGHNAM

BATH

River Severn

CHILTERN HILLS

COTSWOLD HILLS

10 miles

0 5

Map 5 The Oxford area 1644.

Queen Henrietta Maria (1609-1669).
Widely unpopular, partly on account
of her Catholicism, and also because
she was French, the political influence
she was alleged to have over the
King was probably exaggerated by
contemporaries. (Author's collection)

reinforced by 4,200 of the London Trained Bands in order to take Reading, and
they were then to join Essex and capture Oxford.[1]

With these growing threats to consider, the Royalists held a council of war at
Marlborough on 11 April. The Earl of Forth, knowing how it had been impossible
to defend Reading in the previous spring, at a time when the opposing armies
were rather more equal, had already proposed that the town be abandoned, on
the grounds that its garrison might otherwise be lost, and could be better used to
strengthen the Oxford Army. This realistic proposal received unanimous support
from the Council of War, but in the meantime the King deferred to Prince Rupert,
who paid a flying visit to Oxford from his command in the Welsh Marches. Rupert
proposed that Reading and the other garrisons of the "ring" be reinforced with the
remaining Oxford Army foot, with the horse employed as a mobile force to supply
them and disrupt enemy operations until he could march south to join the King.
Whether this was ever a realistic plan may be questioned, and ultimately it would
have resulted in disaster. After a good deal of debate the Council of War prevailed

1   *House of Lords Journal*, VI, pp.546-547.

on the King to reject it. On 16 May the King and the Oxford Army arrived at Reading, but only to evacuate its garrison and supplies, for the defences were already being slighted. Two days later Reading was abandoned and by the 24th the foot were quartered at Abingdon, the horse at Faringdon and the King himself was back in Oxford.

Waller and Essex meanwhile were preparing to take the offensive, the two commanders conferring at Henley on Thames before Essex's men entered Reading on 23 May. There is no question that the evacuation of the town had been the right decision for the Royalists. They had added 3,000 foot to the Oxford Army, without whom it would have been incapable of taking the field. Earlier Stephen Hawkins's Regiment of Foot had been sent to garrison Greenland House, below Henley. As the Parliamentarians crossed the Thames they chased off a small force, sending the Earl of Essex "an insolent message … to desire him to call as he came that way." Essex, with perhaps uncharacteristic heavy humour, replied that he "would not only call but knock."[2]

On 25 April, much more controversially than was the case with Reading, Abingdon was also evacuated by the Royalists. Again, though, there were valid reasons to do so. The garrison consisted only of Sir Lewis Dyve's 500-strong regiment of foot, which would certainly not have been sufficient to have held Abingdon against a determined assault. However, King Charles was "much troubled," as the withdrawal had been carried out without his knowledge or approval. It remains unclear who actually gave the order; Lord Forth is probably the most likely, although Lord Wilmot was later apparently blamed, though not, it seems, until after his disgrace and dismissal in August. The King ordered the immediate re-occupation of Abingdon, but his command came too late.[3]

On the night of 24 May Essex quartered around East Haybourne, six miles south-east of Abingdon, and on the 26th occupied Abingdon itself. Waller, after a quick reconnaissance of his old enemy, Basing House, on 21 May quartered at Basingstoke for three nights, and by Saturday 25 May was also near Abingdon.

Sir Edward Walker later recollected:

> And now the Rebels thought their Game sure, having without a blow got the possession of Reading, Abingdon, and so all Berkshire and therefore enforced His Majesty to draw his Army on the North side of Oxford, there to feed on his own Quarters (the best he could) to keep himself from being bespoilt.[4]

2   *Mercurius Civicus* No.52 (16-23 May 1644), p.511.
3   The King would later blame Lord Wilmot after the latter's disgrace.
4   Walker, p.17.

Sir Edward Walker (1612-1677). Chester Herald in 1638, Walker was Secretary at War to Charles I from 1642-44, and made Garter King of Arms in 1660. He was noted as being a quarrelsome individual. (Author's collection)

On 7 June the King would write penitently to Prince Rupert: "I confess the best had been to have followed your advice."[5] This is debateable, but certainly the Royalists were now in a desperate situation. Initially the Oxford army's foot were quartered at Wolvercote, Marston, Hanborough, Bladon and Woodstock, with the horse across the Thames at Newbridge. This left the approaches to Oxford from the north open to the enemy, but the main concern of the King's commanders was to hold the crossings of the Thames and Cherwell, and prevent the complete encirclement of Oxford.

On the night of 28 May Essex crossed the Thames at Sandford Ferry, three-and-a-half miles below Oxford and next day marched to Islip, six miles to the north of the city, and established his headquarters. On their march the Parliamentarians skirted Oxford on its eastern side over Headington Hill. The Parliamentarians, probably in an attempt to intimidate the enemy, halted on Bullingdon Green, "in full view of the City." Essex:

---

5   Warburton, II, pp.415-416.

himself with a small party of Horse came within Cannon Shot to take a more exact view of the place ... divers parties of his Horse for the greatest part of that day crossed up and down the hill and some of them came very near the Parks and had some slight skirmishes with Ours, but in the height of this bravery three or four great shot was made at them from the works at St Clement's Port which did some little execution, and drove them to their main Body then on their march. His Majesty was this instant was upon the top of Magdalen College Tower where he did exactly view their Order and Motion.[6]

According to Richard Symonds, there was some skirmishing between opposing parties of horse, in which Captain Bennet of Sir Horatio Cary's Regiment of Horse was killed.[7] A Parliamentarian version of events appeared in the *Kingdom's Weekly Intelligencer*:

Wednesday morning His Excellency drew up his Army on Bullingdon Green, within one mile of Oxford, and the whole Army faced Oxford about six hours, they not daring to come out of the City, their whole Army was then in Oxford, and within less than three miles of it, towards Woodstock. They shot off three drakes at a party of our men, which went within less musket shot of the town, but God be thanked did no execution. His Excellency was within musket shot of Oxford to view it, some of our soldiers ran up to the very works, and came off again without any harm, towards night we marched to Islip ... within a mile of the body of the King's Army.[8]

Essex's plan now was to cross the Cherwell and attack Oxford from its northern side; not a particularly attractive option in view of the fortifications, but still the most vulnerable aspect of the town.

On 30 May he attempted to seize the crossing at Gosford Bridge, but the attackers were driven back by Royalist musketeers stationed there. A second attempt was made next day, but by now Jacob Astley was in command there with "a field piece of six pound bullet and certain companies of foot." Astley ... "omitting no part of a valiant and expert commander, raised a breastwork and redoubt for the defence of his men. From whence he did so gall the rebels and played upon them with such advantage, that though they had four pieces of Ordnance on the other side, which made many a shot (the noise and thunder of which was heard in Oxford) yet they

6   Walker, p.16.
7   Symonds, p.7.
8   *Kingdom's Weekly Intelligencer*, No.57 (28 May-4 June), pp.463-464.

did little or no hurt to His Majesty's forces: themselves being shamefully repulsed from their undertaking."[9]

On Saturday 1 June there was a third attempt to seize Gosford Bridge. According to the Royalist version of events:

> The greatest part of this day and the following night was spent about the banks of the River of Cherwell, which the Rebels did attempt in several places but could speed in none. So following their design upon Gosworth Bridge, which they lay hard by all this day. They were most gallantly beaten off by his Majesty's Forces, which made many of them put themselves in Islip Mill, to which His Majesty's soldiers followed them, and played upon them there with such good success, that besides those miserable Rebels whom they killed in the daytime, it was reported next morning that those they had killed in the night [were] above a hundred more at this Bridge and Mill.[10]

The Royalist foot were supported by the King's Troop of the Lifeguard of Horse, although they apparently did not see any action. The Parliamentarian version of events was, perhaps understandably, more low-key: "Thursday and Friday there were some skirmishes, but there was a little brook which hindered our men from coming at them."[11]

Rebuffed at Gosford Bridge, Essex now tried to cross the Cherwell a few miles further north at Enslow Bridge, eight miles from Oxford, and at Tackley Ford another mile-and-a-half further on.

> The Rebels were beaten at more places than one, and therefore ventured for their pass both at Enslow Bridge and Tackley Ford … But His Majesty's Commanders being intent on all occasions, had sent two more small pieces of six pound weight, and a demi-cannon to seize the Bridge, and put some Foot into a mill adjoining the Ford, which were maintained with so great much courage and discretion, that the Rebels were repulsed in both, the ordnance and Musket playing hot upon them; by which a good many of the Rebels were slain and the rest beat off; His Majesty not losing above three men at the most.[12]

9   *Mercurius Aulicus*, p.1002.
10   Walker, p.18.
11   *Mercurius Civicus*, No.54, p.526.
12   *Mercurius Aulicus*, p.1004.

The Parliamentarians said of these encounters:

> On Friday night [31 May] a party was sent forth of his Excellency's own
> Forces, and of the London Auxiliaries, to obtain a passage over Enslow
> Bridge near the mill between Islip and Woodstock between whom and the
> enemy there was that night some single bickerings, but about 4:00 a.m. the
> next morning they began to skirmish very fiercely, and so continued for
> the space of seven hours, till most of our mens' Powder and bullets were
> spent, and then they were relieved by a party of Major General Skippon's,
> who disputed the passage a long time with the enemy, but the enemy
> being on the other side of the river did stand it with much resolution, and
> having advantage of the ground cut off the bridge, and kept the passage
> all that day, and notwithstanding several attempts were made against it, it
> was not taken till the Lord's Day in the afternoon.[13]

The Parliamentarians admitted to the loss of about 40 dead, and Colonel Adam
Cunningham had his arm shot off.

On 2 June Essex wrote from Islip to the Committee of Both Kingdoms:

> My endeavour hath been to fight the King's Army, in pursuit whereof I
> have advanced as far as Islip. My army came not all in until 12:00 a.m.
> on Wednesday night, when for the most part, we have been and are yet
> in skirmish upon the several passes of the river of Cherwell, and some-
> times the service hath been hot. It appears that the enemy declining to
> fight, hath endeavoured to stop us of passing that river, a consequently of
> forcing him to fight or retire further.[14]

The Royalist delaying tactics were proving successful, and were aided by heavy
rain swelling the rivers.

Initially Waller, on the Abingdon side of Oxford, had no more success. On
27 May he tried to cross the Thames at Newbridge, eight miles north-west of
Abingdon, but was "so gallantly received by some of His Majesty's Dragoons, who
lay there of purpose to guard the pass that they were beaten back both with shame
and loss."[15]

Waller had left in Abingdon about 400 horse and 1,000 foot whilst the bulk of
his army was at Sandford. On 29 May he received a scare when a Royalist force
under the Earl of Cleveland made a raid which briefly entered the town, taking
some prisoners. The Royalists for their part admitted to losing Captain Lyne of the

13 *Mercurius Civicus*, No.54, p.506.
14 C.S.P.D. (1644) p.195.
15 *Mercurius Aulicus*, p.1003.

Sir William Waller (1597-1668).
His victories in the early days of
the war won Waller the title in
Parliamentarian news sheets of
'William the Conqueror'. He was
defeated at Roundway Down in July
1643, but, a generally competent
commander, won a partial victory
at Cheriton in the following March.
(Author's collection)

Prince of Wales's Regiment of Horse. In line with their reputation in other places they had occupied, Waller's men did significant damage in Abingdon, wrecking the market cross and smashing stained glass windows in the church.

On Saturday 1 June Waller made a renewed attempt to cross the Thames at Newbridge. The attack was spearheaded by the Tower Hamlets Regiment of the London Trained Bands and the Kentish Horse:

> Notwithstanding the enemy had cut parts of the bridge and made it unpassable, yet our Commanders with a boat or two called Punts and some planks fell on so bravely that they made them forsake the bridge and took 30 prisoners upon quarter and 40 more among whom were divers Irish and a woman who was whipped and turned away.[16]

According to the Royalists, the bridge had been defended by 90 or 100 musketeers or dragoons, who ran out of ammunition and were overpowered when the Parliamentarians crossed below the bridge using punts and took them in the rear.

---

16   Richard Coe, *An Exact Dyarie of the Progress of Sir William Waller's Army* (London, 1644), p.3.

On 2 June the rest of Waller's army crossed, and could perhaps have effectively exploited their success, but Essex ordered Sir William not to advance any further until he received new orders. Nevertheless, with their river defence lines breached, the Royalists were in a critical situation. At 1:00 p.m. on Sunday 2 June the King called a Council of War at Woodstock to discuss the options of standing to fight or attempting to escape to the West. With the details of recent enemy movements still unclear, no decision was reached and it was decided to resume the debate next morning. In the meantime the King attempted to relax by hunting in Woodstock Park, where he killed two bucks, and stayed at Woodstock overnight. However after supper, he received intelligence that Waller was massing his troops at Newbridge, with some horse at least already on the Oxfordshire side of the Thames. With his forces holding the Cherwell crossings now threatened in their rear, Charles ordered them to abandon their positions and decided himself to return to Oxford, where he arrived probably at around 6:00 a.m. on 3 June, having rested *en route* for a few hours in his coach among his troops near Wolvercote.[17] The forces holding the Cherwell crossings had withdrawn under cover of darkness, leaving lighted match in the hedges to confuse the enemy. The crisis was severe, as Sir Edward Walker explains:

> And now in human probability the Rebels had His Majesty, and his Children, his Army, this City and all those who with the hazard of their lives and expense of their fortunes had so long stuck unto His Majesty and the justice of his cause, even in their power and possession, and this was so much apprehended even by some of eminency that at this time His Majesty yield upon conditions to the rebels was proffered him by one, but one of those with whom he privately consulted that evening (which was rejected with scorn) about the Resolution which he then took.

According to one account Charles allegedly responded that "possibly he might be found in the hands of the Earl of Essex, but he would be dead first."[18] However there were only sufficient provisions in Oxford to support the whole army for 14 days, and no prospect of relief if the King's forces were besieged inside the town. So the King took the only alternative to surrender open to him, however desperate and perilous it appeared. He would try to slip out between the closing jaws of Waller and Essex's armies under cover of darkness and head west, both to escape the trap and then depending on events, link up either with Rupert or Maurice.

On 3 June Essex himself quartered at Bletchingdon, with some troops around Woodstock. The King had escaped from there with only a few hours to spare. Waller was still at Newbridge, hesitating as a result of another Royalist feint

---

17   *Mercurius Aulicus*, p.1010.
18   Walker, p.18; Clarendon, VIII, p.47.

towards Abingdon. Having made the decision to leave Oxford, the King would leave behind James, Duke of York, and the bulk of his Privy Council. Day-to-day military command in Oxford would rest with the Governor, Sir Arthur Aston, and a group of military advisers. Orders were issued that "Prayers and Services … be kept up constantly both on Sundays and Tuesdays, as if he himself were present in his royal person."[19]

At 9:00 p.m. King Charles, with the Prince of Wales, the Duke of Richmond and the King's Troop of the Lifeguard rode out of the North Port of the fortifications on the Banbury road. Here most of the horse and foot of the Oxford Army were drawn up. The King ordered that a detachment of 2,500 musketeers, without their colours, should join the 5,000 horse which were to accompany the King on his march. It is most likely that the musketeers were mounted behind cavalry troopers, and as speed was vital, the Royalists took with them no guns and only a few wagons. The remaining 3,500 of the Oxford Army, after making another diversionary feint towards Abingdon, returned to Oxford. Also in Oxford at this time was the newly-raised, and probably incomplete, regiment of horse of the Earl of Peterborough, together with Sir Arthur Aston's horse.

The next few hours would be critical. The odds against the King slipping through the closing Parliamentarian jaws were finely balanced. The Royalists headed first for Wolvercote, then over the road across Port Meadow from Wolvercote, and reached Yarnton by dawn. Much depended upon whether the bridge over the River Evonlode between Bladon and Long Harrow had been secured by the Parliamentarians. But fortune favoured the Royalists; it was found to be unguarded. The Royalists had achieved the first stage of their breakout, but could not immediately rest. They headed on through Milkwood to Northleigh, where they made a brief halt, and then marched on via Holy Oak, Breackwich, Shakeoak Haley and Minster Lovell, in a heavy storm of rain and huge hailstones, reaching Burford at 4:00 p.m., where there was another brief halt to rest exhausted horses and men. Pushing on, the Royalists reached Bourton on the Water at midnight. Here another halt was made, the King resting on a bed in the Rectory, quite possibly fully clothed, for fear of a sudden enemy attack. The Parliamentarians had clearly been wrong-footed, and suggestions made by some writers that Essex had deliberately allowed the King to escape seem unlikely. Once news reached him, Essex ordered a pursuit towards Woodstock, though many of the London Auxiliaries allegedly deserted *en route*. The Parliamentarians were hit by the same storm which the Royalists had encountered, "of thunder, lightning, hail as big as nutmegs and rain," which lasted for two hours.[20] But it is clear that Essex was not moving with the same haste as the Royalists. He halted that night at Woodstock, and only reached Chipping Norton next day.

19   Walker, p.18.
20   *Mercurius Aulicus*, p.1020.

Waller, who at least in theory seems to have been more eager to press the pursuit, had been left partially in the dark about the details of Essex's operations. He had, as we have seen, been told by Essex not to advance any further after crossing the Thames until he heard that Islip Bridge had been taken. News that the Royalists had evacuated their defences there reached Sir William at 12:00 p.m. on the 3rd, and he sent out parties of horse to gain further information, but still awaited further intelligence. It was not until 12:00 p.m. on the 4th that news of the King's march was confirmed, and then Waller seems to have detoured in order to get his wagons across the Thames at Radcot. As a result Waller's army did not reach Witney until midnight on 4 June. Waller himself reached Stow-on-the-Wold on 5 June, by which time the King was at Evesham. The Parliamentarians captured a few exhausted or drunk Royalist stragglers in the streets of Burford, but the King's gamble had, for the moment, succeeded. He was clear of the trap.

Essex and Waller met at Chipping Norton next day (6 June) to discuss their next move. Their decision to divide their forces has received more criticism in hindsight than it did at the time. Essex would march to the relief of Lyme, and possibly defeat Maurice in the process, whilst Waller pursued the King. The decision may well have saved Charles from defeat, or from being forced to go North to join Prince Rupert, with incalculable consequences. In the event, Charles and Waller manoeuvred for several days around Worcester and the Severn Valley without making contact. On 14 June the Royalist Council of War resolved in a meeting at Bewdley to return to Oxford to collect the remainder of their foot and then to attempt to bring Waller to battle.

On 17 June the Royalists were back on the edge of the Cotswolds at Broadway, leaving their opponents "to encounter with their own soul Shadows two days march behind."[21] The Royalist army was somewhat reduced in numbers, having lost, mainly through straggling, several hundred foot in the course of their march. Orders were sent to the Commissioners at Oxford to send to Witney munitions and as many as possible of the foot from the city. Late on the 17th the King was at Burford, and reached Witney, 11 miles from Oxford, next day. Prince Charles and the Duke of Richmond returned to the Royalist capital, whilst the King and his troops remained at Witney for the next three days, and on the 21st, after the reinforcements from Oxford arrived, a general rendezvous was held near Woodstock. The King now mustered between 5-6,000 horse and 4-5,000 foot, a large enough army to face Waller in the right situation with good prospects of success.

The immediate Royalist objective was Buckingham, both to obtain supplies from that area, and by posing the threat of a raid into the Eastern Association, to draw Waller away from Oxford and towards them. The King's forces spent the

21   Ibid., p.1038.

next four days at Buckingham, the Council of War still regarding the situation as "desperate."[22]

Waller, after some convoluted marching, reached Oxhill near Kineton on 26 June. Both armies had shed a good number of their foot in the course of the campaign, perhaps around 1,000 each. But Waller had received some reinforcements from local Parliamentarian forces in Gloucestershire, Warwickshire and Coventry, including around 600 foot, seven troops of horse and 11 guns.

Possibly rather optimistically, some of the Royalist Council of War, probably including Lord Wilmot, had been urging an advance on London, presumably to take advantage of the absence of both Waller and Essex. Realistically, faced still by the bulk of the London Trained Bands behind the protection of strong fortifications, such a move would have stood little chance of success, and would have resulted either in ignominious retreat or the King's forces being trapped between the defenders and Waller. The Commissioners at Oxford strongly opposed the idea, and news of Waller's approach resulted in its being abandoned. Instead the King ordered further supplies of munitions to be sent to Buckingham, and as it seemed that Waller was seeking battle it was decided to seek him out and fight, rather than risk the Parliamentarians gaining an advantage. The Royalists had intended next to march to Daventry, but learning on 28 June of Waller's approach they "marched in good order towards Banbury," and rendezvoused to the east of the town. As the early morning mist cleared, they saw the Parliamentarians drawn up on Hanwell Warren, a mile away on the western side of the town. At the same moment Waller was writing to the Committee of Both Kingdoms: "Thursday in all probability will prove a decisive day … I doubt not we shall render you a good account of our service. We are drawing into the field and therefore I can only give you this short assurance."[23] The two armies manoeuvred all day, seeking the advantage. The Parliamentarians took up position on the high ground of Crouch Hill, one mile south west of Banbury. Typical of Waller's liking for strong defensive positions, it had a ditch in front, and ditches and hedges on each flank. The Royalists were drawn up in the fields on the other side of the Cherwell around Banbury Castle. There was some minor skirmishing in the afternoon, in which 1,000 Royalist commanded musketeers under Colonel Anthony Thelwell who had been posted on the far bank of the Cherwell repulsed an enemy probing attack with loss. That night both armies quartered in the field.

The Royalists had between 4-5,000 horse, organised in the four brigades of Lieutenant General Lord Wilmot, the Earl of Northampton, the Earl of Cleveland and Colonel Sir Humphrey Bennet. Wilmot's brigade probably totalled around 1,000 men, as did Cleveland's. Bennet and Northampton each had at least 800

22   Walker, p.20.
23   C.S.P.D. (1644), p.288.

men. The King's Lifeguard of Horse, perhaps 300-strong, was unbrigaded. The Royalists had about 3,500 foot on the day, the Parliamentarians about 4,000.[24]

Waller had around seven regiments of horse under his Lieutenant General, Sir Arthur Haselrigg. They varied in strength, with Waller and Haselrigg's regiments probably the strongest. There were five regiments of Waller's foot and three London Trained Band Regiments, forming the London Brigade.

At between 3:00 a.m. and 4:00 a.m. on the morning of Saturday 29 June the Royalist army "stood at the bottom near Banbury. Waller and his comrades facing of us on the top of the hills beyond the town."[25] Realising after some hours that Waller was not going to quit his strong position on Crouch Hill in order to fight, the King decided to move on towards Daventry in order to await a better opportunity for battle.

At around 8:00 a.m. the Royalists moved off. The van was commanded by the Earl of Brentford, the King and Prince of Wales marched with the main body and there was a rearguard consisting of Thelwell's commanded musketeers and the cavalry brigades of the earls of Cleveland and Northampton. Walker wrote: "we were no sooner on our March, but the rebels drew off from their ground and coasted us on the other side of the river."[26] The terrain was open and rolling. Waller was moving northwards along the Banbury to Southam road, whilst the King matched him on the western bank of the Cherwell marching along the Banbury-Daventry road, with the opposing armies in full view of each other, from one to two miles apart. About three miles north of Banbury Waller drew up on Bourton Hill. Once again the Parliamentarians were in a strong position, protected by hedges and ditches. Surveying the enemy, Waller wrote again to the Committee of Both Kingdoms:

> The King's army is drawing up the hill, most of the Horse are fallen down towards Cropredy, whether it be to secure their retreat, or to make their passage that way to fight upon more equal ground, is yet uncertain, but we shall quickly know … My present haste will permit me to write no more.[27]

There were three crossings of the Cherwell in the vicinity; Cropredy Bridge, with a ford at its side five miles north of Banbury and another ford just below the bridge at Slat Mill. Beyond Cropredy the Cherwell bends sharply to the north-east and is crossed by the Banbury-Daventry road at Hays Bridge. Cropredy Bridge at the time was probably a narrow "pack horse" bridge, without a parapet.

---

24   See Toynbee & Young, *Cropredy Bridge 1644: The Campaign and the Battle* (Kineton, 1970), chapters 12 and 13.
25   Walker, p.20.
26   Ibid., p.21.
27   C.S.P.D. (1644), p.293.

The Royalists did not expect an attack by Waller "yet to be sure they should not have any advantage, a party of dragoons was sent to keep Cropredy Bridge, until the Army was passed beyond it."[28] The dragoons were probably from Prince Rupert's Regiment, commanded by Colonel Thomas Hooper.

A report was received of 300 Parliamentarian horse, within two miles of the Royalist van, assumed to be further reinforcements intending to join Waller. There seemed a good chance of cutting them off, so the Royalist van and main body increased their pace, opening up a gap between them and the rear. Waller's men "perceiving their advantage," sent a force estimated by Waller at 1,500 horse, 1,000 foot and 11 guns to Cropredy Bridge to force a passage. The Royalist dragoons on guard there quickly retired.[29]

It was said later that there was a gap of a mile-and-a-half between the Royalist Main Body and Rear, and Waller sent two more detachments to seize the Cherwell crossings. A party led by Lieutenant General John Middleton crossed Cropredy Bridge. It included Haselrigg's and Jonas Vandruske's regiments of horse, and about 13 companies of foot, including some of Waller's own regiment. The other party of 1,000 men under Waller himself crossed the ford at Slat Mill "to fall upon the rear of all."

Fighting began at about 1:00 p.m. Waller explained:

> I had a steep hill to mount, and from the top whereof the enemy were drawn up in a strong body. Some of the regiments came up slowly, where- upon I turned back, leaving my regiment to march on, but coming to the foot of the hill, I was advertised that the Lieutenant General had charged the enemy and broken him, and chased them above a mile, the most fair way to have ruined their whole army, but a great body of the enemy having rallied, and charging him broke him and forced him to a quick retreat, not without loss.[30]

Once over the river Middleton's men had charged after the Royalist rear as far as Hays Bridge, but Colonel Thelwall had "overthrown a carriage to barricade the bridge and planted it with Musketeers. This occasioned our retreat back again, being unwilling to so far to engage ourselves, having no Foot within above half a mile of us." The Parliamentarian force involved seems to have consisted of four troops of Haselrigg's Horse.[31] Whilst the Parliamentarians hesitated, the Earl of Cleveland's Brigade launched a counter-charge. Cleveland had drawn his men up on rising ground from whence he saw the body of Parliamentarian horse drawn

---

28   Walker, p.21.
29   Ibid.
30   C.S.P.D. (1644), p.293.
31   Thomas Ellis, *An Exact and Full Relation …* (London, 1644), p.4.

Old Cropredy Bridge. (Author's collection)

up evidently contemplating an attack on the Royalist rear. "Whereupon (not having time to expect either word or Orders from the Lord Wilmot, Lieutenant General of the Horse) he gave his own word (Head and Sword), presently that advancing that Body of Rebels ran."[32] Lord Digby later admitted to Prince Rupert that without Cleveland's prompt action "it was 1,000 to one that our van and main body had been cut off from our rest and all hazarded."[33] It was Waller's body of horse which Cleveland had encountered and at about the same time the Earl of Northampton faced about his own and Lord Wilmot's Regiments and with little difficulty forced Waller's detachment back to Slat Mill. In the meantime Haselrigg's retreating horse had come upon the 1,000 Parliamentarian foot who had followed them across the river in disorderly retreat and cut off from Cropredy Bridge.

King Charles, meanwhile, had halted the march of his van on the far side of Hays Bridge, and from rising ground could see the enemy apparently preparing a second attack on the Royalist rear. So he "commanded the Lord Bernard Stuart [with the King's Lifeguard of Horse] to make haste to the assistance of the rear, and by the way to attempt those two Bodies of the Rebel Horse that faced His Majesty. His Lordship attended by above 100 Gentlemen of the King's Troop (which is ever fullest in time of action) returned instantly over the Bridge and made haste towards those two bodies. Who by this time, seeing their fellows routed by the

32   Walker, p.23.
33   Warburton, II, p.294.

Cropredy Bridge: the battlefield. (Author's collection)

Earl of Cleveland, were advancing to charge him in the flank as he was following the execution."[34]

There seems to have been a sharp skirmish, with the Parliamentarians claiming to have bested the Lifeguard, but the upshot was that Waller's horse fell back. Cleveland had now drawn his brigade up again near "a great Ash" and launched a second charge against Waller's wavering men. According to Walker, Cleveland:

> saw a great Body of the rebels' Horse of 16 Colours (and as many Colours of Foot placed within Hedges) all within Musket shot of him, this caused him suddenly to advance, the Rebels doing the like, and having stoutly stood out their Musket and Carbine shot, he gave the command to charge, and by his singular valour and resolution (seconded by the Officers of his Brigade) he routed all those Horse and foot, and chased them beyond their Cannon all which (being 11 Pieces) were then taken. And two Barricadoes of wood drawn with in each seven small brass and leather Guns charged with case shot.[35]

34   Walker, p.23.
35   Ibid.

Sir Richard Browne (c.1610-1669). After service with the London Trained Bands in 1644 he was made Major General and Governor of Abingdon. A Presbyterian, he would later turn Royalist, becoming Lord Mayor of London and being knighted in 1660. (Author's collection)

Waller admitted that after the Lifeguard were supposedly seen off, they were charged by Cleveland's brigade "with whom we were in no case able to deal, we were necessitated to retreat very disorderly."[36]

Waller's men fell back across the Cherwell, returning to their former position on the high ground of Bourton Hill, leaving foot and dragoons to hold the eastern end of the crossings at Cropredy Bridge and Slat Mill. The Royalists drew up opposite them, and made some rather half-hearted attempts to force the crossings in their turn, but were held off by the Kentish Foot and the Tower Hamlets Auxiliaries supported by two drakes at Cropredy Bridge. The Royalists were able to make a crossing at Slat Mill, but thought better of attempting to attack Waller's strong main position.

With an effective stalemate in place, the King sent Waller a message offering a free pardon, which Waller unsurprisingly rejected, saying that he had no power to treat without the permission of Parliament. At nightfall desultory skirmishing died down.

The opposing armies remained in position throughout the following day, until, learning of the approach of Major General Richard Browne with 4,500 foot from Abingdon, at 4:00 p.m. the Royalist army moved off southwards. Waller made

36   C.S.P.D. (1644), p.293.

no attempt to pursue. Casualties in the engagement were probably fairly light, perhaps 100 dead on each side. Waller was shaken by his defeat, and even more so, personally, when on 30 June, when he was holding a Council of War in an upper room of his quarters, the floor collapsed, and deposited the general and his officers in the cellar under a pile of timber.

Heading westwards, by 3 July Charles was back at Evesham. The untidy action at Cropredy Bridge would prove to have effectively broken Waller's army. From an original strength of 9-10,000 men, by the end of July Waller would only be able to muster half that number. Oxford was for the moment safe, and King Charles could move West to settle accounts with the Earl of Essex.

With the main Royalist field army absent for most of the summer in the West Country, engaged in the operations which climaxed with the surrender of the Earl of Essex's infantry at Lostwithiel on 3 September, operations around Oxford were relatively small-scale. Waller's army remained unfit for action until the autumn, so the only immediate threat to Oxford came from Major General Richard Browne's garrison at Abingdon. Browne's main exploit was the capture in July of the Royalist outpost of Greenland House, after a gallant defence by Colonel Stephen Hawkins and his regiment of foot, who were allowed to make their way to Oxford, where they became part of the garrison.

Browne's horse mounted a number of small-scale raids, on at least one occasion getting as close to Oxford as Wolvercote, but they were a nuisance rather than a major threat.

During the autumn detachments the Oxford garrison under the command of Colonel Henry Gage mounted two daring and successful relief expeditions to Basing House. They earned Gage the enmity of a jealous Sir Arthur Aston, a knighthood, and when Aston, in December, was crippled by a fall from his horse when attempting a display of horsemanship to some ladies, the post of Governor of Oxford.

The Oxford Army, having narrowly avoided disaster in October at the Second Battle of Newbury, returned for the winter to its quarters around Oxford and beyond.

12

Oxford: The Great Fire

There was always a major potential danger of fire in 17th century English towns because of the methods of construction used in buildings, involving the use of easily combustible materials such as timber and thatch, the cramped locations of many in close proximity to each other, and the lack of adequate fire-fighting equipment.

In 1562 Oxford Town Council had ordered that all new houses be roofed with tile or slate with stone chimneys, and that those who failed to observe these regulations would be liable to fines. There would also be a fine of 3/- for any householder whose chimney caught fire.[1] In practice, of course, these regulations proved virtually impossible to enforce, especially in Oxford's period of rapid expansion in the years before the Civil War. The increase in the town population, which roughly doubled between the 1580s and 1630s, meant a rapid growth in poor-quality housing, despite the renewal of the building regulation orders. In 1620 the university complained that the townspeople had built many thatched houses "which were not only unseemly to look to, but also very dangerous for casualties of fire."[2] There was a significant fire in 1640, in Jesus College Lane (now Market Street).

In theory some fire-fighting equipment was available, including a considerable quantity of leather fire buckets and fire hooks on poles to pull burning thatch from roofs. In practice fire ladders and buckets were often misappropriated for other uses, and this misuse increased with the influx of newcomers after the outbreak of war. Overcrowding also increased. In January 1644, for example, 75 houses in St Aldate's each had an average of five strangers lodging in them.[3] The arrival of so many strangers also meant an increase in demand for basic foodstuffs such as bread. Bakers were working much longer hours to meet the need, and bakeries were notorious fire hazards. There were also additional fire hazards from the

---

1   Hobson & Salter, p.109.
2   Stephen Porter, 'The Oxford fire of 1644', in: *Oxoniensia*, Volume XLIX, 1984, pp.289-300
3   Toynbee & Young, *Strangers in Oxford*.

munitions stores and the various other workshops which had been established, and the numerous soldiers quartered in the town were generally more careless about fire precautions than the townspeople. The town authorities had little control over them, and it was clearly only a matter of time before some disaster took place.

It came on the afternoon of Sunday 6 October 1644 when fire broke out, possibly caused by a soldier carelessly roasting a stolen pig in a poorly-built house. The conflagration began on the south side of what is now George Street, outside the medieval walls. There was a stormy strong wind blowing from the north, which quickly spread the flames across the town wall, and burning debris was probably blown across it causing the fire to spread rapidly into the town through North Gate. Particularly serious devastation was caused at the back of the buildings in Cornmarket and New Hall Streets, though even here it seems to have been patchy, and more often it was their outbuildings rather than the houses themselves which were destroyed. However, most of the buildings in Shoe Lane were destroyed, and St Martin's Church damaged. Butcher's Row and the adjoining houses were engulfed, and as the strong wind continued to fan and spread the flames, over 80 dwellings in St Elof's parish were set ablaze "all along irresistibly" where many brewers' houses and stores were burnt as the fire spread south to St Thomas's, but some houses partly protected by long gardens were affected more lightly. It was 12:00 a.m. before the fire began to die down, having spread for a distance of about 1,000 yards. Eight brewhouses, 10 bake houses and perhaps 300 dwellings were destroyed or badly damaged.

It is possible that fire-fighting efforts were hindered by the need to man the defences against any attempt by the Parliamentarians at Abingdon to take advantage of the chaos, and indeed there were inevitable, though certainly erroneous claims that the fire had been started by Parliamentarian saboteurs. In the event, although dramatic, and greatly relished in Parliamentarian newsletters, the fire does not seem to have resulted in any loss of life, and had no real effect on the Royalist war effort. The area affected was mainly one were the common soldiers were billeted, not the court or government officials. Other than the garrison, the bulk of the troops were absent on campaign, but on their return the problems of overcrowding must have been intensified.

Rebuilding did not commence until the spring of 1645, and there must have been difficulty in paying rebuilding costs with so many other financial demands being made on the townspeople. A collection of £100 was made in the city, but reconstruction was still taking place well into the 1650s.[4]

---

4   Porter (1984), p.298.

13

Cromwell's Raid, Spring 1645

During the winter of 1644-45, Prince Rupert, now Lieutenant-General under the nominal command of the Prince of Wales, and replacing the Earl of Forth, attempted a very partial reform of the Royalist armies. Parliament on the other hand, faced with the virtual collapse of their main field armies, replaced them with what is known to posterity as the New Model Army. This was a bold step, with no certainty as to its eventual outcome.

Meanwhile the Parliamentarian garrison at Abingdon remained a major irritant to Royalist Oxford, and on 11 January 1645, Prince Rupert and Sir Henry Gage mounted an attempt to attack the town from two sides. The main Royalist force crossed Culham Bridge, and advanced along the causeway beyond it in the direction of Abingdon itself. But restricted by floodwater to the causeway itself, the bunched Royalists presented easy targets to Browne's musketeers. After three hours of confused fighting in the enclosed country around Culham, the Royalists were forced to withdraw to Oxford. Sir Henry Gage, in the closing stages of the fight, was mortally wounded by a musket shot. He was buried two days later in Christ Church Cathedral, widely mourned in Oxford by most apart from sir Arthur Aston, whose hopes of returning as governor were swiftly dashed by the appointment of Will Legge.[1]

Princes Rupert and Maurice spent the spring on the Welsh Marches, attempting to restore the deteriorating Royalist position there, leaving the King to make preparations in Oxford for the summer campaign. The Parliamentarians were anxious to delay the Royalists until their own New Model Army, training at Windsor, was ready to take the field, and so, on 20 April the Committee of Both Kingdoms instructed Oliver Cromwell:

> Being informed that the enemy have mounted their ordnance at Oxford, and that Prince Maurice is come thither with 1,000 horse to convey his Majesty and those ordnance to join with the forces of the two princes in

1   D.N.B.

Sir Henry Gage (1597-1645), a popular and capable commander with extensive experience before the Civil War in the Army of Flanders.

Oliver Cromwell (1599-1658). (Author's collection)

Hereford and Worcestershire, and considering of what advantage it would be to the public to prevent this design of the enemy we have thought fit to employ in that service your two regiments Col. Fiennes and the rest of that party which went with you into the west. We therefore desire you to take those forces into your charge, and marching the nearest way for interposing between the party from Oxford and the forces about Hereford and Worcester, to hinder the passing of those ordnance and to take all advantages you can against the enemy for the public good. We desire you also to hold correspondence with Major General Browne and Colonel Massey, who will be ready to take all occasions to advance this service.[2]

Massey was told to use his local knowledge to advise Cromwell of enemy movements, and where best to position his forces.[3] Although the Committee of Both Kingdoms' intelligence that Prince Maurice was with the King at Oxford was incorrect, the Royalists were taken completely by surprise. On 21 April Cromwell was at Caversham Bridge, and on the 23rd reached Wallington, where he was joined by Holbourne's Regiment of Horse, giving him a total of 1,500 troopers. Cromwell's command consisted of the Lord General's Regiment, part of Colonel Algernon Sydney's Regiment, five troops which were part of Colonel Vermuyden's Regiment, five troops of Colonel Fiennes, and three from Sir John Norwich's regiment. The Parliamentarians moved on to Wheatley and then to Islip, intending to surprise the Earl of Northampton's brigade of horse, consisting of the regiments of Northampton, himself, Wilmot's (Colonel Aymes Pollard) and the Queen's, in their quarters. However Royalist outposts warned of Cromwell's approach, and Northampton's men hastily retreated. The Royalists recovered from their near surprise, and at dawn next day, Northampton, as Cromwell put it: "came to make an infall upon us." The Parliamentarians seem to have been caught somewhat off-guard. Cromwell described how "Sir Thomas Fairfax's Regiment was the first that took the field, the rest drew out with all possible speed. That which is the general's troop charged a whole squadron of the enemy, and presently broke it. Our other troops coming seasonably on, the rest of the enemy were presently put into confusion, so that we had the chase of them three or four miles, wherein we killed many, and took near 200 prisoners, and about 400 horse." Also taken was a cornet of the Queen's Regiment, "richly embroidered with the Crown in the midst, and 18 fleur de lys wrought out all in gold, with a golden cross on the top."[4]

According to Richard Symonds:

2   C.S.P.D. (1645-7), pp.140-141.
3   Ibid., pp.142-143.
4   W.C. Abbott (ed.), *The Writings and Speeches of Oliver Cromwell* Volume I, p.342.

Cromwell's horse and dragoons ruined some of our horse that quartered about Islip, of the Lord of Northampton's command 27 buried in Islip, 18 men in (-) over against Kidlington.[5]

Some of Northampton's men fled towards Oxford; others headed for the Royalist garrison at Bletchingdon House about three miles north-west of Islip. Cromwell headed in the same direction, and the scene was set for one of the tragic episodes of the Civil War.

Bletchingdon House, five miles north of Oxford and 18 miles east of Woodstock, was a mansion built in the 1630s by Sir Thomas Coghill, a leading member of the local gentry, who had been Sheriff of Oxfordshire in 1632. Despite its proximity to the Royalist capital, Bletchingdon had not until recently been regularly garrisoned. In February it was reported to Sir Samuel Luke that Bletchingdon was held by 160 foot "and there may be great hopes to take it"[6] however the increasing likely threat to Oxford in the coming campaigning season evidently convinced the Royalist command that Bletchingdon should be added to the outer circle of Oxford's defences. Coghill seems to have used his influence to persuade the King, despite previous unfortunate experiences in such situations, to allow him to raise his own garrison for the House. On 15 March the following order was issued to Sir John Heydon by Secretary Nicholas:

> Charles R
> Our will and pleasure is That out of Our Stores remaining in your Charge, you issue and deliver to Sir Thomas Coghill knt, or such as he shall appoint, threescore infixed Muskets, which he (at his own charge)is to fix, for the Arming of his Men raised and designed for the Defence of Bletchingdon House, and for so doing this shall be your Warrent …
>
> Noted 16 March 1644[45] the Muskets above mentioned were delivered by indenture to the above Sir Thomas Coghill.[7]

However it would presumably take some time for Coghill to raise his men, especially as the area had already been thoroughly combed over for recruits. In the meantime, Colonel Francis Windebank was despatched to hold Bletchingdon.

Francis Windebank was born in about 1613, the second son of King Charles's Secretary of State, Sir Francis Windebank. As leading members of the crypto-Catholic faction at Court, the Windebanks, particularly Sir Francis, were increasingly identified with some of the more unpopular aspects of royal policy.

5   Symonds, p.162.
6   H.G. Tibbutt (ed.), *The Letter Books of Sir Samuel Luke, 1644-45* (Bedford, 1963), item 262.
7   Roy, *The Royalist Ordnance Papers Part II*, p.358.

Young Francis Windebank probably gained his first military experience in the Scots War of 1640, captain of a somewhat mutinous Devon company of foot, who he handled with humorous resourcefulness:

> When I first received my men, divers of them swore desperately if they found we were Papists they would soon despatch us; but I finding their humours, upon my first day's march I desired them all to kneel down and sing psalms, and made one of my officers to read prayers, which pleased them not a little, and being very familiar with them at the first, giving them drink and stinking tobacco of sixpence a pound, gained their loves, so as they all swear they will never leave me so long as they live, and indeed, I have not had one man run from me in this nine days' march, but other captains of our regiment are so fearful of their soldiers having much threatened them and done much mischief ... the Puritan rascals of the country had strongly possessed the soldiers that all the commanders of our regiment were papists, so that I was forced for two or three days to sing psalms all the day I marched, for all their religion lies in a psalm ...[8]

Although Windebank came out of the whole sorry affair with some of what little credit there was to be found, his father's fortunes took a turn for the worse when he was among the Catholics dismissed from the Court, and sought refuge in France. From here he penned increasingly disconsolate reproaches to the King alleging lack of support, and became in the process a source of increasing irritation to Charles.

Young Francis, however, found even his brief military experience of value to the Royalist cause as civil war approached. He was commissioned as Major to Charles Gerrard's Regiment of Foot, and served with the Oxford Army throughout the campaigns of 1643. In March 1644 he was present with a detachment at the Battle of Cheriton, where according to the later testimony of Colonel Henry Bard, he "gave a large testimony of his courage."[9] Windebank did not accompany Charles Gerard's regiment to South Wales in the spring of 1644, but resigned his commission for obscure reasons, but possibly connected with his recent marriage to Jane Hopton. Francis remained in Oxford, but was not idle for long. He may have been given a command in the Oxford garrison. In September he led the detachment of foot from the garrison which formed part of Henry Gage's expedition to relieve Basing House.[10]

By the start of 1645 Windebank was being variously styled as "Lieutenant Colonel" and "Colonel." It is unclear whether he was permanently attached to a

8   National Archives SP 16/460/46; 47.
9   C.S.P.D. (1645-47), p.124.
10   C.S.P.D. (1644-5), p.438.

specific unit, though it may be that he had a connection with the Lord General's Regiment, which formed the garrison of Woodstock. On 20 February 1645 one of Sir Samuel Luke's spies reported:

> There come 200 foot thither [to Woodstock] on Saturday night last under command of Col. Windebank. They are fortifying the Manor House, and have made a bulwark over against the gate.[11]

Windebank probably remained at Woodstock until at least 3 March, when Luke reported that 200 foot were fortifying the Manor House and "have pulled down divers dwelling houses and a great stable adjoining it."[12] But by 20 March Colonel Richard Palmer had assumed command at Woodstock, and Windebank had departed to take up command at Bletchingdon.

That day Luke's spy reported:

> Colonel Windebank quarters at Bletchingdon, and has about 30 horse and 50 foot. On Saturday last there fell such a difference between him and his soldiers about pulling down some houses near the garrison, that they cried out 'shoot him, shoot him', which made him fain to fly that night to Woodstock and next day to Oxford, and as yet he hears not of his return to Bletchingdon.[13]

It is likely that this incident had considerable influence on the events which followed. Although details are frustratingly scanty, a probable explanation is that Windebank put forward proposals for improving the defensibility of Bletchingdon House by demolishing some neighbouring cottages and outbuildings, but that his plans resulted in a mutiny by the newly-raised levies of Coghill's garrison. It would be interesting to know what role was played in this by the Coghill family. It is unclear whether Sir Thomas himself was present, but his wife was evidently in the house, probably with his infant daughter and perhaps their other children as well.[14] Windebank evidently felt his position untenable, and headed for Oxford to report to the Royalist command there. The initial reaction seems to have been to remove Windebank, and to make Sir Thomas Coghill responsible for the defence of his home. Luke's spy reported on 27 March:

---

11 Tibbutt (ed.), item 384.
12 Ibid., item 232.
13 Ibid., item 245.
14 Coghill's youngest daughter was baptised in Bletchingdon Church on 16 January 1645 (see J.H. Coghill, *The family of Coghill 1377 to 1879*, (Cambridge, 1879), p.39).

> Colonel Windebank is commanded away from Bletchingdon, and is to march this day with all his forces to Oxford and Sir Thomas Coghill has a commission to raise forces to keep the house in his absence, and caused his drums to be beaten in Woodstock on Tuesday last to that purpose.[15]

The reason that this decision was reversed, or at least modified, is unclear. It may be that Coghill's attempts to raise troops had proved disappointing. And with the approach of the active campaigning season, Prince Rupert may have felt that Coghill should be provided with an experienced military adviser, but considering the evident friction between them, it is perhaps surprising that the choice fell on Windebank. It is fairly clear that Frank Windebank was in an unenviable situation. Though he was evidently regarded as being responsible for Bletchingdon's defence, Coghill's position is unclear. He had evidently left the house by April, but his wife and family were still there, and the bulk of the 200-strong garrison were probably the men raised by Sir Thomas, upon whom Windebank can have placed little reliance.

That all was not well at Bletchingdon can be deduced by Richard Symonds' description of the garrison late in April.[16] No defence works had been constructed, presumably because Windebank was still unable to carry out the necessary demolition work, and the house contained only two or three days' provisions. Windebank was ill-prepared for the crisis which was about to engulf him. It is unclear if Windebank was aware of Cromwell's presence in the vicinity before the fugitives from the action at Islip reached Bletchingdon, although it would be surprising if Northampton had not sent him word. Unfortunately the garrison was singularly unprepared to meet the threat. Apart from being unfortified and unsupplied, Windebank was further hindered by the presence in the house of a number of civilians, including the Coghill family, and perhaps present for a visit, his own wife and her servants. With Cromwell's horse on the loose in the vicinity, there was no prospect of sending the non-combatants off to a place of safety, and their fate in the event of a successful storming of the house was unpleasant to contemplate. Windebank's worst fears were realised, probably late in the afternoon, when Cromwell arrived before Bletchingdon, and summoned the garrison to surrender There were several other officers in the house with Windebank, claimed by the Colonel to be mere visitors, but more probably there from the Woodstock garrison for the purpose of conferring on Cromwell's raid. They included Lieutenant Colonel Hutchinson (probably Edward Hutchinson of the Lord General's Regiment) and Major Richard Earnley of Richard Palmer's Regiment of Horse.[17] They, and the other officers present, seem to have formed Windebank's Council of War.

15   Ibid., item 252.
16   Symonds, p.163.
17   Stuart Reid, *Officers and Regiments of the Royalist Army* (Leigh-on-Sea, n.d.), pp.74, 96.

Windebank's first reaction to Cromwell's summons was to play for time, for Cromwell wrote that there was a "long treaty", and that the defenders were "very dilatory in their answer."[18] But the Royalists had no hope of speedy relief, nor, apparently did they have any confidence that an assault could be repelled. In fact, as Cromwell later admitted "I did much doubt the storming of the house, it being strong and well-manned, and I having few dragoons, and this not being my business, and yet we got it."[19] For this reason Cromwell offered generous terms which, at about 12:00 a.m., Windebank accepted and surrendered.

> Articles of Agreement, upon the Surrender of Bletchingdon House, between Lieutenant-General Cromwell and Colonel Windebank April the 24th, 1645
>
> 1. First, it is agreed, that all officers of horse of commission of the garrison shall march away, with the horse, sword, and pistol.
> 2. That the Colonel and the Major are to march with their horse, swords.
> 3. That all the soldiers in the garrison are to march away, leaving their arms, colours, and drums, behind them; and for such officers of horse as retreat hither for safety, they are to march away with their swords.
> 4. That Mr Hutchinson, Mr Ernley, Mr Edes[20] and Mr Pitts,[21] being gentlemen that had come to visit the colonel, and not engaged, shall march away, with their horses, swords and pistols.
> 5. That all other arms and ammunition shall be delivered up immediately to Lieutenant-General Cromwell, without embezzling, except the above mentioned.
> 6. That a safe conduct be granted by the Lieutenant General, for all the above-mentioned, to Oxford.
> 7. That the Colonel's wife, his two servants, and chaplain, march away along with the Colonel with their horses.
> 8. That the lady of the House shall enjoy her goods as before, without plunder, and all her family.[22]

Cromwell may well not have been taken in by the fiction of the non-combatant status of Hutchinson and the others, but it was a minor point well worth overlooking in return for such an unlooked-for success. Bletchingdon would be garrisoned by Parliamentarian troops from Abingdon for the remainder of the war.

---

18   Abbott (ed.), Volume I, p.341.
19   Ibid.
20   Probably Major Gervase Elwes (Lord General's Foot).
21   Captain Robert Pitt (Palmer's Horse) Pitt may have commanded a 50-strong troop of the Regiment based at Bletchingdon.
22   *House of Lords Journal*, VII, p.340.

For Windebank the surrender proved fatal. He and his party arrived in Oxford early on 25 April, and met with a frosty reception. Windebank and his fellow officers were placed under immediate arrest. The general reaction was summed up by Richard Symonds:

> About 2:00 a.m. or 3:00 a.m. on Friday morning, the colonel valiantly gave up the house and all his arms etc, besides 50 horse that came in thither for shelter, and this without a shot.[23]

The prisoners were brought before a court martial that afternoon. Its membership is unknown, as are the details of its proceedings, but it will have been formed of senior and field officers then available in Oxford, probably including Will Legge, the Governor. The verdict was reached quickly, and in accordance with the penalties laid down in the Orders and Institutions of War, Windebank was "condemned by a council of war to die, and those that were his councillors and advisers, viz. Lieutenant Colonel Hutchinson, Major Earnley, Mr Eides, were disabled for ever bearing arms any more."[24] Sentence on Windebank was to be carried out on the following Wednesday, and in the interim he was imprisoned in the Castle.

There were some among Windebank's fellow officers, perhaps with knowledge of the circumstances at Bletchingdon during the spring, as well of Windebank's previous record, who felt the verdict to be unduly harsh. After all, Richard Feilding had been spared in superficially similar circumstances after the surrender of Reading in 1643. The only real hope of a reprieve lay with Prince Rupert, at present in the Hereford area, though expected in Oxford shortly. He had interceded for Feilding, and perhaps would do the same for Windebank. The colonel was granted a stay of execution pending Rupert's response. Someone in Oxford, perhaps Windebank's wife, wrote to Rupert pleading for mercy, and the letter was forwarded, with his own appeal, by Colonel Sir Henry Bard, Governor of Camden House, a friend of Windebank and a confidante of Prince Rupert:

> The latter enclosed was sent to me from Oxford, to be conveyed with all speed possible, pray God it comes time enough, it concerns a most unfortunate man, Colonel Windebank. Sir, pity and reprieve him; it was God's judgement on him, and no cowardice of his own. At the Battle of Alresford [Cheriton] he gave a large testimony of his courage; and if with modesty I may bring in the witness, I saw it, and thence began our acquaintance. O happy man! Had he ended then. Sir, let him but live to repair his honour; of which I know he is more sensible than the damned of the pains of

---

23 Symonds, p.163.
24 Ibid.

William Legge (c.1607-1670),
a close confidante of Prince
Rupert who did his best to
heal the rupture with the
King in 1645. (National Portrait
Gallery, London)

hell. And sure it will be a perfect means of his salvation. God and your
Highness consult about it.[25]

As this message and the letter enclosed with it were captured by the
Parliamentarians before reaching Rupert, Bard's pleas went unheard. It is impossible to say whether they would have swayed the Prince, but he almost certainly
learnt of Windebank's sentence from another source. In practice, even if he had so
desired (for which there is no evidence) it would have been difficult for Rupert to
overturn a verdict which, under military law, was entirely correct. It would have
been unwise, in any case, to have done so at the start of what was likely to be a
critical campaigning season. Another factor was the alarm and disruption which
Cromwell's raid was causing, and the very different reception he had received when

25   Ibid.

he appeared before Faringdon.[26] These made it still more unlikely that Windebank would be reprieved.

Carrying out the sentence was evidently delayed until Rupert was near enough to Oxford for his opinion to reach the King, but on Saturday 3 May, the day before the Prince arrived in Oxford, in the Castle yard against the wall of Merton College "Colonel Windebank was shot to death."[27] His burial on the same day is recorded in the register of the church of St Mary Magdalen.

In his typical fashion King Charles was later to indicate some remorse for Windebank's death by granting his widow a pension. It is hard to escape the conclusion, that however judicially justifiable his execution was, Windebank was to some extent a victim of circumstance, shot like Admiral Byng in a later war *pour encourager les autres*. It is probably true that Bletchingdon would indeed have been stormed by Cromwell, if he had chosen to do so, and a lighter cost than he anticipated. But, however realistic, Windebank's surrender, and the terms he obtained, could be seen as protecting the interests of his wife and friends at the expense of his duty, and failing to provide the "heroic" example required in a time of crisis. It would have been politically undesirable for the equivocal role of Sir Thomas Coghill in events at Bletchingdon to have been brought to public notice. Windebank, a professional soldier of no particular influence, as well as having a father who King Charles evidently felt to be an annoying reminder of Stuart ingratitude to their servants, provided a suitable scapegoat and warning to others. Francis Windebank was indeed "a most unfortunate man."

Cromwell, meanwhile, marched to Middleton and then towards Witney, seeking to place himself between the King in Oxford and the road to the West and Wales.

In Oxford there was considerable alarm, and efforts made to guard against the threat from Cromwell. On the same afternoon that the Parliamentarians summoned Bletchingdon, horse from Oxford were sent to guard the bridge at Gosford, and that evening they were reinforced by some commanded foot from Oxford and Richard Palmer's Regiment of Horse.[28]

On Saturday, 2 April "Wallingford troops came to Oxford to relieve the Lord of Northampton etc. Some horse and foot from Faringdon from Colonel Lisle's garrison, and all the horse in Oxford were to be drawn out (and many horses were this day plundered upon that pretence) when we had drawn out and marched, news came that the enemy was gone. We returned to our several quarters. At seven

26   C.S.P.D. (1644-5), p.438.
27   Symonds, p.164. It is, of course, just possible that Windebank's execution was deliberately carried out before Rupert could arrive to prevent it – but on balance, it seems more likely that his opinion had already reached the King and that the colonel was shot on the Saturday to avoid a delay until after the Sabbath.
28   Symonds, p.163.

of the clock the Queen's troop of the Life Guard was beat up, and 60 horses taken, but six men."[29] Cromwell learnt of the march of the detachment of Lisle's men:

…which were a commanded party of 300 which came a day before from Faringdon under Colonel Richard Vaughan, to strengthen Woodstock against me, and were now returning. I understood they were not above three hours' march before me. I sent after them, my forlorn overtook them as they had gotten into enclosures not far above Bampton Bush, skirmished with them they killed some of my horses, mine killed and got some of them. But they recovered the town before my body came up, and my forlorn not being strong enough was not able to do more than they did. The enemy presently barricaded up the town, got a pretty strong house. My body coming up about 11:00 p.m., I sent them a summons. They slighted it; I put myself in a posture that they should not escape me, hoping to deal with them in the morning. My men charged them up to their barricadoes in the night, but truly they were of such good resolution that we could not force them from it, and indeed they killed several of my horses, and I was forced to wait until the morning. Besides they had got a pass over a brook, and in the night they strengthened themselves as well as they could in the Stone House. In the morning I sent a drum to them but their answer was they would not quit except that they might march out upon honourable terms. The terms I offered were to submit all to mercy. They refused … I prepared to storm. I sent them word to desire them to deliver out the gentleman and his family, which they did – for they must expect extremity, if they put me to a storm. After some time was spent, all was yielded to mercy. Arms I took, muskets near 200 … besides other arms, though but two barrels of powder, soldiers and officers near 200, besides more slain besides officers, the rest being scattered and killed before. The chief prisoners were Colonel Sir Richard Vaughan, Lieutenant Colonel Middleton, Major Lee, two or three captains and other officers.[30]

Judging by the resistance they had put up it was clear that Lisle's detachment included a number of veteran soldiers, a significant loss for the Royalists. Despatching his prisoners to Abingdon, Cromwell heard of a party of enemy horse marching in the direction of Evesham. He despatched Colonel Fiennes after them, who captured 30 men and 100 horses. Also taken prisoner was a messenger from Lord Digby carrying a letter to George Goring, currently in the Bath area. Digby said that Will Legge had drawn out from Oxford on the

29   Ibid.
30   Abbott (ed.), Volume I, p.343.

Faringdon House. It was fortified with outworks during the war.
(Author's collection)

previous night 700 horse and 500 foot to march to the assistance of Vaughan's men. The Royalists were probably fortunate not to encounter Cromwell, particularly as the majority of the horse were reported to be gentlemen volunteers, all the cavalry available following the rout of Northampton's brigade. The messenger also told Cromwell that Goring, disgruntled from being called away from his operations against Taunton, was on the march towards Oxford with 3,000 horse and 1,000 foot.

Cromwell, who told the Committee of Both Kingdoms that he would be on the alert for Goring's approach, regretted that a lack of dragoons prevented him from taking a number of small enemy garrisons, "for the enemy is in high fear."[31]

On Tuesday 29 April, at about 4:00 p.m., Cromwell appeared before Faringdon. The main strength of the garrison was the castle, and the defenders consisted of the remainder of George Lisle's Regiment, and part of Sir John Owen's. Lisle himself was apparently in Oxford, so command was exercised by Lieutenant Colonel Roger Burges, of Owen's, a soldier of considerable experience. Cromwell immediately sent in a summons to surrender:

> Sir,
> I summon you to deliver into my hands the house wherein you are and your ammunition with all things else there, and persons to be disposed of as the Parliament shall appoint, which if you refuse to do you are to expect the uttermost extremities of war.[32]

31   Ibid., p.344.
32   Ibid.

Burges was plainly unimpressed, and according to *Mercurius Aulicus*:

> The brave men in Faringdon were only afraid that Cromwell would not come near enough to assault (for they were all strongly resolved to welcome him) and therefore Lieutenant Colonel Burges laboured to invite him nearer by this calm civil answer, 'That the King had entrusted them to keep that Garrison, and without special order from His Majesty Himself they could not deliver it.'[33]

According to the Royalist account "this fair answer" gave Cromwell confidence, and advancing into the town itself, he "blustered high in a second summons, which to show his confidence he sent written in such a small shred of foul paper, as if Captain Phips had been given it before it came to the paper mill, his words were these:

> Sir, I understand by 40 or 50 poor men whom you forced into your house that you have many still there whom you cannot arm, and who are not serviceable to you. If these men should perish by your means it were great inhumanity. Surely honour and honesty requires this, and though you be prodigal of your own lives, yet be not of theirs, if God give you into my hands I will not spare a man of you if you put me to a storm.

Cromwell was hoping that Burges would be intimidated in the same way that Windebank had been, but he received an uncompromising reply:

> Sir,
> We have forced none into our garrison, we would have you know you are not now at Bletchingdon: the guiltless blood that shall be spilt God will require at your hands that have caused this unnatural war. We fear not your Storming nor will have any more Parlies.
> Your servant,
> Roger Burges.

This response, the writer of *Mercurius Aulicus* crowed gleefully: "heated Cromwell's face seven times more red than ordinarily."[34] The Parliamentarians had by now been joined by a detachment of foot despatched somewhat unwillingly by Richard Browne at Abingdon, and at around 3:00 a.m. on 30 April, Cromwell began his assault. For details we are largely reliant on the account in *Mercurius Aulicus*:

33   Quoted *Mercurius Aulicus* (30 April 1645), p.1570.
34   Ibid., p.1571.

He first fell upon the Sconce on the South-west side, where Captain Canon reared up the first ladder, and ascended himself, but was welcomed by the gallant Lieutenant Colonel Burges, who with a pike thrust Canon into the Ditch, where crying for quarter he came up the ladder and was received in. After this, the Rebels never offered to scale, but left all their Ladders rear'd before the Workes; besides this Sconce they assaulted at two other places (all three at once) on the north-west side and north, where the greatest part of the storm fell, though it proved so fruitless, that they killed but two Common Soldiers and hurt four, not any officer so much as touched, though the storm lasted full three hours, wherein the rebels lost 200 Officers and Souldiers killed in the place, and great numbers wounded. Captain Canon taken prisoner, with an Ensign, and eight common souldiers, 100 arms, besides some clubs with spikes (called Roundheads) made for the New Model; with all the pillage of the rebels' bodies within musket shot of the works, most whereof had ropes swaddled about their middles (you may guess why) though the rebels who were lately prisoners had quarter and fair useage.[35]

The garrison had prepared piles of stones, which they also hurled at the attackers, evidently to good effect. Royalist claims of Cromwell's losses are probably inflated, but the Parliamentarians had suffered a serious reverse, as evidenced by a somewhat chastened letter which Cromwell sent to Burges soon after the failure of the attack:

Sir,
There shall be no interruption of your viewing and gathering together the dead bodies, and I do acknowledge it as a favour, your willingness to let me dispose of them. Captain Canon is but a Captain, his Major is Smith so far as I know, but he is a stranger to me, I am confident he is but a Captain. Master Elmes but an Ancient, I thank you for your civility to them, you may credit me in this, I rest,
Your servant, Oliver Cromwell
If you accept of equal exchange I shall perform my part.[36]

Cromwell now had a problem. He allegedly blamed the poor performance of the Abingdon foot as the reason for the repulse, and talked of dismounting his

---

35　Ibid., pp.1571-1572. The writer was presumably claiming that the attackers were roped together to prevent them from running away.
36　Ibid. Cromwell's lack of knowledge regarding Captain Canon suggests that the assault had been made mainly by the Abingdon foot.

George Lord Goring (1608-1657). Arguably the most capable of the Royalist cavalry commanders, though increasingly undermined towards the end of the war by ill-health, drink and intrigue, he died in exile in Spain. (Author's collection)

troopers to make a renewed assault. But he was also aware that time was short. He knew that Goring had been ordered to assist Lisle, but evidently didn't intercept the letter which Lord Digby sent to Goring on 28 April, in which he reported the action at Bampton in the Bush, and expressed concern that unless he came in strength, Goring might be defeated. "Be suddenly here with such strength as may safely convey the King and his train within reach of Prince Rupert's horse; for upon the reputation of Cromwell's successes hereabouts the Rebels are swarming out of London in hope to besiege the King here in Oxford."[37] As well as his other operations, Cromwell was rounding up as many horses as he could from the Oxfordshire countryside, and Goring was instructed to bring as many draught horses as he could to move the Royalist siege train in the coming campaign.[38]

37   Bodleian Library, Clarendon MSS 26, f.134.
38   Ibid.

George Goring was confident of success, telling Lord Colepeper of the Council in the West that he would "give a good account of Fairfax even if Cromwell be joined with him."[39] On 30 April he set out from Wells with 3,000 horse and dragoons, and reached Marlborough the same night. He intended to be between Oxford and Faringdon next day.

On 2 May some of Fairfax's men, who had now reached Newbury, captured some of Goring's troopers, who confirmed that Goring was planning to attack Cromwell at Faringdon. Cromwell was with Fairfax when the news arrived, and hurried back to alert his own troops, but Goring, moving with the speed which could be a characteristic of his, arrived sooner than expected. A series of skirmishes followed in the vicinity of Radcot Bridge. A Parliamentarian patrol encountered Goring's vanguard, under Colonel Adrian Scroop. Cromwell reinforced his men with a party under Major Christopher Bethell, and a sharp action followed. As usual, the opposing sides differed on the details. The fullest account, which magnifies the extent of the Royalist success, appears in *Mercurius Aulicus*:

> The Earl of Brentford's Regiment (under the command of Lieutenant Colonel Scroop) going upon the guard near Bampton on the Bush, hearing the Rebels had passed some men over the water, found about 100 horse, drew up to them, gallantly repulsed them, killed nine and took 30 prisoners. Upon this Alarm the Rebels drew over near 1,000 horse more, and the Lord Goring hearing the Guard was engaged, got what horse he could in a readiness before the rest could be had together, and came up as Major General Digby (who had been to visit the Guards) and Lieutenant Colonel Scroope were retiring in excellent order before the Rebels, who followed them in very great bodies; The Lord Goring was not in all full 400 horse, (an no Dragoons) when the Rebels drew three great bodies up to a narrow passage (where his Lordship faced them) and sent their Major Bethell another way with 300 horse to fall upon his Lordship's flanks. A small party of the Prince of Wales' Regiment was ready to expect Bethell and his 300 Rebels, but falling into a bog as they were going to charge, forced them to wheel about in some disorder; the Rebels pursuing this small party with great shouts and fast though in no ill order, but then the Lord Goring presently brought up to their relief part of his own Regiment, and of Colonel Richard Neville (commanded at that time by his gallant Lieutenant Colonel Standish, Sir Bernard Gascoigne, Captain Metcalf and some other officers) with these his Lordship so dealt with the Rebels, that though their body was twice as strong as both his, he broke them all to pieces, though with some difficulty, and that part of the Prince of Wales's Regiment which was forced to wheel, turned back soon enough to share in

39   Ibid. f.130.

Radcot Bridge. (Author's collection)

beating them,. There were very many of them killed and wounded, Major Bethell himself (who commanded in chief) taken prisoner, two colours of horse, and divers common soldiers, the rest saved themselves in the dark. The lord Wentworth in the interim with a very small number stopped the Rebels other bodies from coming over at the Pass; no more of His Majesty's horse coming up in many hours after. And in all this action his lordship's horse received no loss, but Captain Metcalf slightly hurt, lieutenant Hall and some few common soldiers hurt, and not one killed or taken that we can yet hear of.[40]

The Parliamentarians minimised their casualties, and indeed they were probably light, but the Royalists were left firmly in control of Radcot Bridge. With Prince Rupert and Prince Maurice approaching, the odds against Cromwell were now too great, and he raised his blockade of Faringdon and fell back to join Fairfax.

The great raid was over. Although it had not accomplished everything Cromwell had hoped for, he had taken one small garrison, mauled the Royalist forces around Oxford, and by driving off so many of the valuable draught horses, imposed on a significant delay on the King's campaign plans.

40   *Mercurius Aulicus*, p.1571.

14

The Summer Campaign 1645

As in the previous year, before leaving Oxford on 7 May at the start of his summer campaign, the King appointed a "Council for the preservation and well ordering of the City and University of Oxford, the counties of Oxford, Berks, and Bucks, and the garrisons therein, during the King's absence, with ample instructions and authority for fortifying, sequestrating, levying contributions, raising forces of horse and foot, impresting horses, carts and carriages, deciding controversy, suppressing confederacies and issuing money out of the Exchequer by warrants signed by them, for the King's service."[1]

The Commissioners were mainly leading officials of the court, household and Royalist administration, though some of them, principally Prince Rupert, Charles Prince of Wales, Lord Digby, Lord Hopton and Sir Edward Hyde, were not in the city. Rupert and Digby were with the King and the field army, and Prince Charles, Hopton, Hyde, Colepeper and Capel were in the Prince's Council in the West. James, Duke of York was still too young to play any active role in deliberations, and leadership was evidently mainly exercised by Sir Edward Nicholas, as Secretary of State, and Will Legge as Governor, though a quorum of three Commissioners was stipulated to be required for any decision to be valid.

When the King and his army reached Stow-on-the-Wold on 9 May, it was agreed that Goring and his cavalry should for the moment return to the West, to resume operations against Taunton, and watch the movements of Sir Thomas Fairfax and Parliament's New Model Army, whilst the King and Rupert marched north, the relief of Chester their first objective, but enemy intentions were still unclear. So far as the Oxford area was concerned, the first orders from the Committee of Both Kingdoms were to Major General Richard Browne at Abingdon to garrison Bletchingdon House, where Colonel Fiennes's Regiment of Horse, still in the area after Cromwell's raid should base itself at Bletchingdon, and from there "hinder the carrying of provisions into Oxford."[2]

---

1   C.S.P.D. (1644-5), p.467.
2   John Rushworth, *Historical Collections* (London, 1680-1701), Volume 6, p.42.

Sir Edward Nicholas (1593-1669), a
capable administrator who was a
Secretary of State to Charles I and later
to Charles II. (Author's collection)

In Royalist Oxford the leadership for the moment seemed confident; on 12 May
Sir Edward Nicholas told Lord George Digby that Cromwell with 5,000 horse and
foot together with the local forces of Hertfordshire and Buckinghamshire was
believed to be heading for the Eastern Association. "We are here very diligent in
putting this garrison into good order, and I assure you the Governor is very labo-
rious in it."[3]

It was probably as another result of Cromwell's raid that the Royalists had
evidently not had time to fully provision Oxford before the King's departure on
campaign. This might not have mattered too much, had not the Committee of
Both Kingdoms on 17 May ordered Fairfax to lay siege to Oxford, "out of a desire
to put an end to this miserable war we do think it fit that siege be laid to the City
of Oxford, for the taking of it, it being the centre of our troubles."[4] Cromwell was
ordered to link up with Fairfax, making a night march from Coventry towards
Daventry, and then to Brackley, where he arrived on 21 May, reaching Marston
next day.

3   W. Bray (ed.), *Memoirs of John Evelyn* (London, 1827), Volume 5, p.65.
4   Ibid., p.127.

Fairfax was opposed from the start to the idea of tying down the New Model in a long and quite possibly fruitless siege of Oxford at a time when the King and his field army were at large, but had no option but to obey the instructions of the C.O.B.K. There was some skirmishing as the Parliamentarians approached. Captain Thomas Gardner of Legge's Regiment of Horse was sent with a party of horse and foot to harass the enemy advance, but was repulsed, with probably exaggerated claims of 200 prisoners being sent to Abingdon.

On 22 May Fairfax established his headquarters at Marston, whilst Cromwell and Browne took up their quarters on the west side of Oxford, at Wytham and Wolvercote.

Legge and the Commissioners, as we have seen, had been given authority over all the neighbouring Royalist garrisons except Banbury, and on 23 May Legge ordered that the outpost at Godstow House be abandoned and burnt. It was set ablaze, but a party from Colonel Thomas Sheffield's New Model Regiment of Horse arrived in time to extinguish the flames, recover some powder and shot, and take a few prisoners.

On the same day the C.O.B.K. wrote to Walter Strickland, their representative in the Low Countries:

> We have designed the besieging of Oxford to be the first and chief action of this summer's service, and require to be furnished with instruments fit for such a service. We find greatest want here of good engineers, and we conceive they may be had with you [in the Low Countries]. We therefore desire you to inquire for a good and sufficient engineer, who has no particular interests in the other [Royalist] party, also two skilful conductors of works for carrying on of approaches and the like service, and having agreed with them for their entertainment send them over hither with what speed you can, as we intend to proceed with that work with all expedition.[5]

It was clear that the decision to lay siege to Oxford had been arrived at in some haste. As well as a lack of engineers, Fairfax was also without an adequate siege train, which would take at least a fortnight to reach him. In the meantime he could do no more than blockade Oxford. Sir Samuel Luke, no friend to the Independent party in Parliament, whose creation he regarded the New Model as being, wrote "Sir Thomas Fairfax is before Oxford with such strength as is not so considerable as I could wish for such work, the enemy in the out garrisons being very bold – no whit daunted."[6]

5　C.S.P.D., p.328.
6　Tibbutt (ed.), p.295.

Sir William Dugdale, in besieged Oxford, recorded enemy movements. On 27 May "Two Regiments of the Rebels, the white and the red, with two guns" marched via Godstow to the Hinckley area, where they established their quarters.[7] Two days later, on the 29th, "This Evening a bullet of six lb weight shot from the rebels' warning piece at Marston fell against the wall on the north side of the Hall at Christ Church." On the same day 600 foot and 200 horse under Colonel Thomas Rainsborough attacked the small Royalist garrison at Gaunt House near Newbridge on the Thames. Around 30 of the garrison were absent, foraging, and the remaining 21 surrendered two days later.[8] It was now that the first doubts regarding Oxford's ability to hold out began to surface. Chief among the doubters was Lord Colepeper, nominally one of the Commissioners, though actually at Bath with the Prince of Wales. On 26 May he told Lord Digby:

> Both yesterday and Saturday I wrote very earnestly to you concerning the speedy relief of Oxford, yet I cannot give over urging it until we have your resolution sent to us touching that business. Yet I would not be understood as if I apprehended that this new raw army could storm Oxford, or be master of it by approach without at least 24 days' time, less that it is possible they within should be so ill-provided with victuals as to be starved out of it at a month's warning. I fear not either of these if there were nothing else in the case, but when I consider the temper of those within the town, the disaffection of the townsmen, the necessities of the soldiers, and the vast importance of the place and persons within the town, I should dissemble if I were to say that I am without apprehensions. Neither is it fear alone that ought to put wings to the relief of it, accidents on the way ought to be considered, and hope may very justly tender you counsel that way when fear cannot. I say the hope to visit those "Hogen-Moghens" when they have their bellyful of knocks and duty, and to fight with them when they shall find themselves in the same condition their fellows were at Newark, when Prince Rupert bestowed his favour on them. If that should fail and they will not give you leave to surprise them, they must when the King shall come near, either advance and fight with him or retreat. The former, in my opinion (if His Majesty have joined with him Goring and Gerard) is not to be declined: a battle we must have, and I know not how it can be struck upon better terms,; or if they will not fight they must retreat, in which case (without the spirit of prophecy) I dare affirm their army is broken, and all the east of England, at the least, will be the reward of this relief of Oxford. On the other side if they take that place they will immediately

---

7   Hamper (ed.), p.34.
8   Ibid.

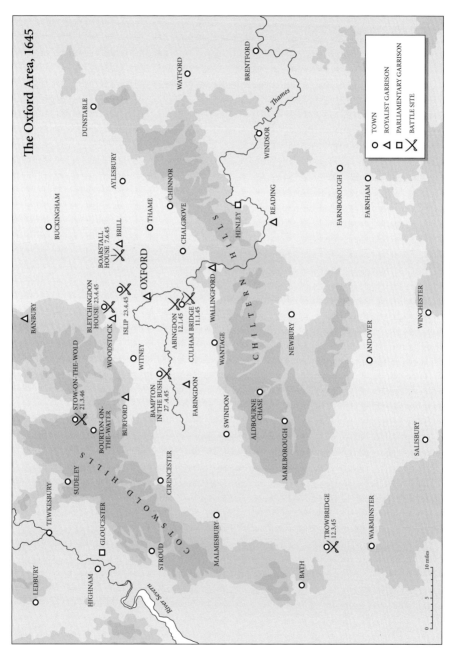

Map 6 The Oxford area 1645.

pursue the King with an army of 20,000 men if they desire so many, and the reputation of such a prize would equally dismay all the King's friends as the loss of a battle would. What you resolve in this business must be speedily acted; send us orders, and expect from hence all that is possible. The ends of the besiegers are apparently to surprise the place before relief can come, to divert the designs of the King if His Majesty shall attempt their succour, and to oppress him with power if he should come near them. The second is not to be answered but balanced, and speed with united strength may satisfy the first and third. I shall impatiently expect your answer; in the meantime, if you resolve to succour them, send them multiplied lotions of hope, and if there be a little tincture in them it will be never the worse."[9]

It seems that Colepeper's fears had a considerable effect upon some among the King's advisers, notably probably on the "civilians," George Digby and William Ashburnham. It is also true that not everyone felt these worries to be justified. Sir Edward Hyde, also with the Prince of Wales in the West, and presumably privy to the same intelligence as Colepeper, wrote to Prince Rupert on 27 May: "We receive strange alarms every day from Oxford, but if such a town cannot endure the face of an army for some time I would dwell hereafter in the fields and villages, and think no more of fortifying towns."[10]

On the face of it, Hyde's verdict seems more justifiable, but there were certainly doubts about the reliability of at least the Town Regiment in Oxford. The University Regiment was loyal, as it was hoped were any other units in the town. At the moment these probably consisted of part of the Lord General's and the Queen's Regiments of Foot, and the Lord Treasurer's and William Legge's Horse. It was certainly questionable whether they would be sufficient both to quell rebellion within Oxford and a co-ordinated assault by the enemy. However, there was nothing to suggest that such a mutiny was likely. As one didn't occur even in the far more hopeless circumstances of the siege in the following year, it was unlikely to have been a serious possibility now.

Although later Prince Rupert's opponents would express fears that Legge and the Prince's followers in Oxford were plotting to betray the city to the Parliamentarians, there is nothing to suggest that such rumours were current at this stage. More likely to have been the real concern was those voiced by Sir Henry Slingsby, who was with the King's army and had received from Oxford "some intimation that the town was not so well provided for a siege, which stopped the King in his march and turned his thoughts how to relieve it."[11] There may well have been

9   C.S.P.D., p.522.
10 Ibid., p.520.
11 Sir Henry Slingsby, *The diary of Sir Henry Slingsby of Scriven, Bart.* (London, 1836), p.146.

John, 1st Lord Colepeper
(c.1600-1660). Possessing some
pre-war military experience, he
was made Master of the Rolls in
1643 and sat on the Council of
the West in 1645. Colepeper was
an opponent of Prince Rupert.
(Author's collection)

some truth in this. We know from Sir Edward Nicholas's earlier report that Legge had been trying to bring in supplies, but he had only a short time in which to do so, from an area already finding it difficult to meet the demands of the army and town, and which had just been suffering from the effects of Cromwell's raid. The arrival of the New Model may well have ended these efforts before Oxford was fully provisioned, and caused alarm among some of the court at least, who Legge might well have had difficulty in imposing rationing on.

There was clearly no way in which the Royalists could risk the loss of Oxford. Although a considerable part of their arms manufacturing capacity had by now been transferred to Bristol, much remained at Oxford, and it was still the King's administrative capital, with his son, the Duke of York, and many prominent Royalist supporters there.

The King and his Council were unaware at this stage how ineffective Fairfax's operations were proving to be. On 2 June the garrison made a sortie at about 3:00 a.m., some horse and foot, led by Will Legge in person, falling on the Parliamentarian quarters at Headington Hill taking them by surprise, and, according to the Royalists, killing 50 of the enemy, and taking 96 prisoners. On the same day the besiegers gained some compensation when they captured 50 cattle which had been grazing just outside the East Gate.[12] At the same time that they attacked Gaunt House, the Parliamentarians also began operations against Boarstall House. The besiegers opened up a brisk bombardment of "granadoes" and cannon shot, which went on for several days. Fairfax also summoned Boarstall's Governor, Sir William Campion, to surrender:

> Sir,
> I send you this Summons, before I proceed to further extremities, to deliver up to me the House of Boarstall you now hold, with all the Ordnance, Arms and Ammunition therein, for the use and service of The Kingdom, which if you shall agree unto you may expect civilities and fair respects, otherwise you may draw upon yourself those inconveniencies which I desire may be prevented. I expect your answer by this trumpet within one hour. I rest
> Your servant,
> Thomas Fairfax[13]

Sir William rejected the summons ending "I am therefore ready to undergo all inconveniencies whatever, rather than submit to any, much less to these so dishonourable and unworthy Propositions. This is the resolution of your servant, W. Campion."[14]

Fairfax's men now assaulted Boarstall. Sir Thomas brought according to a Royalist estimate about 1,200 foot from Marston with ladders and "that night Skippon caused the House to be stormed, but the Moat being much deeper than they expected, the Assailants were beat off with Loss, and so the next day they raised that Siege also … " The Royalists made a wildly inflated claim to have killed some 400 of the attackers.[15]

Meanwhile, concern for the plight of Oxford had caused the King to change his plan of campaign, as it would ultimately prove, with fatal consequences. Postponing the planned advance into Yorkshire, the King's army swung eastwards, and on 28 May stormed Leicester. The outcome had been what Fairfax had feared. Whilst the New Model had been spending its time fruitlessly before Oxford, the King's army had been at liberty to create havoc across the Midlands. On 2 June Fairfax received preliminary orders from the C.O.B.K. to begin preparations to raise the siege and move to protect the Eastern Association, and on the 4th these orders were confirmed. The local Parliamentarian forces from Northampton, Newport Pagnell and Aylesbury which had reinforced the New Model were to be placed

---

12   Hamper (ed.), p.34.
13   Eddershaw, p.140.
14   Ibid.
15   Rushworth, p.236.

in garrison at Abingdon, and Fairfax was to join Cromwell and Vermuyden and the Eastern Association horse and after that "We desire you to attend the King's motions in such way as, being at the place, you may judge to be best."

Fairfax demolished the bridge he had thrown across the Cherwell, and the troops from the opposite side of the River Ray were ordered to rendezvous with the rest of the army at Islip. The Royalists, at least according to their version of events, continued to harass the besiegers as they prepared to depart, claiming to have taken 100 prisoners who were exchanged for Royalists captured at the beginning of the siege.

By 5 June the New Model was on its way north, and the immediate threat to Oxford at an end. But this does not seem to have been appreciated in the Royalist camp. On 3 June Sir Edward Nicholas had written to the King in some alarm, telling him that the town council had had to open the magazine of food stored in order to supply corn to some of the poorer people whose own food stocks were running out. It was also felt that before the Royalists could resume their northwards march, it was necessary to ensure that Oxford was well enough provisioned to minimise the danger of the same threat arising again. The King told Nicholas on 4 June that he intended firstly to march south to the vicinity of Market Harborough, in order to gather supplies, especially cattle and sheep, to be sent into Oxford. In the meantime he urged Nicholas to send out as many non-essential civilians as possible, because without Goring and Gerard's men with him, he felt his army too weak to challenge Fairfax in an attempt to relieve Oxford unless there was no alternative. Based around Daventry, the Royalist cavalry spent the next few days rounding up large numbers of sheep and cattle, probably over-estimated by the Parliamentarians at 30,000 sheep and 8,000 cattle.[16]

On 8 June a convoy of 1,200 horse set off to take the provisions to Oxford, and did not return until the 12th, when they brought back with them some munitions, probably mainly granadoes to replace those expended in the storm of Leicester. Two days later, the Royalist army was crushingly defeated by Sir Thomas Fairfax at Naseby.

Although retrospectively, Naseby spelt the doom of the Royalist cause, this was not immediately apparent. Fairfax and the New Model headed for the West Country, to deal with the other remaining significant Royalist field army under George Goring, and Oxford was not for the moment under threat.

Whilst the King entertained hopes of raising a new force of infantry in Wales and the Marches, it was clear that his capital would sooner or later come under attack again, and the summer and autumn saw renewed work on strengthening Oxford's defences.

On 1 August Lord Digby, with the King at Cardiff in South Wales, wrote to Sir Edward Nicholas, painting a gloomy picture of Royalist prospects: "I hope

16   Bray, pp.130-131.

George, Lord Digby (1612-1677). Commanded a regiment of horse until 1643, when he became a secretary of state. He was briefly lieutenant general in the North in 1645, before retiring to France. Often characterised as an ambitious intriguer, he was increasingly at odds with Prince Rupert. (Author's collection)

the generality at Oxford will be found very firm and sincere, and though I must confess that such a torrent of misfortunes hath quite overbourne my sanguine complexion, yet it is supplied by faith, that god will not wholly desert us in so just a cause."[17]

There was however, growing unease in Oxford, hinted at in a letter of 7 August from Sir Edward Nicholas to John Ashburnham:

Some displeasure being conceived against Lord Colepeper's servant he being captain-lieutenant in that regiment of volunteers here, which was the lord keeper's, and is now, against my understanding, the Duke of York's, occasion was taken against him for some foolish words and behaviour, and upon a trial at a court of war the captain was condemned to be shot to death for endeavouring to raise a mutiny, which is so ill-taken that

17   C.S.P.D., p.632.

Prince Rupert (1619-82), a charismatic
commander who fell foul of the King
for his surrender of Bristol in 1645.
(Author's collection)

Prince Maurice (1620-1652),
younger brother of Prince Rupert
and a capable soldier, though
unpopular at court. He drowned at
sea. (Author's collection)

the Auxiliaries are like to desert, but the Lords have taken order for the reprieving of the captain. I hope this business will be now quelled with as little prejudice as may be, but this gives occasion to talk more loudly of the great favour that is shown here in certain quarters. I wish the discontent were not so visible as it is.[18]

At least part of the problem lay in the increasingly strained relations between Lord Digby's supporters, and the followers of Prince Rupert, headed by Will Legge. Legge had rebutted angrily a letter from Digby, in which the latter had inferred that Rupert had been to blame for the decision to fight at Naseby. But it was clear that the animosity between Rupert and Digby had deepened, and the supporters of both were reacting. On 12 August Digby received a letter from Edward Walsingham, the Royalist propagandist who was also Digby's agent in Oxford:

Our condition in Oxford is like summer ale, the faction grows every day more insolent and high, and the Governor [Legge] since the favour he did Mr Felton is pleased daily to show his teeth plainer to you and yours, and has already expressed as high ingratitude, to give it no worse a character, towards you as his discretion can well manage, and I am deceived if he do not afford his Majesty the like honour, when a fit occasion comes. Prince Rupert salutes him almost daily from Bristol with epistles beginning Brother Governor etc, which are communicated daily to the Junto you know of, and thence the ill humours dispersed abroad. Prince Rupert in general obloquy with all sorts of people except Wm. Legge, and some few others of that stamp well known to you. Now every one desires his absence and discarding; his Majesty has had sufficient experience both of his wilfulness and ignorance, if of no worse. Yourself have spelled him over enough for your own particular, and these and many other circumstances considered, and which I need not suggest, you cannot but conclude that now is the time to take the bridle out of Phaeton's hands and permit him not a third time to burn the world, which, if not prevented, my friend who urges me (in a letter I must not send) to tell you this believes it will one way or the other of necessity come to pass. Something extraordinary is in hand is evident by the daily letters which pass between here and Bristol continually yet so as they are smothered as much as may be and disavowed. Tis sure now time to provide for the security of Oxford, for I am certain that many things are done which will not bear examination both within and without the line. Alderman Legge applies himself to none but such as most men doubt as citizens and malcontents, the number whereof

18 Ibid., p.34.

he seeks to augment and incorporate. The strength and danger of which party cannot well be long evaded if Oxford be not committed to the care of some able man, and Sir [Thomas] Glemham is generally desired, as I doubt not the Lords have ere this signified, and if he be not spared here are both Sir John Cansfield and Sir John Heydon with Nevill, all able, stout and worthy men … If Oxford be lost it is not all the noble treatings and endearments in the world will make his Majesty reparation.[19]

Just how much basis there was to Walsingham's allegations is difficult to determine. Certainly the disaster at Naseby was attributed by many to Prince Rupert, who had always at least as many opponents as friends, largely due to his own doing. Digby is invariably portrayed as a malevolent force, set on Rupert's downfall, yet this is an over-simplification of a complex situation. It is probably safest to assume that there was a good deal of ill-will and suspicion between supporters in Oxford of the opposing camps. Legge was an enthusiastic supporter of Rupert, but Walsingham's suggestion of a plot to betray Oxford to the enemy, or to stage some kind of coup, is certainly a product of malice, or a reflection of the panic in Oxford following news of Naseby and Langport. Lord Digby certainly affected to believe much of what Walsingham told him, and on 27 August told Lord Jermyn, in Paris with Queen Henrietta Maria:

I hope that it is not possible they can in anyways endanger Oxford before the winter relieve it [But] I do not think it will be in the King's power to hinder himself from being forced to accept such conditions as the rebels will give him, and that the next news you will have, after we have been one month at Oxford, will be, that I and those few others who may be thought by our counsels to fortify the King in firmness to his principles shall be forced or torn from him; and you will find Prince Rupert, Byron, Gerard, Wm. Legge and Ormond are the prime instruments to impose the necessity upon the King of submitting to what they and most of the King's party at Oxford shall think fit.[20]

Whatever the differences among the Royalist leadership, the garrison of Oxford continued to strike at neighbouring Parliamentarian outposts when they saw opportunity. Learning that Colonel Greaves with a party of Buckinghamshire Parliamentarian horse were quartered at Thame, and not particularly on the alert, Will Legge:

19 Ibid., p.65.
20 Ibid., p.87.

...Resolved to beat him up; and therefore sent 400 horse from Oxford commanded by Colonel David Walter (the High Sheriff of the County) and Colonel Robert Legge the Governor's brother. These (with 60 musketeers of the Governor's Regiment commanded by Captain Burgh) marched forth this afternoon, and before they came near Thame divided into two bodies, the Van Colonel walter, and Col. Rob. Legge had the rear. They found the Town very strongly barricaded at every Avenue, notwithstanding which, Major Medcalfe, (major to Colonel Robert Legge) gallantly led up the Forlorn Hope, charged the Rebels' guard, and maintained his ground so handsomely, that (major Aglionby coming up to his assistance) the Rebels were beat off the Guards, so as Major Medcalfe with seven Troopers leapt from his horse, and removing the Carts opened the Avenue. This done, the two gallant Majors charged the rebels up through the street, doing execution to the Market place, where Colonel greaves himself stood with about 200 horse drawn up; but Colonel Walter being ready with the other Troops (his own, Colonel Tucker's and Major Trist's) gave the rebels such a charge as made then fly the town, and after pursuing the fugitive Rebels, drove them above half a mile from Thame. In the meantime Colonel Legge (who with the rear guarded the town and Avenues) lest others of the Rebels (being in all 800) should break in and defeat the whole) now drew into the Town, that others might have secure time to search Houses and Stables. Orders were given and 'twas done accordingly, after which they all drew out of the town and marched away with their horses and prisoners. Before they had gone two miles, at least 200 Rebels were got in their Rear, but then Colonel Legge charged them so gallantly, that the Rebels ran back much faster than they came on; Yet far had they not gone before these vexed Rebels came on again, and then also Colonel Legge beat them so far back that they never attempted to come on again. In this last charge that most gallant hopeful young Gentleman Captain Henry Gardiner (son to Sir Thomas Gardiner His Majesty's Solicitor General) was unfortunately shot dead; a youth of such high incomparable courage, mixed with such abundance of modesty and sweetness, that we cannot easily match him unless with his brave Brother (young Sir Thomas Gardiner) which two are now buried in the same Grave, whither they were brought with so much universal sorrow and affection. Besides this gallant Gentleman, no Officer was killed, and but three common Soldiers, nor scarce any hurt, only Major Medcalfe shot in the arm. The Rebels dropped plentifully in the street and fields; Colonel greaves himself escaping very narrowly, being run into the body, and at first thought to have been slain. The rebels being thus beaten, His Majesty's Forces brought away those prisoners they had taken, which (besides common Troopers) are 27 Officers, amongst which are their Adjutant General Puide, their Provost Marshal General and their Engineer, four Captains, and seven Lieutenants, three Cornets, besides

13 Sergeants Quartermasters and Corporals. A great deal of money was found in the Rebels' pockets (they had lately received Advance money) many Arms taken, betwixt two and 300 good Horse and three Colours.[21]

The skirmish was witnessed by an excited young Anthony Wood, who, it will be remembered, had been sent to school at Thame from Oxford as likely to be a place of greater safety. He added a few details of the action:

This alarm and onset was made by the cavaliers from Oxford about break of day on Sunday morning 7 Sept before any of the rebels were stirring. But by the alarm was taken from the sentinel that stood at that end of the town leading to Oxford, many of them came out of their beds in the market place without their doublets; whereof Adj. Gen. Puide was one, who fought in his shirt. Some that were quartered near the church, as in Vincent Barry's house between it and the school, and those in the vicar's house (wherein A.W. then sojourned) fled into the church (some with their horses also) and going to the top of the tower, would be peeping thence to see the cavaliers run into the houses where they quartered, to fetch away their goods.

There were about six of the Parliament soldiers (troopers) that quartered in the vicar's house; and one being slow and careless, was airing and warming his boots, while they were fighting in the town: and no sooner he was withdrawn, into the garden I think, but some of the cavaliers who were retiring with their spoil towards Boarstall (for they had separated themselves from those that went to Oxford) ran into the vicar's house, and seized on cloaks and goods of the rebels, while some of the said rebels (who had lock'd themselves up in the church were beholding out of the church windows what they were doing.

On the day before (Saturday) some of the said rebels that lodged in the said house had been progging for venison, in Thame park I think; and one or two pasties of it were made, and newly put into the oven before the cavaliers entered into the house. But so it was, that none of the said rebels were left at 11 of the clock to eat the said pasties, so their share fell among the schoolboys that were sojourners in the said house.[22]

The action at Thame was Will Legge's last success as Governor, for devastating news now reached Oxford. Rupert had been besieged at Bristol by Fairfax and the New Model Army, and had been confidently expected to hold out for several weeks, whilst the King desperately attempted to mount a relief effort. But on 10

21   *Mercurius Aulicus*, pp.1734-1736.
22   Wood, pp.120-121.

September, acknowledging the futility of further resistance, the Prince had made terms and surrendered Bristol.

To Edward Walsingham in Oxford the news seemed to confirm all his worst fears. He wrote on the 14th to Lord Digby, forwarding a message allegedly received from an agent in London:

> Sir, I am extremely sorry that you made no better use of my frequent informations concerning Prince Rupert and his creature Legge. Now that you are there more than undone. I hope you will repent your error. Pray God it be not too late, for the Dunkirk of your Flanders is gone, nay wilfully cast away. I am so angry at the King that he would take no other course, that I have no pity almost left for him, but I cannot so divest myself of my loyalty as to omit to tell you that Oxford also will be lost, so he will have soon to seek a new land, if some extraordinary course be not taken soon we are ruined … Deceive yourselves not any longer if you desire not to be ruined. I have seen transactions of the bargain [possibly for the surrender of Oxford?] already, and there is no prevention but by an immediate repair of his Majesty thither, and changing the Governor, putting that city into the hands of some worthy man, … but whilst his Majesty is solicitous for this I would not by any means have him neglect his own personal safety, upon which he need have an extraordinary cautious and watchful eye, for I hear a whisper as if something ill were intended him, and your master Lord Digby. Either send us a new pastor, or the wolf will devour us. Prince Rupert is at Burford with scarce 500 men, who must there part with their arms, according to the agreement, as we hear.[23]

Whether or not Walsingham had himself fabricated all of this is unclear, but he urged Digby to persuade the King to come to Oxford, if only for one night. "You must not else at all depend now on that force which we still have, there is no power left to give any assurance of preserving Oxford, for Prince Rupert is hourly expected here with his train, which will so curb the endeavours of all honest men with a prevalent number that if necessity require it, it will be mere madness to attempt anything."

In a postscript, Lady Digby added:

> Dear heart, in this letter is contained all I had to say; for God's sake lose no time in the deciphering of it, for it concerns you infinitely much. Let me to conjure you to lose not a minute of time in giving a speedy answer to this business. I wish Sir Thomas Glemham may bring it.[24]

---

23 C.S.P.D., pp.107-108.
24 Ibid.

On 14 September a furious King Charles stripped Prince Rupert of all of his commands, and ordered Legge to be removed as Governor of Oxford and placed under arrest. Rupert reached Oxford on 15 September and two days later "by letter from the King, the Lords [Commissioners] discharged the Prince of his Generalship, cashiered his Regiments of Horse and Foot his Troop and firelocks. That day was Colonel Legge discharged of his Government of Oxford, and confined to his house."[25] It was left to Sir Edward Nicholas, as Secretary of State, to put these orders into effect, as he reported to the King on 18 September:

> I went immediately to the Lord Treasurer [Cottington] and having there delivered to Lieutenant Colonel Sir James Hamilton your warrant to take charge of Oxford in the absence of Sir Thomas Glemham, we thought fit to send for Colonel Legge thither, who came presently, and readily submitted himself prisoner to your commands. This being thus despatched, I went to Colonel Legge's house, where Prince Rupert dined, and desiring to speak privately with him in the withdrawing room, I presented to him first his discharge, and after that your letter, to which he humbly submitted, telling me he was very innocent of anything that might deserve so heavy a punishment. After this I forthwith assembled the Lords of Your Majesty's Privy Council, where the Duke of York was pleased to be present, and there acquainted them with the contents of Your majesty's letter, and your gracious care of them and this place, for which they are very thankful, and presently gave orders to the Lieutenant Governor and the officers here to have an especial care of their several charges, whereunto they very cheerfully applied themselves, so as I am confident your Majesty will find that this great alteration will not in this place anyways disturb your affairs. This day the Lords intend to dispose of the horse and foot which came from Bristol into several garrisons and quarters hereabouts as shall be requisite; most of the horse we think fit to send to the parts about Banbury. Their Lordships hope your Majesty will hasten hither, as soon as may be, Sir Thomas Glemham himself for their better assistance in military affairs in these parts.[26]

There had been some consideration of a suggestion that Sir John Cansfield, formerly colonel of the Queen's Regiment of Horse, be made Governor of Oxford, but Cansfield, a Lancashire man, was a Roman Catholic, and it was evidently thought undesirable to risk a repetition of the controversy which had followed Sir Henry Gage's appointment at the end of 1644. Lieutenant Colonel Hamilton, for the moment acting as Lieutenant Governor, was most probably John Hamilton,

25 Hamper (ed.), p.39.
26 C.S.P.D., p.134.

a Buckinghamshire, an otherwise obscure figure, but presumably not felt to be tainted as a supporter of Prince Rupert.

Sir Edward Nicholas made his own sympathy with Rupert fairly clear in his letter to the King:

> And now I may not omit to acquaint your Majesty that I hear Prince Rupert hath not £50 in all the world, but is reduced to so great extremity as he hath not wherewith to feed himself or servants. I hear that Colonel Legge is in no more plentiful condition, which I held it my duty to mention, as not unfit for your consideration. Your Majesty will herewith receive a letter from Prince Rupert, who I believe will stay here till he hears again from you, for that he cannot, without leave from the rebels, go to embark himself, and without your Majesty's licence I hear he will not demand a pass from the rebels.[27]

The immediate concern of the Lords Commissioners was the disposal of the troops who had come from Bristol. It was ordered on 18 September that the foot, under Colonel Henry Tillier, who had been Major General to Rupert, be added to the Oxford garrison. Sir Horatio Cary with the horse from Bristol, including apparently the remnants of Rupert's own Regiment and his scarlet-coated fire-locks, were to march to Worcester. There was evidently some concern about the attitude of some of the officers, especially of Rupert's Lifeguard, because it was emphasised that:

> Those officers and soldiers of Sir Horatio Cary's brigade, and those of Prince Rupert's troop, and also those belonging to sir Charles Lucas which came from Berkeley Castle, are hereby in his Majesty's name commanded to repair to their colours, and to march according to orders given.[28]

However Rupert's horse at least seem to have been in a discontented mood, presumably hanging around the inns and taverns of Oxford, for on 19 September a further order was issued:

> Order made this day at the meeting of the King's Privy Council at Oxford. Whereas commandment has already been given, that all the horse which came from Bristol should repair to their colours and march according to orders, Captain Grimshaw's only excepted, which order we now under-stand is not obeyed, divers officers and troopers still remaining in this town. These are to signify to them all that it is again commanded that they

---

27 Ibid.
28 Ibid., p.146.

forthwith repair to Woodstock, and from thence to march as is already ordered. If any shall still remain in this town their horses will be taken away, and themselves proceeded against. Hereof the Lieutenant Governor is desired to take notice, and to see this order punctually observed.[29]

Prince Rupert remained in Oxford until 10 October, when he set off with Prince Maurice and a band of supporters on his eventful dash to Newark, where a stormy meeting with the King took place. At Rupert's request, the King reluctantly agreed to a court martial, which cleared the prince of any wrongdoing with respect to the loss of Bristol. But it did not lead to any immediate reconciliation between Charles and his nephew, and Rupert retired to Woodstock, with some of his more devoted followers, where he remained for some weeks, whilst Will Legge, released from house arrest in Oxford, worked to bring about some form of reconciliation.

Sir Thomas Glemham took up his post as Governor of Oxford on 2 October. A Suffolk man, born in the 1590s, Glemham was a professional soldier of considerable European experience, who was knighted in 1617, and served as an MP and JP, though politically he seems before the outbreak of the civil war to have been somewhat opportunistic. A colonel of foot in the Earl of Newcastle's Northern Royalist army, Glemham was governor of York from April to July 1644, and then of Carlisle, which he held stubbornly against the Scots army until July 1645. With a reputation as a capable governor of garrisons under threat, and a competent soldier, Glemham was the safe pair of hands which Oxford needed. It was not, in fact, under immediate threat. Following the fall of Bristol it was agreed by the Committee of Both Kingdoms that Fairfax and the New Model should concentrate on the probably prolonged task of mopping up the remaining Royalist forces and garrisons in the West of England. In the meantime it was recognised that "we are not furnished for the moment with forces to oppose those at Oxford." It was estimated on 22 September that there around 2,000 horse and dragoons in Oxford. These were reinforced early in November, when the King and his Lifeguard and a few other horse made a perilous march through the enemy forces from Newark back to Oxford. The Committee of Both Kingdoms told Fairfax that:

The forces of Oxford are much augmented by those come from the surrendered garrisons, that Abingdon is not so good a condition as formerly. That the King with 3-400 horse is come from Newark, also to show the necessity of having forces in therse parts for their defence … and leave it to him to send such forces hither as he can spare.[30]

29   Ibid.
30   Ibid., p.158.

Fairfax detached Colonel Edward Whalley's brigade of horse, consisting of two regiments, but these were insufficient to do more than hinder Royalist operations, as highlighted in a letter of 27 November from Whalley to the Committee:

> We have now received intelligence that a party of the King's horse from Oxford, Woodstock and Banbury, about 1,000 or 1,500, are marched toward the Eastern association, and went yesterday night through Leighton Buzzard in Beds. We have given orders to the forces of Aylesbury, Newport and Herts and to the regiment of horse and regiment of dragoons of London [stationed at Thame] to follow them. We desire you, with all the forces under your command, to march after that party and to endeavour a conjunction with the rest of our forces appointed for that service, and to follow the enemy wherever they go till you shall receive further order, by which means we trust there may be a very good account given of that party.[31]

The Royalists evidently evaded the Parliamentarian forces in what was one of a number of far-reaching raiding and foraging expeditions mounted that winter. They can have done little to boost morale among King Charles and a court facing Christmas in Oxford almost without hope.

31   Ibid., p.397.

15

The Last Battle: Stow-on-the-Wold 1646

By the end of 1645, the Royalist cause was desperate. The Oxford Army was a broken remnant, plans for new recruitment in Wales and the West had been shattered by the defeat of Goring at Langport and the loss of Bristol. The reverse suffered by Montrose at Philliphaugh in September would prove fatal to any hopes the King had of assistance from Scotland. However, the King's horse were still capable of raids, as the Oxford Horse under Sir John Cansfield demonstrated that winter:

> About this time were come together all the Horse Forces of our Garrisons of Oxford, Banbury, Wallingford, Borstal and Faringdon, making a Body of 1,200 Horse under the command of Sir John Cansfield, and made journeys with them into Bedfordshire, Wiltshire and other Places without any great Advantages but only for their present Subsistance.[1]

The Parliamentarian garrison of Abingdon continued to be a major annoyance to Royalist Oxford, and a renewed attempt was made by Sir Thomas Glemham to recover it. The plan got off to a bad start when a cart carrying materials broke down on the way. However Royalist horse and foot led by Captain Mead got into an enemy sconce, and many of the Parliamentarian defenders ran out on the other side. But their horse made a stand and drove the Royalists out again. Walker complained:

> This Misfortune was the greater, we being so near the contrary, and four Shots to have made way for those who had done the Business. Sir Stephen Hawkins who commanded the Party was much blamed for the Oversight. Prince Rupert attempted it two days after, but then it was too late. Had we got the Place, and the Lord Astley come up without Interruption, we

---

1   Walker, p.145.

might for some time have been Masters of those Counties, but this failure and Banbury being besieged, we were brought to some Straits.[2]

Clarendon summed up the position:

There were yet some garrisons which remained in his obedience, and which were like, during the winter season, to be preserved from any attempt of the enemy; but upon the approach of the spring, if the King should be without an army in the field, the fate of those few places was easy to be discerned. And which way an army could possibly be brought together, or where it should be raised, was not within the compass of the wisest man's comprehension. However the more difficult it was, the more vigour was to be applied to the attempt.[3]

Apart from the South-West, only in the southern Marches of Wales did the King still possess a significant foothold. The city of Worcester retained links with the remaining Royalist garrisons of Wales and the West Midlands. Its proximity to Wales, from where there was still a faint hope of new levies, and where a few still hoped that Irish Confederate assistance might land, also made it vital.

Various desperate schemes were aired in Oxford that winter. In December, it was proposed that James, Duke of York should be sent to Ireland and the Prince of Wales to France, and a plan suggested earlier by Sir Richard Willys, the former Governor of Newark, was revived when it was proposed to concentrate the garrisons of Worcester, Exeter, Newark, Chester and Oxford at Worcester after they simultaneously demolished their fortifications on 20 February. By this means it was hoped to raise a force of 3,000 foot and 2,500 horse, to be reinforced by 2,000 recruits raised along the Welsh Border during the winter. This army could either march into the West to link up with the remaining Royalist forces there, advance into Kent and Sussex in the faint hope of triggering a Royalist uprising, or support the landing of the oft-promised but almost entirely imaginary foreign mercenaries supposedly being recruited by the Queen. One major objection to the scheme, even if it had been possible to unite the troops from such widely separated garrisons without them being intercepted by the enemy, was that it would involve the abandoning of Oxford, the Court and the logistical and administrative resources of the Royalist capital. In any event, it was too late for the scheme to have any prospects of success. By February, with resistance in the West on the point of collapse after Hopton's defeat at Torrington, Charles was thinking instead of a dash into Kent at the head of 2,000 horse and dragoons in an attempt to secure the port of Rochester. At the same time Charles was making foredoomed offers to go to

2   Ibid.
3   Clarendon, Book IX, p.161.

Sir Jacob (later Lord) Astley
(1579-1652), who commanded
the Oxford Army Foot from 1642
to 1645. (Philip Mould Gallery,
London)

London to discuss with Parliament terms for a peace settlement, providing he was allowed to retire to Worcester by 20 February.

Royalist military hopes rested with 67 year-old Jacob, Lord Astley. On 6 December 1645 Astley was effectively placed in command of all the remaining Royalist forces outside of the West of England, with the title of Lieutenant General of Worcestershire, Staffordshire, Herefordshire and Shropshire. The post of Lieutenant General of Horse was given to Sir Charles Lucas, an excellent fighting commander, who had the unenviable task of trying to reorganise the disorderly remnants of the Royalist horse. There were delays in Astley taking up his command, and by the time he reached Worcester on Christmas Day, the Royalist position in the Welsh Marches had suffered another serious blow with the loss of Hereford. More time was then spent in fruitless attempts to relieve Chester, so it was not until that garrison fell on 3 February 1646 that Astley was at last able to concentrate on mustering his forces to join the King. Even then his first task lay in trying to reconcile the quarrelling Royalist commanders in the area, and reorganise the chaotic local Royalist administration.

As spring approached, he began to call in every available man from the outlying garrisons. In Oxford, however, King Charles was continuing to hesitate over his next move. He lacked any coherent strategy, and his desperation in early 1646 is summarised by Clarendon:

> If he could by all possible endeavours have drawn out of all his garrisons a force of 5,000 horse and foot (which at that time seemed a thing not to be despaired of) he did more desire to have lost his life in some signal attempt upon any part of the enemy's army than to have enjoyed any conditions which he foresaw he was ever like to obtain by treaty.[4]

The plan which now evolved was for the King, with the Oxford Horse, to:

> Join himself with the Lord Astley, and either to endeavour to relieve Banbury or to retire to Worcester and there take new Resolution. To this end Lord Astley had order march with all his Horse and Foot out of Worcestershire and over Avon to come to Stow, and so to Chipping Norton, where his Majesty with about 1,500 Foot drawn out of Oxford and other Garrisons intended to meet him.[5]

On 18 February, Secretary Nicholas wrote to the Marquis of Ormonde in Dublin:

> We are here busy in gathering the King's forces together, the King intending by the beginning of next month to take the field and we hope he will have 5,000 horse dragoons and foot ready to march with him by that time.[6]

Astley, so short of funds that he had to borrow for his own needs from Bridgnorth town council, gathered men from all available garrisons, which in some cases were abandoned. He held a general rendezvous at Bridgnorth prior to commencing his hazardous march. Astley's army included many reminders of the great days of the Cavaliers. Among his 700 horse were the remaining fragments of such once redoubtable regiments as those of Lord Byron and Prince Maurice, the remnants of Gerard's and Vaughan's forces and many reformadoes, including the colourful Lorraine mercenary, the Comte de St Pol, formerly Major General of Horse to Lord Byron. The foot were drawn from an equally diverse range of sources, including in their ranks the survivors of Prince Rupert's Lifeguard of Firelocks, those of his brother, Prince Maurice, the last of Sir Michael Ernley's Regiment of Foot from the army in Ireland, and 60 men of Sir Charles Lloyd's Denbighshire regiment which

---

4   Clarendon, p.163.
5   Walker, p.145.
6   Thomas Carte, *History of the life of James, duke of Ormonde, from his birth in 1610 to his death in 1688* (Oxford, 1853), Volume 6, p.354.

had first seen action at Edgehill and had made their way back to Bridgnorth after a gallant defence of Devizes. These veterans were joined by other experienced troops from the garrisons of Worcester, Bridgnorth and Ludlow, though apparently by very few of the hoped-for new levies. It was a band of unpaid and desperate men, for the most part diehard Royalists, who were staking their all on a last throw.[7]

Astley's task was a formidable one. Thanks to captured letters and despatches, the enemy were aware of his intentions and already moving to trap him. On the fall of Chester the Committee of Both Kingdoms ordered that a total of 1,200 horse and 1,800 foot of the army of Sir William Brereton should be sent to besiege Lichfield.[8]

There was some debate as to whether the Parliamentarians should concentrate their forces against Astley before laying siege to Lichfield, but although it was accepted that Brereton should concentrate on Lichfield, he was ready to detach horse in pursuit of Astley. On 7 March Brereton was given command of the forces of Cheshire, Staffordshire, Shropshire, Worcestershire, Warwickshire, Derbyshire, Herefordshire and Gloucester "now drawn together for following the enemy in the field," and to "attend the motion" of Astley's forces.[9] Troops from Hereford and Gloucester, under Colonel John Birch and Major General Thomas Morgan, "a diminutive, fiery, resolute Welshman," were also poised to intercept the Royalist march. Nearer to Oxford, the New Model horse of Colonel John Fleetwood were ready to block any juncture with the King.

From Bridgnorth Astley marched his 700 horse and 2,300 foot via Kidderminster to Worcester, where he halted for a few days to make his final preparations. The passage over the River Avon at Evesham was in enemy hands, so the Royalists would have to find other means to cross the river. Then they must deal with or evade, Birch and Morgan, who, with a force slightly smaller than their own, lay across the likely Royalist line of march at Broadway, on the edge of the Cotswolds. Fortunately for Astley, Sir William Brereton, moving with some lack of haste with about 1,000 Cheshire, Shropshire and Warwickshire horse, was heading south from Lichfield. On 17 March Brereton reached Coleshill in Warwickshire, and remained there next day, exchanging messages with Morgan. Colonel Sanderson's Regiment, which was under Brereton's command, but quartered possibly at Droitwich, eventually joined Fleetwood at Woodstock. Morgan and Birch had rendezvoused at Gloucester on 15 March, and then marched to Evesham, where they were reinforced by 600 of the garrison, so placing a force of about 2,300 Parliamentarians across Astley's likely path. The Royalist commander's hopes of beginning his march undetected,

---

7   The units in Astley's army can be identified in part from the prisoners listed in *A True and Fuller Relation of the Battell Fought at Stow in the Wold March 21 1646* (London, 1646) and Symonds, pp.72-80.

8   C.S.P.D. (1645-7), pp.330, 342.

9   Ibid., p.359.

and being well on his way on his way to join the King before the enemy reacted, had been dashed. Nevertheless, the old general's first moves were both skilful and successful. Leaving Worcester on 19 March, Astley sent Lucas and some of the horse in a feint towards Evesham, whilst his main body marched north along the Droitwich road. The Parliamentarians were left in doubt whether Astley's objective was Oxford, or if after all he planned to attempt the relief of Lichfield, and the ever-cautious Brereton reacted by abandoning his intended rendezvous with Birch and Morgan and marched back northwards to Wooton Wawen, and then to Knowle, south-east of Birmingham, in order to stay between Astley and Lichfield. Having thus temporarily disposed of one of his opponents, early on 20 March Astley swung south-east in a night march across country via Feckenham and Inkberrow, and reached the Avon at Bidford. Here he sprang another surprise. The Royalists had with them a bridge of boats, possibly some of the equipment manufactured in Oxford in the previous spring, or perhaps a simpler construction, and crossed the river before marching on along the old Roman Buckle Street through Honeybourne and Chipping Campden up into the Cotswolds, brushing past the flank of Birch and Morgan, who were still at Broadway.

Neither side was anxious to bring on an immediate battle; the Parliamentarians wanted to await Brereton, whilst Astley saw joining the King as his priority. By late afternoon on the 20th, the Royalists had reached the crest of the Cotswolds near Broadway and were pushing on across the downlands towards Stow-on-the-Wold, their rearguard skirmishing with parties of Morgan's horse who were attempting to slow down the Royalists until Brereton came up. As dusk fell, with still no sign of Sir William, Morgan called off his men, though he continued to follow Astley at a distance. It may be that the Royalist commander assumed that he had deterred Morgan from attacking, or simply that his own men were exhausted after marching without respite since the previous night, covering in some cases as much as 25 miles. Whatever the reason, he "early begins to draw into quarters" around the village of Donnington, about two miles from Stow. Astley might have been better to have occupied the town itself, which offered more defensible positions.

The Parliamentarians, meanwhile, were recovering from being outmanoeu-vred. Brereton had still been hesitating in the Birmingham area when, on the morning of the 20th, he received news that the Royalists were laying their bridge of boats across the Avon. Morgan reported that he intended to engage Astley in the Cotswolds, and asked for urgent assistance. Even now Brereton only reached Stratford "about the going down of the sun" and where another message arrived from Morgan reporting him to be within three miles of the enemy, with the forlorn hopes already engaged, "and if Sir William made not haste they would be gone, for he himself should be too weak to engage all their Forces … "[10]

10   *True and Fuller Relation.*

A bridge of boats.
(Author's collection)

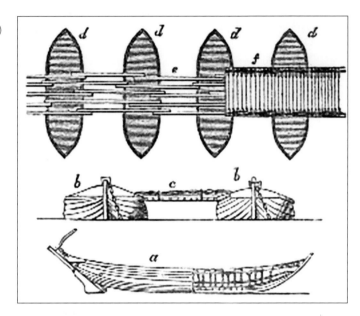

Sir William
Brereton (1604-
1661), Parliament's
commander in
Cheshire. He was
more notable as an
administrator than
combat commander.
(Author's collection)

Whereupon [according to the account of one of his officers] Sir William gave a strict command, that none should stay in Stratford, but all march away presently, notwithstanding the constant marches before. The Bridge at Stratford being pulled down, we could pass over but one at a time, yet we made all the haste that possibly we could, and came to Camden hills by 12:00 a.m. that night. Colonel Morgan with his party were advanced by 11:00 p.m., and still sent posts to Sir William to follow, and he would do what possibly he could to engage Astley to stay. Sir William, not delaying any time, but marched as fast as possibly might be, desiring him by constant posts to engage the enemy if possibly he could, whilst he came up, which he promised to do with all speed. And between 1:00 a.m. and 2:00 a.m. on Saturday morning, after we had marched backward and forward 30 miles since Friday morning, we overtook Colonel Morgan, and then, being joined we marched about a mile.

Realising that he could not avoid battle, and possibly still hoping to be rein-forced by troops from Oxford, Astley for the last time drew up a Royalist army in battle array, taking up position on a steep hillside about quarter of a mile west of Donnington, an area now partially occupied by Horsington Plantation.

Both sides seem to have drawn up in conventional fashion. Astley and his foot were in the Royalist centre, with about 350 horse under Lucas on the right, and the remainder, probably led by Sir William Vaughan, on the left. Brereton commanded the Parliamentarian right, though he seems to have left Morgan to take overall charge of the battle. Birch was in the centre and Morgan on the left. Deployment complete, a pause followed as the Parliamentarians awaited daylight before launching their attack. It may have been at around 6:00 a.m. when the final Battle of the First Civil War began. It was fiercely contested, the Parliamentarians shouting their watchword of "God be our Guide," the Royalists replying with "Patrick and George."

The initial Parliamentarian attack on the left, made by Morgan with 400 horse and 200 firelocks, was twice thrown back by the counter-attacks of Sir Charles Lucas and his horse, during which Lucas was unhorsed and briefly captured, but rescued by a party of Royalist firelocks. In the centre the struggle was equally intense, Birch having his horse killed under him, and, as his secretary wrote, "Hard it was for a while, their reformadoes standing stoutly to it." However on the Parliamentarian right Brereton "most bravely going on with the Right Wing of the Horse, and, at least, 200 Firelocks fiercely charge the [Royalist] left, both of Horse and Foot, and totally routed them." Vaughan's horse were no doubt inferior in quality to Brereton's men, as well as being outnumbered two to one and Vaughan himself "hardly escaped but not without some wounds."

Brereton's success here was decisive. He turned his horse against the flank of Astley's stubbornly resisting foot, whilst Lucas's cavalry were either routed or

Sir Charles Lucas (1613-1648). He fought as a cavalry commander at Marston Moor. Though evidently capable, he was given no senior command by Prince Rupert. Lucas was shot on the surrender of Colchester in 1648 for breaking the terms of his parole. (Author's collection)

made off. Sir Charles himself took refuge in a nearby wood, where at daylight he was captured by Parliamentarian troops searching for stragglers.

Astley attempted to make a fighting retreat with his foot into Stow to stage a last stand. Here some were cut down in the streets by the Parliamentarian horse, whilst most of the remainder were surrounded in the market place. Astley was taken prisoner by a trooper of Birch's cavalry. The old soldier accepted the inevitable philosophically. He ordered his men to surrender, and, himself 'being somewhat wearied from the fight was given a drum to sit on by his captors, to whom he remarked wryly: "you have done your work, boys, and may go play, unless you fall out among yourselves."[11]

The battle had cost the Royalists about 100 dead, with 67 officers and 1,630 men taken prisoner. They were confined for the night in St Edward's Church, and then taken to Gloucester.

---

11 There are several slight variations in different accounts, but this is the most generally accepted version of Astley's comment.

Stow-on-the-Wold market place, the scene of Astley's surrender.
(Author's collection)

Astley's words were both prophetic and accurate. The King summed up the situation in a letter of 26 March to the Earl of Ormonde:

> Our condition is now very low and sad … by the defeat given to the Lord Astley and the forces he was to bring from Worcester to join with such as we have in these parts, so as we have no face of an army left …

He added defiantly to Lord Digby: "If I cannot live as a King, I shall die like a gentleman."[12]

12   Carte, Volume 6, p.358.

16

The Fall of Oxford

The defeat at Stow-on-the-Wold, and the surrender of Hopton's army in the West on 14 March spelt the end of Royalist hopes. All that remained was to decide the fate of King Charles and to reduce the still numerous garrisons which still held out in his name. Chief among these, of course, was Oxford.

For the moment the New Model Army was besieging Exeter, but Parliamentarian forces began tightening the net around Oxford, initially concentrating on its outlying garrisons. In January Colonel Edward Whalley had begun operations against Banbury Castle, but he complained that his operations were constantly hindered by lack of supplies and guns and harassed by constant sorties by Sir William Compton and his garrison, and by raids by the Royalist horse based at Woodstock and Oxford. He was also diverted for some time by the need to guard against Astley's force from the Welsh Marches, and it was clear that the siege of Banbury would be both difficult and protracted.

Parliamentarian forces were also besieging Donnington Castle, which fell at the end of March; Colonel Thomas Rainsborough laid siege to Woodstock in the middle of the month. Once again lack of ordnance hindered the Parliamentarian forces. The defenders of Woodstock, under Captain Fawcett (probably of the Ordnance Office) were determined, and Rainsborough was still held up early in April, when the Committee of Both Kingdoms wrote to Whalley, still besieging Banbury:

> We are assured by Colonel Rainsborough's letter that if he had cannon and a mortar piece he would in four days take in Woodstock Manor, which if it were effected would leave a good part of those forces at liberty to take quarter at Wheatley, which we have determined to do, and thereby block up Oxford close on that side. If the guns and mortar piece be come to you from Northampton send them with their equipage to Woodstock, when that service is accomplished they shall be returned to you again. In order that Col. Fleetwood may be the better able to watch the movements of the enemy every way, send him all the horse, both of your own

regiment, the Northampton regiment, and the Compton horse, that they may receive his orders, reserving only with you one troop.[1]

On 3 April the Committee told Colonel Dalbier, the chief engineer of the New Model, who had been in command at the siege of Donnington, that, his work there being completed, he was asked to consider occupying Wallingford town, in order to put pressure on the Castle. Rainsborough, who had complained of a shortage of powder, was to be sent 50 barrels from Banbury, "with match and bullet proportionable" and Major General Richard Browne at Abingdon was to send another 30 barrels of powder. Rainsborough was also to be reinforced by 700 foot from Northampton.[2]

On 10 April, Colonel Thomas Sanderson, with the Warwick forces, was ordered to blockade Radcot.[3] The tempo of operations at Woodstock were stepped up with the arrival of the ordnance from Banbury as well as a mortar and two whole culverins which Dalbier had been using at Donnington, The governor of Malmesbury was to send 300 foot to blockade Faringdon.[4] For the moment, however, the main efforts were focussed on Woodstock. For several days the sound of the bombardment could be heard clearly in Oxford, and on 15 April:

> This morning the cannon played hard against Woodstock House, and in the evening about 6:00 p.m. they stormed it, but were beaten off with the loss of at least 100 men all their scaling ladders, divers wounded. Of the house only five hurt.[5]

But this success could only delay the inevitable. Some civilians, among them Mary, Duchess of Richmond, the reputed lover of Prince Rupert, left Oxford whilst they still could. On the same day Prince Rupert's troop was disbanded, though it seems that he and Maurice raised an ad hoc volunteer troop almost immediately. Recognising that Woodstock was doomed, commissioners headed by the Earl of Lindsey went out to Woodstock to negotiate with Rainsborough. Terms were agreed, and on 26 April Woodstock was surrendered. Its garrison was disarmed but allowed to retire to Oxford. On the same day 700 foot from recently surrendered Exeter, under its former Governor, Sir John Berkeley, arrived in Oxford. There were probably die-hards from other surrendered garrisons still trickling into Oxford.[6]

---

1   C.S.P.D. (1645-7), p.371.
2   Ibid., p.384.
3   Ibid.
4   Ibid., p.387.
5   Hamper (ed.), p.63.
6   Ibid.

The King's escape from Oxford, 1646. (Author's collection)

It was clear, now that organised resistance in the West of England was virtually at an end, that the Royalist capital would be the next target for Fairfax and the New Model Army. King Charles was now pinning his hopes on dividing his opponents by reaching an agreement with the Scots, whose army was currently besieging Newark. So, on 27 April, disguised as a servant, and with three other men who addressed him as "Harry," but declining Prince Rupert's offer to be one of his companions, the King slipped out of Oxford for the last time, via its North Gate, and eventually made his way across country to reach the Scottish camp at Newark. Ahead lay months of intrigue and debate, whose complexities lie beyond the scope of our story.[7]

During the previous summer many of the Royalist courtiers in Oxford had been glad of the King's absence, reasoning that it made it less likely that the enemy would focus their attention on the city. They had no reason for such hopes now. Morale was generally low. The Lords Commissioners were once again in control, with Sir Thomas Glemham acting to some extent under their orders. The attitude of the townspeople was at best ambivalent. In March, as in previous years, the Town Council had renewed the agreement made in previous years which granted the King the first hay crop from Port Meadow, but this time with the significant

7   Varley (1932), pp.133-134.

proviso that if the war should end and the garrison be disbanded before the crop was ready, it should revert to the use of the town. For the townspeople, with concerns for their families' homes and livelihoods in the event of a siege, and the soldiers and die-hard Royalists, with perhaps little left to lose there was an obvious potential source of conflict.[8]

On 1 May the horse of the New Model Army were sighted in the hills east of Oxford. The siege was about to begin.

Although the Royalist cause was now beaten beyond hope of recovery, Oxford retained huge symbolic importance. As Joshua Sprigge, the historian of the New Model Army, put it:

> It had been from the beginning of the Wars the King's headquarter and Garrison, his Chief place of residence and retreat where his Council, and most of the Nobility that had left the Parliament attended him. Its place being almost in the Centre of the Kingdom, gave it no small advantage for the sending out of Parties upon any Design.

Oxford's ring of garrisons were "as so many outworks unto it," whilst its rivers made it very defensible. By the addition of flooding, Oxford could be rendered absolutely unapproachable on three sides, and the northern side of the town was strongly defended with fortifications. The Parliamentarians estimated that there were in Oxford 5,000 "good foot, most of them of the King's old Infantry, which had served him from the beginning of the war."[9] This was an over-estimate, for although the defenders might in theory be approximately that total, they were a very mixed bag indeed.

However, after viewing the defences and considering the information he had regarding the garrison, Fairfax had concluded "that this was no place to be taken at a running pace, but likely rather to prove a business of time, hazard and industry."[10]

There were a number of other probable reasons for the decision made by Fairfax and his council of war to proceed methodically, and he may have exaggerated the difficulty of the task facing him deliberately. With the war effectively won, there was little appetite for incurring heavy casualties, whilst Sir Thomas, it has been suggested, may have wished to avoid unnecessary damage to the fabric of the University of which he was himself a member. He also had a more conciliatory attitude to his opponents, now that peace seemed at hand, than did many of his colleagues. An inflated estimate of the difficulty of the task involved in capturing Oxford might make it easier politically for Fairfax to offer generous terms.

---

8   Eddershaw, p.141.
9   Joshua Sprigge, *Anglia Rediviva* (London, 1647), pp.249-250.
10   Ibid., p.250.

Sir Thomas (later Lord) Fairfax (1612-1671), general of the New Model Army from 1645. A capable and moderate soldier, he made his name in the fighting in the North. (Author's collection)

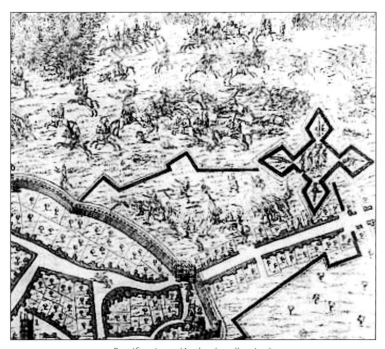

Fortifications. (Author's collection)

Fairfax established his own headquarters at Garsington, and during the next few days his foot took up quarters in the villages around Oxford.

The Committee of Both Kingdoms had ordered major preparations for the siege. The list of material to be provided included 1,200 wooden spades and shovels, 300 steel spades and 500 pickaxes, 200 sets of horse harness and 20 provision wagons, 500 barrels of gunpowder, 1,000 granadoes, 600 mortar shells, 30 tons of shot, 40 tons of match, and 200 scaling ladders.[11]

The Parliamentarians' first task was to build fortified encampments for the besieging troops. It was agreed to build an encampment to hold 3,000 men on Headington Hill, which was completed in three or four days, with a bridge of boats across the Cherwell linking the rest of the army to another fortified camp at Marston where troops under Thomas Rainsborough were stationed. A third encampment was under the command of Colonel John Lambert, and a fourth under Colonel Herbert. An entrenchment was to be dug linking the fortifications near St Clements. With most of the foot deployed on the northern side of Oxford, the train of artillery was placed at Elsford Forge. With the outlying garrisons of Faringdon, Radcot, Wallingford and Boarstall all blockaded, and horse sent to sever any remaining links with Royalist-held Worcester, on 11 May Fairfax decided the time was ripe to summon Sir Thomas Glemham to surrender:

> Sir,
> I do by these summon you to deliver up the City of Oxford into my hands, for the use of the Parliament. I very much desire the preservation of that place (so famous for learning) from ruin, which inevitably is like to fall upon it, except you concur. You may have honourable terms for yourself and all within that garrison if you reasonably accept thereof. I desire the answer this day, and rest your servant
> Thomas Fairfax.[12]

On the same day the Parliamentarians began constructing more siege works, and in response Prince Rupert, without any formal command, but serving as volunteer in the garrison, led a sortie out of the North Gate:

> Prince Rupert, and with him near a hundred Horse, went forth of Oxford on Colonel Rainsborough's side to take the air (Prince Rupert riding without Boots, in his shoes and stockings) a Party of our men marched up towards them, and fired upon them; in which skirmish Prince Rupert

---

11   C.S.P.D., p.406.
12   Sprigge, pp.253-254.

The siege of Oxford, a largely imaginary impression painted by Jan de Wyck.
(Author's collection)

had a shot in the right shoulder, (but pierced no bone) whereupon they retreated to Oxford.[13]

On the 13th the first cannon shot fired by the besiegers fell harmlessly in Christ Church Meadow. It was probably intended as a warning of what might follow.

Glemham was not, of course, a free agent, but had to consult with the Lords Commissioners in Oxford before responding to Fairfax. He replied to Fairfax's summons:

> Sir,
> I have received your letter, summoning me to surrender the City, which was given in trust for His Majesty's use. But in respect there are many persons of Eminency I must desire you to receive for an Answer a Request that you will be pleased to send a safe conduct for Sir John Monson and Mr Phillip Warwick to repair unto you at such a time and place as you shall appoint, by whom you shall understand what for the present is desired … [14]

13 Ibid., p.256.
14 Ibid., p.254.

The Royalist commissioners asked for leave to send a message to the King to learn his wishes, whilst their Parliamentarian counterparts tried to persuade them "of the vanity" of resistance "advising them rather to take the present opportunity lest they afterwards fell short of these terms they might now have by present compliance." However Glemham claimed that more time was needed to consult with the Royalist leadership in Oxford.[15]

Sir Thomas and his officers felt that Oxford was defensible, and there was clearly some difference of opinion among the Lords commissioners, for both the Earl of Dorset and Lord Hatton dissented from the instructions sent to Glemham to begin negotiations. At the same time the destruction of the documentation regarding the Oxford Parliament and other records of the Royalist administration began. Sir Thomas Glemham wrote to the Lords Commissioners enquiring upon what authority they acted in the King's absence in ordering him to open negotiations for terms:

> My Lords,
> I conceive I have in obedience to Commands, and absolutely against mine and all the Officers opinions in point of time, begun a treaty with the Rebels, which I can neither justify in honour, nor well answer the same. And therefore desire, seeing your Lordships fid yesterday declare that in his Majesty's absence your Lordships, as his Council, had the Sovereign power residing in you, that for my justification you will declare under your hands, that you have the power to raise and disband forces, to fortify and give up Garrisons, and to do other warlike actions. And to give me command in pursuance of that power, to proceed with the Treaty. Otherwise I must proceed according to my discretion upon the power and trust reposed by his Majesty.[16]

To some extent Glemham may have been protecting himself against the fates which had befallen other governors such as Feilding and Windebank, but a letter of the following day, sent to the Lords Commissioners, displays the strength of feeling of the military commanders in Oxford:

> We the Officers of the Garrison of Oxford, who have here underwritten our names, do hereby declare upon our several reputations that it is absolutely against our wills and opinions to treat at this present with Sir Thomas Fairfax. But upon the Governor's intimation of order received by him from the King to observe what the body of the Privy Council should determine in his absence, have in obedience to his Majesty under

---

15   Ibid.
16   Quoted Hamper (ed.), p.64.

him enforced by the lords of the Privy Council should determine in his absence, have in obedience to his Majesty order been enforced by the Lords of the Privy Council to this treaty And do further declare to the world, that what inconvenience soever may arise to the King's cause or his friends upon this Treaty, is not in our hands to prevent.

"T[homas] Glemham, Steven Hawkins, Richard Hamilton, Richard Gosnold, Thomas Shirley, Henry Tillier, Richard Gerard, W Rose, Richard Clayton, Henry Crompton, Clement Martin, R Hall, W Horwood, Reginald Moy, W. Smith, Robert Meade, John Sisson, Edward Masters, M Prideaux, Thomas Graham, Francis Hall, John Cressy, Adam Rock, Hannibal Bagnell, John Hughes.[17]

Also on the 18th negotiations began, but broke down over the first article proposed by the Royalists, which was to have permission to send a message to the King to ascertain his wishes regarding the surrender of Oxford. Talks were adjourned until 22 May.

In the meantime, although it is unclear when or if it reached the defenders of Oxford, the King, now effectively a prisoner of the Scots at Newark on 18 May sent a letter to Glemham, which was intercepted by the Parliamentarians:

Trusty and well-beloved we greet you well. Being desirous to stop the further effusion of the blood of our subjects, and yet respecting the faithful services of all in that City of Oxford which hath faithfully served us and hazarded their lives for us, we have thought it good to command you to quit that City, and disband the forces under your charge there, you receiving Honourable conditions for you and them.[18]

Similar messages were sent to the other Royalist garrisons still holding out, but on balance it seems unlikely that the contents were passed on to the Royalists in Oxford. They were however still in occasional contact with the outside world by means of disguised messengers, and it is very possible that the gist of the King's orders reached Oxford. Although both sides now realised that terms would be struck eventually, the outcome was neither certain nor easy. There were a number of details which proved difficult to agree upon. On the 23rd talks were again broken off when the Parliamentarians said that Royalist demands were too high, and they would prepare their own set of proposals. For several days low-key military operations continued.

Around 24 May the Royalist outpost at Radcot surrendered "after it had endured great extremity by our Granadoes, one whereof falling on the top of a Tower, made

17   Ibid.
18   C.S.P.D., p.412.

fearful work, tearing it into a thousand pieces, and sending it several ways, and at last falling into the Cellar, let out all their Beer. There were a hundred men in it, who were to go to their several homes, leaving their Arms behind."[19]

On 30 May Sir Thomas Fairfax sent a trumpet to Oxford with his terms, the House of Commons having rejected those first out forward by the Royalists. Talks were resumed, and continued over the next few days. In the meantime, on the evening of 31 May the Parliamentarians weakened the water defences of Oxford when the Isis was diverted back into its old course near Hinckley and Botley.

On 3 June:

> A sally made out at the East gate by about 100 horse, with purpose to have driven in cattle, which were grazing near Cowley, but the Rebels' Horse coming down prevented the same by skirmishes, wherein one Captain Richardson and two more were slain.[20]

The Commissioners of the two sides were still meeting daily at Marston, with some details still to be resolved. On 9 June Fairfax called another Council of War to review his options. Once again the strength of the defences and the garrison were considered and the reputation that Sir Thomas Glemham had of holding out in his previous commands with such determination.

> So according to this account, consider what expense of time and blood would have issued in carrying on the approaches for the reducement by force; December being a month they might very well have reached unto, which must necessarily have engaged the army into so much winter, water, cold and difficulty, as that the issue might in reason of War proved as sad for the Besiegers, all things considered, as for those in the City; three months time would have been the least; and when all things had been ripe for enforcing, the hazard of how many honest, gallant men against earth and walls, against Lines and Colleges?
>
> But surely we flow not with good men in the Kingdom, that we should be so indifferently prodigal of those we have, if victories may be purchased cheaper, and at an easier rate, besides the spoil and firing of Colleges, and it may be, of that famous Library, which how it would have stood with the Reputation of this State, to destroy places of Arts so freely, let others judge.[21]

19 Sprigge, p.258.
20 Hamper (ed.), p.64.
21 Sprigge, p.279.

Sprigge's version of the conclusions of the Council of War were, of course, written some time later, following widespread criticism that the terms agreed at Oxford were too lenient, but it probably fairly accurately reflected the conclusions of Fairfax and his officers.

There was still grumbling within Oxford. Some of the gentlemen and clergy complained that their interests were not being adequately represented in the negotiations, and the military, as we have seen, were still unhappy. But there seems to have been a general feeling that the talks were in their closing stages. This was perhaps reflected on 10 June when Fairfax sent into Oxford as a gift for James, Duke of York a "Brace of bucks, two muttons, two veals, two lambs and six capons."

It may have been that the die-hards among the military in Oxford decided on a final gesture of defiance, for:

> A few days before the Treaty ended, when the Enemy perceived it was like to succeed, they played with their Cannon day and night into our Leaguers and Quarters, discharging sometimes near 200 shots on a day, at random, as was conceived, rather to spend their Powder than to do any great execution, though they showed good skill, in that they levelled their pieces, so as they shot into the Leaguer on Headington Hill (and on that side Lieutenant-Colonel Cosworth was slain with a great shot) and likewise into the Leaguer on Colonel Rainsborough's side, where they killed with their shot a sutler and others in their Tents: Our Cannon in recompence, played fiercely upon the enemy, and much annoyed them in their Works and Colleges, till at last, a cessation of great shot was agreed to on both sides.[22]

By now discipline among the garrison seems to have been breaking down, with opposing factions not far from violence. On 17 June, following the exchange of cannon fire, there was a general cessation of arms, with increasing fraternisation among the ordinary soldiers of both sides. "Divers enemy soldiers came to the Ports, and drank with ours."[23]

Diehard Royalist reformadoes, however, were still apparently hostile to the truce negotiations, because the Privy Council was unable to meet in the Audit House, as it usually did, " in regard of the mutinous soldiers, especially reformadoes," and the 19th the Privy Councillors kept their swords at the ready, in case of attack.[24] But the publication on Oxford, on 17 June, of the King's letter commanding the Oxford commanders to make reasonable terms may have played a part in cooling tempers, for on 20 June the articles of Surrender for Oxford were signed by the

---

22   Ibid., p.259.
23   Hamper (ed.), p.65.
24   Ibid.

Commissioners of the Privy Council and Glemham for the Royalists, and Fairfax for the Parliamentarians. The town and its defences were to be handed over to the Parliamentarians at 10:00 a.m. on 24 June. The Duke of York was to be taken to join the other royal children in London. Princes Rupert and Maurice, with their entourage, probably including Bernard de Gomme and Bartholomew La Roche, were given passes to remain in the country, though not in London, for six months before being given passes to leave the country. The Great Seal and other symbols of royal authority, were to be handed over to Fairfax. The articles included extensive provisions for the troops of the garrison. Glemham and his men, including what remained of the Oxford Army:

> … shall march out of the city of Oxen with their horses and complete Arms that properly belong unto them, proportionable to their present and past commands, flying Colours, trumpets sounding, Drums beating, Matches lighted at both ends, Bullet in their mouths, and every Soldier to have 12 Charges of powder, Match and Bullet proportionable, with Bag and Baggage, to any place within 15 miles of Oxford, which the Governor shall choose, where such of the common Soldiers as desire to go to their own homes, or Friends, shall lay down their Arms, which shall be delivered up to such as the General Sir Thomas Fairfax shall appoint to receive them.[25]

There were extensive provisions for those officers and men who wished to seek employment abroad, for it was obviously in the interests of Parliament that those who remained unreconciled to the new order, especially the professional soldiers, should be out of the country. The Auxiliary Regiments of the town and university should disband and return to civilian life. Apart from those already exempted from pardon by Parliament, there would be an amnesty for all actions committed during the war, and the large number of civilian refugees in Oxford would have leave either to remain, or to compound with Parliament for their estates and properties elsewhere. The rights and privileges of the university and colleges were confirmed and their property "preserved from defacing or spoil" and the privileges of the Corporation were similarly guaranteed.

> All Ladies, Gentlewomen, and other women now in Oxen, whose husbands or friends are absent from thence, may have Passes and Protections for themselves, servants and goods to go to and remain at the houses of their husbands, or at their friends, as they shall desire; and to go or send to

25 Sprigge, pp.237-238.

London, or elsewhere, to obtain the Allowances out of their husbands' or parents' Estates, allowed them by the Ordnance of Parliament.[26]

The King's servants were to be permitted to move his property and possessions to Hampton Court Palace, and remain there with them, pending further developments.

As agreed, the Royalist troops began to march out of Oxford on 24 June, although the process could not be completed in one day. Those with homes to the north of Oxford marched out by the North Port, whilst 900 more left via Magdalen Bridge, over Headington Hill, past the great Parliamentarian redoubt, between the ranks of the New Model Army, whose behaviour unlike that of their opponents on similar occasions was faultless. The troops marched to Thame, where they were disbanded, and given a pass in the following terms:

> You are to suffer the Bearer _____ who was in the City and Garrison of Oxford at its Surrender, and is to have the full benefit of the Articles etc, quietly and without interruption to pass your Guards with his Servants, horses, arms and goods, and so to repair to London or elsewhere upon his necessary occasions. And in all places where he shall reside or remove, he is to be protected from violence to his person goods or estate according to these Articles, and to have full liberty within six months to go to any convenient port, and to transport himself with his servants, goods and necessaries beyond the seas, and in all other things to enjoy the benefit of the said articles.[27]

On 25 June the keys of the city were handed over to Sir Thomas Fairfax, and he sent in three regiments of foot to preserve order until the remaining Royalist troops had gone. Sir Thomas also, typically, issued another prompt order:

> The first thing … was to set a good guard of Soldiers to preserve the Bodleian Library. Thus was there was no hurt done by those Cavaliers [formerly of the garrison] by way of entering it of cutting of chains of books … He was a lover of learning, and had he not taken this special care, that noble Library had been utterly destroyed.[28]

Oxford, with some trepidation, awaited its new masters.

26   Ibid., p.280.
27   Ibid.
28   Aubrey, p.129.

17

Aftermath

Although the majority of the citizens of Oxford greeted the surrender with relief, mixed with trepidation, King Charles, at least in retrospect, reacted with some annoyance to the news. He commented in July:

> I have not written concerning the yielding of Oxford, not having been fully (as now I am) informed thereof, but now I must make my observations to thee upon it. In a word, all that had any directing power (except the Governor, Secretary Nicholas, Dorchester and Lord Hatton) did look only upon themselves,, without regard to my honour, and interest, but this mean failing in friendship looks so seriously that it rather animates than discourages me, in being firm to all who will not forsake themselves, which there was, I assure thee, many in Oxford.[1]

The remaining garrisons in the "ring" around Oxford surrendered one by one. Banbury Castle had already surrendered, on generous terms on 8 May. At Faringdon, the governor Thomas Blagge, a professional soldier of strong character, refused to negotiate, even after the fall of Oxford, without the King's permission. Parliamentarian reinforcements were brought up to tighten the blockade, but it was only after receiving the King's general order to his garrisons to surrender that on 27 July Blagge accepted similar generous terms to those which had been granted to the Oxford garrison.

In Oxford, as in other formerly Royalist-controlled towns, a number of councillors and other officials known or suspected of being supporters of the King were barred from office. The council, with a keen eye to political reality, promptly rescinded the resolution which had been imposed on them in 1643 expelling a number of Parliamentarian supporters, who were now reinstated. The most prominent of them, John Nixon, was elected as Mayor.

---

1   F.J. Varley, *A supplement to The Siege of Oxford: An account of Oxford during the Civil War, 1642-1646* (Oxford, 1935), p.1.

The following year there was "a great difference" among the councillors; the House of Commons intervened to quash the election of a Royalist mayor, and in 1648 the County Committee removed four members of the mayor's council and at least 12 other councillors. Two of the exiles of 1643 were then elected mayor and bailiff, and a third joined the mayor's council. The purge was completed in 1649 by the replacement of the high steward, Thomas Howard, Earl of Berkshire, by Bulstrode Whitelocke, Oxford's recorder since 1647 and one of the Lords Commissioners of the Great Seal.[2] Political purges during the Interregnum included the dismissal by the council of an alderman in 1651, and the removal, by order of the Committee for Indemnity, of five common councillors in 1653. Among the proposed replacements was a leading Baptist, Richard Tidmarsh, whose reluctance to serve, either then or later, did not save him from being treated as a political pawn during the upheavals of the next 30 years. In 1658 the Council of State refused to accept the election of a delinquent mayor, but withdrew after a petition from 98 councillors testified to his integrity.[3]

The university, with its amply attested Royalist sympathy, might have been expected to have fared badly under the new order. But it also had many supporters among the Parliamentarians, and was able to hold on to most of its privileges, and soon resumed its long –standing disputes with the town council. These came no nearer to being resolved under the new regime than they had under the old one. So far as material damage was concerned, Oxford suffered less severely than towns such as Chester which had sustained prolonged bombardment. The greatest damage resulted from the Great Fire of 1644, along with the demolition of suburbs, particularly on the northern side of the town, when Oxford was fortified. It was estimated that around a quarter of the houses in the town had been either destroyed or dismantled. The fortifications themselves were slighted in 1647-8, the work mainly being organised by the Council. Oxford retained a military garrison and governor for several years, particularly during times of active Royalist plotting and insurrection. However the town was not involved in any further fighting. A Royalist plot in 1648, during the Second Civil War, came to nothing so far as Oxford was concerned. The castle was garrisoned in 1651, during the invasion of England by Charles II with a Scottish army, but that was crushed at the Battle of Worcester. In 1655 local forces were again mustered on the outbreak of another minor Royalist uprising. But on the whole life in Oxford seems to have returned quite quickly to a peacetime routine. Rebuilding was well under way by the mid-1650s, and trade recovered steadily. This did not mean, however, that the university, in particular, had shed all of its Royalist inclinations. In September 1658, on the death of Oliver Cromwell, the mayor and council officials, with a military escort, when proclaiming at the Carfax Oliver's son Richard

2   Eddershaw, p.127.
3   Ibid.

as the new Lord Protector, were pelted with carrots and turnips by some of the scholars.[4]

The Restoration of Charles II in 1660 was warmly welcomed, not least by the university. A maypole forbidden under the Commonwealth was set up in a gesture of defiance on 1 May and Restoration Day, on 29 May was celebrated long into the night. With some justice the new King Charles would reckon Oxford amongst his most loyal cities.

4   Wood, p.259.

Bibliography

Unpublished materials

Bodleian Library, Oxford:
  Clarendon MSS 26.
British Library, London:
  Harleian MSS 6851.
National Archives, Kew:
  SP 16/460/46; 47.

Contemporary newsletters etc.

Anon., *A True and Fuller Relation of the Battell Fought at Stow in the Wold March 21 1646*, London, 1646.

Anon., *His Highness Prince Rupert's late beating up of the Rebels' quarters at Postcomb and Chinnor*, Oxford, 1643.

Coe, Richard, *An Exact Dyarie of the Progress of Sir William Waller's Army*, London, 1644.

Ellis, Thomas, *An exact and full relation of the last fight, between the Kings forces and Sir William Waller. Sent in a letter from an officer in the army to his friend in London. Printed to prevent mis-information*, London, 1644.

Kingdom's Weekly Intelligencer, London, 1643-46.

Mercurius Aulicus, Oxford, 1643-46.

Mercurius Civicus, London, 1643-46.

Printed primary sources

Abbott, W.C. (ed.), *The Writings and Speeches of Oliver Cromwell*, Cambridge MA: Harvard University Press, 1937-47, 4 volumes.

Atkyns, Richard, 'Vindication', in Peter Young (ed.) *Military Memoirs: the Civil War*, London: Longmans, 1967.

Aubrey, John (ed. Oliver Lawson Dick), *Brief Lives*, London: Secker & Warburg, 1949.

Bray, W. (ed.), *Memoirs of John Evelyn*, London: Henry Coburn, 1827, 5 volumes.

Calendar of State Papers Domestic Series.

Carte, Thomas, *History of the life of James, duke of Ormonde, from his birth in 1610 to his death in 1688*, Oxford: Oxford University Press, 1853, 6 volumes.

Clarendon, Earl of (ed. W.D. Macray), *History of the Rebellion and Civil Wars in England begun in the year 1641*, Oxford: Oxford University Press, 1888, 6 volumes.

Fanshawe, Lady Anne, *Memoirs of Lady Fanshawe, wife of Sir Richard Fanshawe, Bart., Ambassador*, London: Forgotten Books, 2012.

Firth, C.H. (ed.), 'The Journal of Prince Rupert's Marches, 5 Sept. 1642 to 4 July 1646' in: *English Historical Review*, Volume 13 Number 52 (October 1898), pp.729-741.

Green, M.A.E., *Letters of Queen Henrietta Maria including her private correspondence with Charles the First*, London: Richard Bentley, 1886.

Hamper, William (ed.), *The life, diary, and correspondence of Sir William Dugdale ... With an appendix, containing an account of his published works, an index to his manuscript collections, copies of monumental inscriptions to the memory of the Dugdale family, and heraldic grants and pedigrees*, London: Printed for Harding, Lepard, 1827.

H.M.C. Portland MSS, I.

Hobson, M.G., & Salter, H.E. (eds.), *Oxford Council Acts Volume II: 1626-1665*, Oxford: Clarendon Press for the Oxford Historical Society, 1933.

Larkin, F. (ed.), *Stuart Royal Proclamations*, Oxford: Oxford University Press, 1983.

Lloyd, David, *Memoirs of the lives, actions, sufferings and deaths of those noble personages, that suffered by death, sequestration, decimation, or otherwise, for the protestant religion from 1637 to 1660 continued to 1666. With the life and martyrdom of King Charles I*, London, 1668.

House of Commons Journal.

House of Lords Journal.

Phillip, I.G. (ed.), *The Journal of Sir Samuel Luke*, Oxford: Oxfordshire Record Society, 1947-53, 3 volumes.

Roy, Ian (ed.), *The Royalist Ordnance Papers*, Oxford: Oxfordshire Record Society, 1964, 1975, 2 volumes.

Rushworth, John, *Historical collections of private passages of state, weighty matters in law, remarkable proceedings in five Parliaments beginning the sixteenth year of King James, anno 1618, and ending ... [with the death of King Charles the First, 1649]*, London: Printed by J.A. for Robert Boulter, 1680-1701, 8 volumes.

Slingsby, Sir Henry, (ed. D. Parsons), *The diary of Sir Henry Slingsby of Scriven, Bart.*, London: Longman, 1836.

Sprigge Joshua, *Anglia Rediviva, or Englands recovery, being the history of the motions, actions, and successes of the army under the immediate conduct of His Excellency Sr. Thomas Fairfax, Kt., Captain-General of all the Parliaments forces in England*, London: Printed by R.W. for John Patridge, 1647.

Symonds, Richard (ed. C.E. Long), *Diary of the Marches of the Royal Army during the Great Civil War*, London: Camden Society, 1859.

Tibbutt, H.G. (ed.), *The Letter Books of Sir Samuel Luke, 1644-45*, Bedford: Bedfordshire Historical Society, 1963.

Toynbee, Margaret (ed.), *The papers of Captain Henry Stevens, waggon-master-general to King Charles I*, Oxford: Oxfordshire Record Society, 1961.

Walker, Sir Edward, *Historical collections of several important transactions relating to the late rebellion and civil wars of England not publish'd in my Lord Clarendon's history, or any other*, London: Printed by W.B. for Sam. Keble, at the Turk's Head in Fleetstreet, 1707.

Warburton, Eliot, *Memoirs of Prince Rupert and the Cavaliers*, London: Richard Bentley, 1849, 3 volumes.

Warner, G.F. (ed.), *The Nicholas papers: correspondence of Sir Edward Nicholas, secretary of state*, London: Camden Society New Series, 1886-1920, 4 volumes.

Wood, Anthony à, (ed. Andrew Clark), *The life and times of Anthony Wood, antiquary, of Oxford, 1632-1695, described by himself*, Oxford: Printed for the Oxford Historical Society at the Clarendon Press, 1891-1900, 5 volumes.

Secondary sources

Adair, John, *A Life of John Hampden, the Patriot, 1594*-1643, London: MacDonald & Jane's, 1976.

Adair, John, *Roundhead General: The Campaigns of Sir William Waller*, Stroud: Sutton Publishing, 1997, 2nd ed.

Barratt, John, *Cavaliers: The Royalist Army at War 1642-1646*, Stroud: Sutton Publishing, 2000.

Barres-Baker, M.C., *The Siege of Reading, April 1643*, N.p.: ebooksLib, n.d.

Besly, Edward, *Coins and Medals of the English Civil War*, London: Seaby in association with the National Museum of Wales, 1990.

Carleton, Charles, *Going to the Wars: The experience of the British civil wars, 1638-1651*, London: Routledge, 1992.

Chance, Eleanor et al, *A History of the County of Oxford: Volume 4, the City of Oxford*, London: Victoria County History, 1979.

Coghill, James Henry, *The family of Coghill 1377 to 1879. With some sketches of their maternal ancestors, the Slingsbys, of Scriven Hall 1135 to 1879*, Cambridge: Printed at the Riverside Press, 1879.

Eddershaw, David, *The Civil War in Oxfordshire*, Stroud: Sutton Publishing, 1995.

Goldman, Lawrence (ed.), *Oxford Dictionary of National* Biography, London: Oxford University Press, 2004.

Edwards, Peter, *Dealing in Death: The arms trade and the British Civil Wars, 1638-52,* Stroud: Sutton Publishing, 2000.

Foard, Glenn, *Naseby: The Decisive Campaign*, Whitstable: Pryor Publications, 1995.

Gruber von Arni, Eric, *Justice to the maimed soldier: nursing, medical care, and welfare for sick and wounded soldiers and their families during the English Civil Wars and interregnum, 1642-1660*, Aldershot: Ashgate, 2001.

Hutton, Ronald, *The Royalist War Effort 1642-1646*, London: Longman, 1981.

Hyett, F.A, 'The Last Battle of the First English Civil War' in: *Transactions of the Bristol and Gloucestershire Archaeological Society* Volume 16, 1891-92, pp.61-67.

Kemp, Anthony, 'The Fortification of Oxford during the Civil War' in: *Oxoniensia*, Volume XLII, 1977, pp.237-246.

Lattey, R.T. et al, 'A Contemporary Map of the Defences of Oxford in 1644' in: *Oxoniensia*, Volume I, 1936, pp.161-172.

Longmore, Sir T. & Leon Banov, *Richard Wiseman: surgeon and sergeant-surgeon to Charles II – a biographical study*, London: Longmans, Green & Co., 1891.

Morrah, Patrick, *Prince Rupert of the Rhine*, London: Collins, 1974.

Newman, Peter R., *Royalist Officers in England and Wales 1642-1660: A Biographical Dictionary*, New York: Garland, 1981.

Porter, Stephen, 'The Oxford fire of 1644', in: *Oxoniensia*, Volume XLIX, 1984, pp.289-300.

Porter, Stephen, *Destruction in the English Civil War*, Stroud: Alan Sutton, 1994.

Reid, Stuart, *Officers and Regiments of the Royalist Army*, Leigh-on-Sea: Partizan Press, n.d., 5 volumes.

Roy, Ian, 'The Royalist Council of War 1642-46' in: *Bulletin of the Institute of Historical Research*, Volume 35, Issue 92, November 1962, pp.150-168.

Stevenson, J. & Carter, A., 'The Raid on Chinnor and the Fight at Chalgrove Field, June 17th and 18th, 1643' in: *Oxoniensia*, Volume XXXVIII, 1973, pp.346-355.

Taylor, A.J., 'The Royal Visit to Oxford in 1636' in: *Oxonensia*, Volume I, 1936, pp.151-158.

Toynbee, Margaret & Young, Peter, Crop*redy Bridge 1644: The Campaign and the Battle*, Kineton: Roundwood Press, 1970.

Toynbee, Margaret, & Young, Peter, *Strangers in Oxford: A side light on the first Civil War, 1642-1646*, Chichester: Phillimore, 1973.

Varley, Frederick John, *Mercurius Aulicus: A diurnall communicating the intelligence and affaires of the court to the rest of the Kingdome*, Oxford: Oxford University Press, 1930.

Varley, Frederick John, *The Siege of Oxford: An account of Oxford during the Civil War, 1642-1646*, Oxford: Oxford University Press, 1932.

Varley, Frederick John, *A supplement to The Siege of Oxford: An account of Oxford during the Civil War, 1642-1646*, Oxford: Oxford University Press, 1935.

Index

INDEX OF PEOPLE

INDEX OF PLACES

For locations and buildings within Oxford (e.g. All Souls College) *see* 'Oxford (specific locations)'.

INDEX OF MILITARY UNITS

INDEX OF MISCELLANEOUS/OTHER TERMS